THE BALKANS

MINORITIES
AND
STATES IN
CONFLICT

Minority Rights Publications

For Prue

Minority Rights Group is an international, non-governmental organization whose aims are to secure justice for minority (and non-dominant majority) groups suffering discrimination by:

1. Researching and publishing the facts as widely as possible to raise public knowledge and awareness of minority issues worldwide.

2. Advocating on all aspects of the human rights of minorities to aid the prevention of dangerous and destructive conflicts.

3. Educating through its schools programme on issues relating to prejudice, discrimination and group conflicts.

If you would like to know more about the work of the Minority Rights Group, please contact Alan Phillips (Director), MRG, 379 Brixton Road, London SW9 7DE.

m

Minority Rights Publications is a new series of books from the Minority Rights Group. Through the series, we aim to make available to a wide audience reliable data on, and objective analyses of, specific minority issues. The series draws on the expertise and authority built up by the Minority Rights Group over two decades of publishing. Further details on MRG's highly acclaimed series of reports can be found at the end of this book. Other titles in the book series are:

Armenia and Karabagh: The Struggle for Unity
edited by Christopher J. Walker (1991)

forthcoming titles will cover:
Refugees in Europe
The Kurds

THE BALKANS

MINORITIES
AND
STATES IN
CONFLICT

by
Hugh Poulton

Foreword by
Milovan Djilas

m

Minority Rights Publications

© Minority Rights Group 1991

First published in Great Britain
in 1991 by
Minority Rights Publications
379 Brixton Road
London SW9 7DE

British Library Cataloguing in Publication Data
A CIP catalogue record of this book is available from the British Library

ISBN 1 873194 05 6 paper
ISBN 1 873194 25 0 hardback

Library of Congress Cataloguing in Publication Data
CIP Data available from the Library of Congress

Designed and typeset by Brixton Graphics
Printed and bound by Billing and Sons Ltd

Cover photo –
Christian Vioujard / Gamma

CONTENTS

FOREWORD

by Milovan Djilas

Of all various publications on minorities of the world which Minority Rights Group (MRG) has published, this latest one on minorities and states in conflict in the Balkans is worthy of special attention, both for its treatment of the subject and for the obvious relevance of the subject itself. The conflict among Balkan states because of minorities could turn, as it actually has so many times in the past, to an open armed clash. This publication, the first in the new book series from Minority Rights Publications, comes at the right time: the friction caused by minorities in the Balkans is getting sharper each day, and this information based on scientific research and impartial observation is very welcome to all those who care for peace and peaceful settlement of problems.

As a Yugoslav and a Balkan, I know quite a lot about Yugoslavia, and surely something about the Balkans. But I am simply amazed by the thoroughness of this text and the enormous endeavour which Mr. Hugh Poulton has invested in it. Even if the text were bereft of all its other virtues, it undoubtedly remains a precious and detailed manual to people interested in political relations in the Balkans and the position of many minorities in the Balkans who are still deprived in various aspects.

By its very title, this publication from MRG hits the core of the problem: conflicts among states because of minorities. And indeed, the kernel of conflict in the Balkans either takes place among the states, or rather nations, parts of which are minorities in other states, or could be found in aspirations – as in the case of Macedonians – to nations, to whom then any specific national characteristics and right to a state of their own are denied. Those minorities who are scattered throughout the Balkans, such as the Roma or Vlahs, have no states of their own, and have only rarely been the cause of disputes among Balkan states. So have their concerns: the time of awakening and of political and cultural constitution of these discriminated nations is still to come.

In its impartial presentation of facts and its summarizing of historical events, *The Balkans: Minorities and States in Conflict* points to potential and existing dangers, some of which have already become apparent in relations among Balkan states in the first place in Yugoslavia.

This book offers no proposals and solutions – to do so is not the objective of the Minority Rights Group. However, by its content and its thorough treatment of its subject, it suggests that the solutions can no longer be sought in the old ways – war, conflicts and state hegemonisms. Thus the book, indirectly, reaches the conclusion: ways forward from Balkan ethnic diversities and ethnic entanglements should only be sought and found, even if it can only be achieved over the long run, in strict implementation of human rights, patient settlement of disputes, in open democratic societies and non-aggressive, non-hegemonistic state policies.

In this way, this publication goes beyond its informative and analytical task and makes a significant contribution to the study and endeavours which are finally to open roads to agreements and cooperation of ethnic groups and states in the Balkans too.

Milovan Djilas

Milovan Djilas is a writer, dissident and former politician. He was a leading member of Tito's post-war government and, for a time, Vice-President of Yugoslavia before his dissident views resulted in two periods of imprisonment in the 1950s and 1960s. He is the author of over 20 books on Eastern European history and politics and was honoured with the Freedom Award in 1968.

INTRODUCTION

The peoples of the Balkans; the legacy of the Ottomans and the Hapsburgs; and the rise of local nationalism

The Balkan peninsula in south-east Europe is one of the most ethnically, linguistically and religiously complex areas of the world. Its geographic position has historically resulted in it being disrupted by invaders moving from Asia Minor to Europe or vice-versa. The three oldest peoples in the area under study are the Greeks, the Vlahs (descended from the original Thracians), and the Albanians who claim descent from the ancient Illyrians.

The Slavs, an Indo-European people originating in east-central Europe had begun to cross the Danube into the Balkans by the 6th Century AD. In the 7th Century combined assaults by Slavs and Proto-Bulgarians, a Turkic people from the area between the Urals and the Volga who had come via the steppes north of the Caspian Sea, led to the founding of the first Bulgarian state in 681. In 864 under the direction of their leader Boris, the Proto-Bulgarians converted en masse to Christianity and this greatly helped them to coalesce with the Slavs, who had already been converted, and by the end of the 9th Century they were as one people speaking a Slav-based language (Yugoslav historians claim that the Macedonian Slavs have always been a separate people from those in Bulgaria).

From the 10th Century onwards Roma (Gypsies), originating from northern India, began to move into the region. In the 7th Century Slavs settled in the northern area of present-day Yugoslavia. The Croats established an independent state which lasted until 1102 when they were first incorporated into the Kingdom of Hungary, and then into the expanding Hapsburg Empire which included the Slovenes and came to dominate central-eastern Europe. The Hapsburg territories included present-day Slovenia, Croatia, the Vojvodina, and, after 1878, Bosnia-Hercegovina. The Dalmation coast of Croatia, for the most part, geographically cut off from the hinterland by impassable mountains, retains to this day strong Venetian influence readily visible in its

1

architecture. By the end of the 13th Century the Serbs, another Slavic people, were establishing hegemony over much of the Balkans and in 1282 King Milutin took Skopje from the Byzantium Empire and opened the way for Serbian penetration into Macedonia. Disunity in the Balkans allowed the Ottoman Turks, an Asiatic people who had gradually eroded away the ailing Byzantine Empire, to invade the peninsula from Asia Minor in the 14th Century through Macedonia and the Maritsa valley. The gradual Ottoman conquest culminated in the defeat of the Serbs at Kosovo Polje in 1389 and opened the way for complete Ottoman conquest of the Balkans and the fall of Constantinople in 1453 saw the end of the Byzantine Empire. Large numbers of Serbs moved northwards from Kosovo to escape Ottoman domination and settled on the borders of the Kingdom of Hungary in present-day Vojvodina.

Ottoman rule was to last for almost five centuries over much of the Balkan peninsula. However despite at one time advancing almost to Vienna and looking to threaten Western Europe, the Ottoman Empire began to decline and by the early 19th Century the empire was in a state of decay with its economy stagnant, the once efficient bureaucracy corrupt, and the army demoralized. Simultaneously, and to an extent because of this degeneration, there appeared the awakening of the Balkan peoples aided by the intervention and interest of the Great Powers especially Russia and Austria-Hungary.

Geographically the Balkan peninsula is very mountainous and communications are difficult and this has resulted in communities tending to be compartmentalized as opposed to unified. Although there were inevitably some people who accepted the religion of the new rulers – the majority of Albanians, the Pomaks of the Rhodope mountains, and the Bosnians in central Yugoslavia – the Ottoman rulers were non-assimilative and multi-national without the technological and institutional facilities for integrating and unifying the subject peoples – unlike in Western Europe where the new 'nation-states' were able, for the most part, to transcend regional loyalties. As a result the peoples of the Balkans managed to retain their separate identities and cultures as well as, for many of them, retaining a sense of a former glorious history when they controlled a particular area, which with the national awakenings in the 19th Century they once more claimed – often at the expense of their neighbours who likewise made historical claims to the territory in question.

Thus, the national awakenings which saw the beginnings of the crumbling of Ottoman power in the Balkans by the mid-19th Century with the establishment of the Serbian state, in the north around Belgrade, and the Greek state, in the south around Athens, often gave rise to hostility between the previous Ottoman subject peoples – a hostility that was to reach its zenith in the struggle for Macedonia at the beginning of the 20th Century.

The Ottoman Empire was until the last quarter of the 19th and first part of the 20th Century a theocratic empire whose population was divided not along linguistic lines but by religious affiliation – the *millet* system – and religion has traditionally been one of the main factors in differentiating between various groups. The concept of nationality as expounded in the ideology of nationalism was a late arrival to the Balkans as well as to Turkey.

In the case of the Bulgarians, after the Ottoman invasion, the separate Bulgarian church and the attendant education system were placed under the control of the Greek Orthodox Church and the Greek Patriarch in Istanbul. Thus, until the Bulgarian national revival in the 19th Century it can be argued that the Bulgarians faced as big a threat of assimilation from the Greeks who controlled the religious services and education both of which were held in Greek, as from the Ottoman Turks. This is illustrated in an old Bulgarian proverb 'Save us Lord from the Bulgarian who becomes a Greek and from the Gypsy who becomes a Turk'.

Indeed a crucial factor in the growth of Bulgarian national consciousness was the establishment of the national church, the Exarchate, in 1870 by the Ottoman authorities following a long movement which began in 1820. In 1867 Patriarch Gregory VI had offered an autonomous Bulgarian church but one not to be extended to the parishes in Macedonia. The Bulgarians had refused and called for the populations of the relevant dioceses to decide. The decree of 1870 gave the Exarchate in only 17 dioceses but allowed parishes by two-thirds majority vote of all adult males to choose whether to join and have church services in the vernacular or continue in Greek.

This struggle for a national church was a political rather than a religious struggle. The parishes which opted for the vernacular comprised the so-called Greater Bulgaria which was to come into existence following the Treaty of San Stefano in 1878 at the end of the Russo-Turkish war of 1875-8. However, the Great Powers, notably Britain and Austro-Hungary both of whom feared that such a large Bulgaria dominating the Balkans and straddling the Bosphorus would be a client-state of Russia, forced its abandonment and its replacement instead by a severely truncated state at the Treaty of Berlin.

The loss of what most Bulgarians then, and still today, consider to be their natural territory is an important factor in the Bulgarian national psyche and the anniversary of the San Stefano Treaty is still celebrated in Bulgaria with greater official pomp than the anniversary of the Treaty of Berlin which followed. Although Bulgaria did succeed in regaining Eastern Rumelia in 1885 much of the 'lost territories' remain outside her borders and are now in present-day Yugoslavia and Greece.

The experience of the Catholic Croats and Slovenes (and also the Vojvodina Serbs) of the Hapsburg Empire was very different. The frontier between the two rival empires was heavily fortified on the Hapsburg side by garrison towns. In the 1848 revolutions which swept across the Hapsburg Empire, the authorities used the Croats and Serbs to help put down Hungarian attempts at independence. However, the short-lived attempt in the 1850s to homogenize the increasingly (compared to the newly emerging 'nation-states' of Western Europe) ramshackled empire on a German basis was an abject failure and the authorities were forced into a compromise with the Hungarians resulting in the *Ausgleich* of 1867.

The second half of the 19th Century saw the empire increasingly suffer from internal strife as, under the growing influence of nationalism, the various ethnic groups competed with each other and the two centres for national rights. The inability of the Hapsburg Empire to deal with its minorities, especially the Serbs, was a major factor in increasing tension with the new state of Serbia and one of the causes of World War I – the initial spark being the assassination in Sarajevo of Archduke Franz Ferdinand (who ironically favoured the triune empire with the South Slavs as the third component) by a Bosnian Serb.

4

1

YUGOSLAVIA IN OUTLINE

Of all the countries in Europe, the Socialist Federal Republic of Yugoslavia (SFRJ) is the least homogenous. It is a multi-national federation with a three-tier system of national rights as follows:

(i) the 'Nations of Yugoslavia', each with a national home based in one of the republics – this is an important point in denying the Albanians republican status in Kosovo as their national home is outside Yugoslavia (see below). There are six officially recognized 'Nations of Yugoslavia': Croats, Macedonians, Montenegrins, Muslims (an ethnic category recognized as a nation since the 1971 census), Serbs and Slovenes;

(ii) the 'Nationalities of Yugoslavia' which are legally allowed a variety of language and cultural rights. There are 10 ethnic groups officially recognized as 'Nationalities', the largest being the Albanians and the Hungarians concentrated in Kosovo and the Vojvodina, respectively, with the others as Bulgarians, Czechs, Gypsies, Italians, Romanians, Ruthenians, Slovaks and Turks;

(iii) 'Other Nationalities and Ethnic Groups' which are the remaining ethnic groups – Austrians, Greeks, Jews, Germans, Poles, Russians, Ukrainians, Vlahs and others including those who classify themselves as 'Yugoslavs'.

Yugoslavia came into existence in December 1918 as the Kingdom of Serbs, Croats and Slovenes at the end of World War I. It united the former Austro-Hungarian territories of Slovenia, Croatia-Slavonia, the Vojvodina, Dalmatia and Bosnia-Hercegovina, and the kingdoms of Montenegro and Serbia (including territories corresponding approximately to present-day Macedonia and Kosovo).

In 1941, during World War II, Yugoslavia was invaded by the Axis powers. The following years saw fierce resistance to the occupying forces accompanied by bitter civil war. At the end of the war, in which military and political ascendancy had been gained by the communist-led resistance movement (the Partisans) under Marshall Tito, the king was deposed and the Federal People's Republic of Yugoslavia was proclaimed in January 1946.

Under the constitution of 1974, the Socialist Federal Republic of Yugoslavia (SFRJ), as the country was renamed in 1963, was a federal state comprising six constituent republics: Bosnia-Hercegovina (of which the capital is Sarajevo); Croatia (Zagreb); Macedonia (Skopje); Montenegro (Titograd); Slovenia (Ljubljana) and Serbia (Belgrade) – which incorporates the two 'autonomous provinces' of the Vojvodina (Novi Sad) and Kosovo (Pristina). The federal capital is Belgrade.

Succeeding constitutions have been carefully worded so that while the 'right to self-determination, including the right to secession' of each of the 'Nations of Yugoslavia' is mentioned, it is asserted that these nations 'on the basis of their will freely expressed' during World War II have united. This meant that constitutionally the nations made a binding decision and the right of secession no longer applied.

However, rapid political changes beginning in 1989 saw the complete breakup of the old constitutional system. The growth of Serbian nationalism fuelled Serb discontent with the 1974 constitutional arrangement whereby the Autonomous Provinces of the Vojvodina and Kosovo were de facto republics within the Republic of Serbia. In March 1989 Serbia pushed through constitutional changes which limited the provinces' autonomy. In response to the possible threat of Serbian hegemony, and the continuing economic and political crisis which gripped the country, separatist tendencies began to emerge in Slovenia and revive in Croatia. On 27 September 1989 the Slovene Assembly overwhelmingly endorsed amendments to the Republic's Constitution which explicitly allowed the Republic to secede. The 1974 Constitution was no more.

Victory for the Croatian nationalist party in elections in Croatia underlined the split between the more prosperous Roman Catholic northern Republics of Slovenia and Croatia with their Hapsburg legacy, and the others, predominantly Serbia. On 23 December 1990 Slovenia held a plebiscite on whether the Republic should remain within what was left of the Yugoslav framework, or declare independence. The Slovenes overwhelmingly voted for independence and it seemed probable that Yugoslavia would soon cease to be.

Religion

Religion and the state were separate under the 1974 Constitution. The main Christian denominations are the Serbian and Macedonian Orthodox Churches with an estimated eight million adherents, and the Roman Catholic Church with some six million adherents, mainly Croats and Slovenes. There is also a large Muslim community, believed to number about four million, including ethnic Slavs in Bosnia-Hercegovina, most Albanians and the Turkish minority. There are over 30 other, often very small, religious communities, mostly Protestant.

Religion has historically played an important role in Yugoslavia, with Roman Catholicism, Orthodoxy and Islam meeting head on. In Bosnia, where Latin and Greek Christendom met, there emerged the Bogumil heresy – akin to the Albigenses. By the time of the Ottoman conquest in the 15th Century, Bosnia had largely reverted to Roman Catholicism mainly due to Franciscan missionaries, while Hercegovina and the extreme eastern part of Bosnia was mainly Orthodox. Bogumilism remained concentrated in northern Hercegovina where changes of faith were frequent. The new creed of Islam attracted many from all classes, especially the Bosnian nobility.

The Orthodox church traditionally has been a 'state' church and largely receptive to whatever government is in power. In Slovenia, the Catholic church was very influential in the main inter-war political party, the Slovenian People's Party. In Bosnia, the Yugoslav Muslim Organization also became a force in pre-war politics, but neither of these two inter-war religious based parties could escape their essential localism and emerge as a national force. By contrast, in Croatia in the inter-war period, the main political party, the Croatian Peasant Party (HSS), was anti-clerical.

However, after World War II, the position of the Catholic Church vis-a-vis Croatian nationalism radically changed. The Roman Catholic Church (in contrast to the Orthodox Church which has traditionally tended to be a state church) due, in no small part to its centre of allegiance, Rome, being outside the country, was seen by the new communist authorities as a dangerous rival and a full scale attack on it was mounted in 1946 with the trial of Archbishop Stepinac of Zagreb. This had the result for the first time of turning the Catholic Church in Croatia into one of the symbols of Croatian nationalism.

Despite the initial ideological frontal attack on religion of all types by the new authorities, the census of 1953 recorded that only 12.6% of the population registered as 'without religion'. Islam has also lately emerged as a potent force in Bosnia, potentially for Albanian

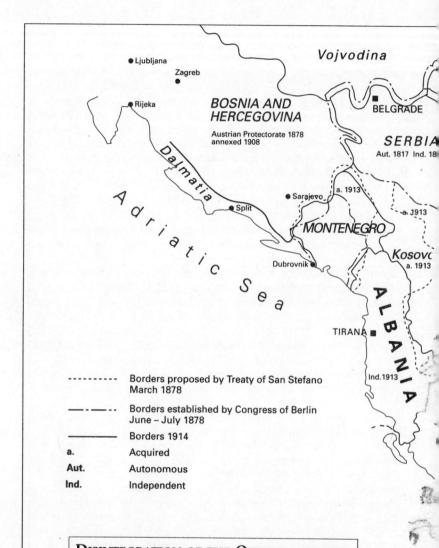

Borders proposed by Treaty of San Stefano
March 1878

Borders established by Congress of Berlin
June – July 1878

Borders 1914

a.   Acquired

Aut.   Autonomous

Ind.   Independent

DISINTEGRATION OF THE OTTOMAN EMPIRE IN THE 19TH AND EARLY 20TH CENTURY

W a l l a c h a
Aut. 1829 Ind. 1878
■ BUCHAREST
a. 1878

R O M A N I A

a. 1913

B U L G A R I A
Aut. 1878 Ind. 1908

Dobrudzha

● Varna

● Stara Zagora
Aut. 1878 To Bulgaria 1885
● Burgas

B l a c k
S e a

■ SOFIA

Eastern
Rumelia

a. 1913

● Plovdiy
(Philippopolis)

● Edirne

a. 1913

ISTANBUL ●
(Constantinople)

8

JE
ub)

a. 1913

a. 1913

T h r a c e

● Kavalla

Sea of Marmara

stir (Salonika)
Thessaloniki

A e g e a n
S e a

Ottoman
Empire

TURKEY

● Larissa
a. 1881

a. 1913

aly
a. 1830

C
E

85 MILES

135 KILOMETRES

The maps in this book are based on the Peters projection.

9

nationalism despite some observers view that religion is taken lightly by the Albanian people. An opinion poll on religious belief carried out in November 1985 in all the Yugoslav republics and autonomous regions gave the following results: Kosovo 44%; Croatia 33%; Slovenia 26%; Macedonia 19%; Bosnia and Hercegovina 17%; Serbia 11%; Vojvodina 10%; Montenegro 10%. (*Interview*, Belgrade, 28 March 1986.)

It is interesting to note that Kosovo has the highest figure, with 25% of party members declaring themselves to be believers and even 4% declaring themselves to be religious activists. Another poll (*NIN* 25 May 1986) recorded 94% of Communist Party members to be non-religious but 30% of Kosovo Communist Party members declared themselves to be religious. Albanian, Croatian and, in the latter part of the 1980s, Slovenian nationalism, appear to have correlation in religious activity and belief. The resurgence of Serbian nationalism in the late 1980s may well be reflected in a rise from the recorded low figures in 1985.

Politics

Until the momentous changes beginning in 1989, the League of Communists of Yugoslavia (SKJ) was the sole authorized political party. It controlled political life through its domination of key 'socio-political organizations' especially the Socialist Alliance of Working People of Yugoslavia (SSRNJ). After the death of President Tito (who was President of the Republic, president of the SKJ and Commander-in-Chief of the Armed Forces), the SKJ was headed by a 23-member collective leadership, the Presidium of the Central Committee, the presidency of which rotates annually. The functions of the head of state were exercised by a nine-member collegial body, the Presidency of the SFRJ, comprising representatives of each republic and autonomous province and *ex officio* the president of the SKJ Presidium. The presidency of this body rotated annually also.

In all the main legislative bodies, as in other federal bodies, the principle of equal representation of all republics and proportional representation of provinces prevailed. Thus, the Yugoslav federation was based on the principle of national equality, not ethnic proportionality and each republic practice internally a policy of national quotas – for example, in late 1989 the head of the Croatian party was a Serb. Each republic and autonomous province, in addition to its own assembly, had its own governmental apparatus and judiciary.

However, in 1989, the beginnings of political pluralism became evident, especially in Slovenia where a more liberal climate prevailed, with non-communist groups entering the SSRNJ, and the issue became widely discussed elsewhere. Parallel with the extraordinary changes taking place in neighbouring erstwhile communist states, political change in Yugoslavia accelerated with awesome speed.

Republican communist parties, usually changing their names in an attempt to distance themselves from past failures, for the first time since the war faced growing opposition from rival, non-communist, predominantly nationalist, parties. Although the growth of new parties in all republics was phenomenal – over 30 in Serbia alone – the contest rapidly became, in this first initial post-communist phase, a fight between the old communist parties (however, they were now named) and usually one main nationalist party for each ethnic group, with the Prime Minister Ante Markovic's Alliance of Reformist Forces (SRS) attempting, usually with little success, to play the united Yugoslavia position.

In republic after republic, as free elections were allowed to take place during 1990, the nationalists eclipsed the former ruling communist parties. The exceptions were Serbia (and also Montenegro) where the resurgent Serbian nationalism was initially led by the Party under Slobodan Milosevic and the socialists/communists held their ground in the face of challenges from more extreme nationalist parties. An attempt to revive the fortunes of Yugoslavia as a whole, was led by Ante Markovic, the popular Prime Minister who had some success in stabilizing the hyper-inflation and campaigned on a non-national Yugoslav basis but was not able to stem the nationalist tide.

As indicated above, Yugoslavia was always a complicated country in nationality terms, and has become even more complex as it entered the 1990s. It can be argued that as there is no majority ethnic group, all are minorities and should be treated as such and this book has attempted to cover all main groups. However, it could equally be argued that given Yugoslavia's current situation, or even the situation post-1974, the republics should be treated as separate states and thus, for example, the Slovenes in Slovenia should be seen as a huge majority rather than as a minority in Yugoslavia. In this study, special attention has been given to the most explosive, or potentially explosive, minority issues. These are:

1. **The Albanians** – both in Kosovo, where they are an overwhelming majority, and Macedonia where they form a large compact minority. Large numbers of Albanians also live in compact groups in Montenegro and Southern Serbia. The size of the minority and its conflicts,

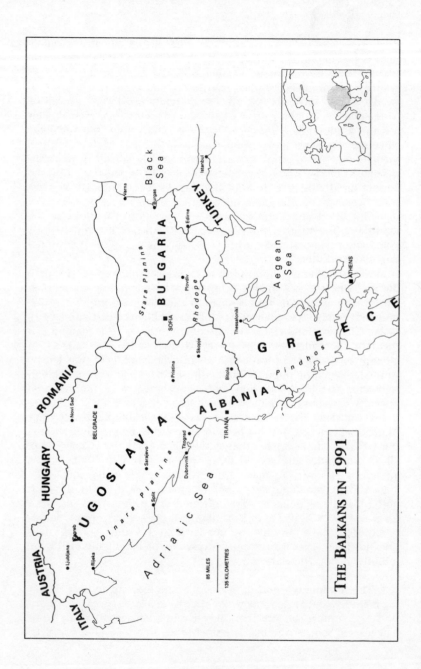

especially with the Serbs but also the Macedonians, and its geographic position bordering on Albania makes the Yugoslav Albanian question perhaps the most urgent and problematic.

2. The **Serbs** – as a minority. Although the Serbs are the largest ethnic group and form the majority in the republic of Serbia (including Vojvodina – where they are a majority – and Kosovo-Metohija), they are a small minority in Kosovo-Metohija when considered separately. There are also large vocal compact Serb settlements in Bosnia-Hercegovina and Croatia, and the problems raised by these minorities (in Kosovo-Metohija, which is technically part of the republic of Serbia, they formed a minority within a minority) further complicates the picture.

3. The **Macedonians** – are also given extensive study due to the continuing controversy as to whether they are indeed a separate people at all or merely an invention of Tito's Yugoslavia. Hostility to the idea of Macedonians as a separate Slav people has been constant in both Bulgaria and Greece and has now apparently revived also in Serbia. If Yugoslavia, which seems at least possible and even probable at the time of writing, breaks up, 'The Macedonian Question' may again be centre stage and Macedonia again become the 'cockpit of the Balkans.'

4. The (Slav) **Muslims** – pose a similar problem as to whether they are a separate nationality or not, and to any postulates about their future, if Yugoslavia does break up. There are large Muslim minorities in southern Serbia (the Sandzak) and Macedonia, as well as being the largest, but not the majority group, in Bosnia-Hercegovina.

5. The **Roma** (Gypsies) – who, in neighbouring states especially Romania, Bulgaria and Hungary, similarly form a large minority at the bottom of the social scale but who are beginning to become more active, will certainly be an important future factor.

2

THE LARGEST NATION – SERBS

The background

The largest single Yugoslav national group, although still a minority, are the Serbs. According to the 1981 census there were 8,140,507 Serbs in Yugoslavia or 36.3% of the total population of 22,427,585. Serbs live mainly in the Republic of Serbia, where they made up 85.4% of the population, without taking into consideration the Autonomous provinces of Kosovo and Vojvodina where they constituted 13.2% and 54.4%, respectively in 1981, and also in the republics of Bosnia-Hercegovina and Croatia where they constitute 32% and 11%, respectively, of the population.

Serbs settled in the Balkan Peninsula in the 7th Century. By the 12th Century the Serbs established their own state which reached the height of its power in the 14th Century based in the present-day territory of Kosovo, which although today is populated overwhelmingly by Albanians, remains emotionally part of the Serbian heartland. From the mid-15th Century until the early 1800s Serbia was occupied by the Ottoman Turks and large numbers of Serbs migrated northwards to the Vojvodina, then part of the Kingdom of Hungary in the Hapsburg empire, to escape Ottoman domination. The Vojvodina was a mosaic of 10 ethnic groups due to the desire of the Hapsburg Empire to settle different national groups there to create a bulwark against the Ottomans.

After a series of bloody uprisings, Serbia was granted autonomy within the Ottoman Empire in 1815, and in 1878 it became formally independent. However, the placing of Bosnia-Hercegovina with its large Serb population under the Hapsburg Protectorate in 1878 meant that the fledgling Serbian state, denied expansion to the north-west, looked south instead. The insistence by the Great Powers, notably Austria-Hungary, of the Ottoman Empire retaining the Sandjak of Novibazar (the Sandzak) so as to prevent Serbian unification with the Principality of Montenegro, further pointed Serbian aspirations at Macedonia.

15

After the Balkan Wars of 1912/3, Serbia expanded its territory. Following the assassination of Austrian Archduke Franz Ferdinand in Sarajevo in June 1914, Serbia defied an Austrian ultimatum and was attacked by the central powers, triggering off World War I. After great loss of life Serbia emerged as one of the victors when the new map of Europe was drawn up after the war.

Their experience of independence and heritage as well as being the largest single group, allowed the Serbs to dominate the new kingdom which became known as Yugoslavia. This led to considerable tension, especially with the Croats and after World War II there was a consistent effort to limit Serbian dominance of the new state. This was especially so after the fall in 1966 of Alexander Rankovic, a Serb, Vice-President of Yugoslavia and chief of the powerful state security police, leading eventually to the constitution of 1974 which truly made Yugoslavia a federation and, some even say, a confederation.

However, since 1988/9, especially as a result of the situation regarding the Albanians in Kosovo, there has been a Serbian backlash against what many Serbs see as discriminatory measures in the Yugoslav federation which adversely affected them, most notably the powers granted to the autonomous provinces under the 1974 constitution despite their ostensibly being part of the Serbian Republic. Also many Serbs regard the distinction between Serbs and Montenegrins as artificial.

The leadership of the League of Communists of Serbia, appealing to this resurgent national sentiment, has committed itself to reasserting Serbian control over the autonomous provinces, and also Montenegro, and in 1988 there were mass demonstrations and rallies throughout Serbia and in certain other parts of the country in support of these aims. A result of this pressure was the unprecedented downfall in 1988 of party leaderships opposed to Serbian aspirations in the autonomous provinces and in the republic of Montenegro.

Within the republic itself, the resurgent nationalism was used by the Communist Party led by Slobodan Milosevic. The growth of democracy enabled Albanian nationalist aspirations in Kosovo to move away from the sphere of 'illegal' groups to the mainstream Albanian political and cultural life. Faced with the prospect of the overwhelming majority of the province voting for at least autonomy for the Albanians (and almost certainly more in the form of equal – ie. republican – national rights for the two million strong minority) the Serbian authorities clamped down hard. In this they were supported by Serbian public opinion and the majority of Serbian opposition parties were, if anything, even more anti-Albanian and nationalistic than Milosevic and his party.

There is no doubt that Kosovo (or Kosovo-Metohija as the province was renamed by Serbia in 1990 in a symbolic reinforcement of Serbian claims on the territory) occupies a place in the Serbian national psyche which at times defies rationality. The claim that the Serbian minority in the province (a minority within a minority) was subject to Albanian repression (see below) was taken up by the Serbian intelligentsia in the mid-1980s. They and the Serbian Orthodox Church began to use the highly emotive term of 'genocide' to describe the alleged atrocities committed against Serbs, of which the most highly publicized was the case of Djordje Martinovic in May 1985 who claimed to have had a beer bottle forcibly pushed up his anus by Albanian attackers. In the ensuing climate, any inter-ethnic incident, especially rapes of Serbian women, fuelled the nationalist fires[1].

It is especially regrettable that the Serbian intelligentsia has played such a prominent role in whipping up ethnic tension which politicians like Milosevic have used for their own ends. In comparison to Bulgaria where the authorities' attempt to forcibly discriminate against the ethnic Turks (the Bulgarians' traditional enemy) has been publicly criticized by leading members of the Bulgarian intelligentsia, in Serbia the reverse appears to be the case, with the laudable exception of some noteworthy individuals such as the Yugoslav Helsinki Federation member, Tanya Petovar.

Two examples of this trend are Vuk Draskovic, the renowned novelist and leader of The Serbian Renewal Movement whose Serbian nationalism is not only directed at Kosovo Albanians but also at Macedonia which he classifies as South Serbia in line with pre-war Great Serb policies, and Vojislav Seselj – a Serb who was sentenced in Sarajevo in 1984 to six years' imprisonment for his courageous stand against local Stalinist bureaucracy, but who has since his release shown himself to be an extreme nationalist and leader of the Serbian *Chetnik* movement, with similar views to Draskovic on the Yugoslav national question.

The Belgrade intellectuals' petition of January 1986

While it is unfair to paint the whole Serbian intelligentsia with the Draskovic/Seselj brush, intellectual opponents of the rising tide of Serbian nationalism have increasingly become politically marginalized. An important point in this process was the 'genocide' petition of January 1986. This crucial document signalled the real beginning of the rise of Serbian nationalism which Slobodan Milosevic has been so successful in riding.

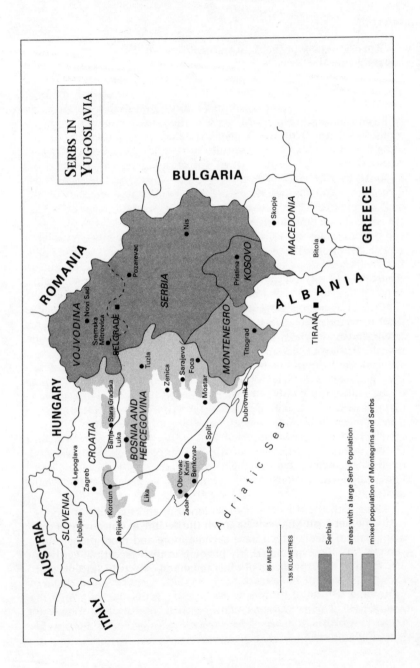

SERBS IN YUGOSLAVIA

AUSTRIA

ITALY

SLOVENIA

Ljubljana

HUNGARY

CROATIA

Lepoglava

Zagreb

Kordun

Rijeka

Lika

Zadar

Obrovac
Knin
Benkovac

Split

Banja
Luka

Stara Gradiska

BOSNIA AND
HERCEGOVINA

Zenica

Mostar

Tuzla

Sarajevo
Foca

Dubrovnik

ROMANIA

VOJVODINA

Novi Sad

Sremska
Mitrovica

BELGRADE

Pozarevac

SERBIA

Nis

BULGARIA

MONTENEGRO

Titograd

KOSOVO

Pristina

MACEDONIA

Skopje

Bitola

GREECE

ALBANIA

TIRANA

A d r i a t i c   S e a

85 MILES

135 KILOMETRES

Serbia

areas with a large Serb Population

mixed population of Montegrins and Serbs

18

The petition, signed by some 200 prominent Belgrade intellectuals constituting a highly representative cross-section of the Belgrade intelligentsia and professional middle classes including Orthodox priests and retired army officers, was sent to the Yugoslav and Serbian national assemblies. It accused the authorities of condoning national treason and 'genocide' against the Serb minority in Kosovo.[2] Among the signatories were Zaga Golubovic, Mihajlo Markovic and Ljubo Tadic, soon to be joined by Milan Kangrga – all former editors of *Praxis*, the theoretical Marxist publication which hitherto had been so critical of nationalism. In the late 1960s these same editors had roundly condemned the Croatian *Maspok*. Their signatures on the petition along with people like Dobrica Cosic, the renowned Serbian novelist, gave a clear signal that Serbian nationalism was a force to be reckoned with and encompassed the whole political spectrum of the Serbian intelligentsia. Its clear call not only for protection of the Serb minority in Kosovo, but also for changes in the relationship between Kosovo and the Vojvodina and Serbia, presaged the future limiting of the autonomy of the provinces.

As noted above, there is some justice in the Serb claim that the position of the autonomous regions as defined in the 1974 constitutional arrangement was anomalous. Likewise the claims of Seselj and others that the nations of Moslems, Montenegrins and even Macedonians are artificial and work to the disadvantage of the Serbian nation – there is perhaps more to such claims as regards the Montenegrins, less regarding the Muslims of Bosnia and very little regarding Serb claims over Macedonians (see CHAPTER 4). However, this cannot justify the almost 'laagar' mentality which has become prevalent among Serbs which manifests itself in almost complete disregard for anyone else – even to the extent of apparently not caring about the adverse publicity caused by local Serb officials in Kosovo arresting and expelling international human rights observers like those from the International Helsinki Federation.[3]

Along with the rise of Serbian nationalism and the political domination of Slobodan Milosevic has been the decline in objectivity of the main Serbian media which have become more and more propaganda vehicles for Milosevic and rabidly pro-Serb in their reporting. Partly as a reaction to this, the media in other republics, especially Slovenia and Croatia, has tended to become more and more anti-Serb but has not fallen to the levels of the Serb media. The decline in standards of newspapers like the *Belgrade Politika* and the weekly *NIN* following Milosevic's takeover of the Serbian political apparatus in the second half of 1980s, can only be regretted and the almost hysterical tone of their reportage have helped keep Serbian nationalist passions used by Milosevic at fever pitch. Belgrade's journalists have protested at the blatant editorial manipulation, and in December, a week before Milosevic was re-elected president of Serbia, journalists from Politika and Belgrade's main radio and television stations demonstrated for the immediate dismissal of their editors – a hopeful sign.

However, the overwhelming success of the former Serbian Communist Party, now called the Socialist Party of Serbia (SPS) led by Milosevic in the December 1990 elections – the SPS won 194 of the 250 seats with Draskovic's party, the Serbian Renaissance Movement coming second with 19 – and Milosevic's successful re-election as president does not bode well for the immediate future. Milosevic appears to have ridden the nationalist tiger and subjugated the Serbian press in an almost Stalinist manner. It is likely that he will continue to play the demagogue to Serbian nationalism, and unsubstantiated stories with headlines like 'Fascist Terrorists Sent to Subjugate Serbs' will continue to feature in the main Serbian media and further inflame passions.[4]

Milosevic quickly showed his attitude to the Yugoslav federation in December 1990 by passing a secret law enabling the unauthorised issue of over $18 million worth of money – an amount almost half of all the loans to banks in the country – planned to be raised from the money issue in 1991. This measure was roundly condemned by the Federal Executive Council and obliged the Yugoslav National Bank to take measures to combat it.[5] On 30 January, a group of Serbia's leading opposition figures initiated the formation of the Pan- Serbian Council for National Salvation which called for either an integral Yugoslavia with no republican border or a united Serb state of Serbia, Montenegro, Bosnia-Hercegovina and parts of Macedonia[6] showing again the strength of Serbian nationalism.

The Serbs as minorities

Serbs living outside of the republic of Serbia in 1981 in every case except Montenegro had a higher percentage of Communist Party members than their percentage of the population. Taking 100 to indicate parity between the two percentages, the figures for Serbs and Montenegerins were as follows:[7]

Republic Province	Serbs	Montenegrins
Slovenia	255	(n/a)
Croatia	200	343
Macedonia	122	(n/a)
Bosnia-Hercegovina	129	313
Montengro	61	120
Vojvodina	125	258
Kosovo	148	279
Serbia (proper)	96	237

Another way of putting it is that one out of every four Montenegrins was a Communist Party member, nearly one out of every six Serbs, one out of every six or seven 'ethnically uncommitted' (ie. those declaring themselves to be Yugoslavs), similarly for Macedonians, then every seventh or eighth Muslim, every 10th or 11th Croat, every 11th Albanian and Slovene, and finally less than every 12th Hungarian.[8]

Similarly in the JNA (the Yugoslav army) professional command, Serbs and Montenegrins predominate. Taking into account the similarity between Serbs and Montenegrins it is hard to escape the conclusion that the post-war communist Yugoslav state was supported by Serbs (and Montenegrins) more than by other groups. The success of the Communist Party in Serbia and Montenegro and its failure elsewhere reinforces this view.

Serbs in Kosovo

The situation of the Serb minority in Kosovo, and repeated petitions and demonstrations by Kosovo Serbs in Belgrade has, as detailed above, been instrumental in the rise of Serbian nationalism and has acted as a catalyst to Serb sensibilities. The constitutional changes which have reduced the autonomy of the province and effectively incorporated it into the body of the Serbian Republic have turned the legal position of the Serb minority there into that of part of the majority of Serbia. However, Serb (and Montenegrin) emigration from Kosovo continues despite political leaders' statements of mass repatriation of Serbs back to Kosovo to counter the swelling Albanian presence there.

Within Kosovo itself a Serb nationalist group, *Bozur*, led by Bogdan Kecman and based in Kosovo Polje outside Pristina, is attempting to put these words into action and aims at a 50% ethnic split in Kosovo between Serbs and Albanians.[9] Such policies appear to be totally unrealistic even with the possible implementation of the Serbian government's proposal to settle some of Romania's 50,000 Serbs from the Banat in Kosovo, and little more than empty rhetoric from the likes of Milosevic to his Serbian audience. It is as likely that Serbs (and Albanians) are emigrating for economic reasons – Kosovo being extremely backward with high unemployment – as for reasons of ethnic tension although these must surely play a part.

The Serbian Orthodox Church has been in the forefront of alleging outrages against the local Serbs by ethnic Albanians[10] often with little attempt at impartiality – any offence which involves the two nationalities however trivial, is seen as part of a deliberate anti-Serb Albanian master plan of 'genocide'. While in the deteriorating climate in Kosovo it would be ingenuous to say that there have been no provocations by ethnic Albanians against Serbs, there appears to be no basis for the highly emotive charge of 'genocide'. The current situation whereby the ethnic Albanians are denied all autonomy and the province is under effective Serbian-dominated military rule with local Serbs in control cannot last indefinitely, and seems certain to make any rapprochement between ethnic Albanians and Serbs in Kosovo even harder in the future. Appeals to ancient history are not sufficient. If and when the ethnic Albanians in Kosovo are allowed their real autonomy, it is likely that the exodus of the Serb minority will accelerate, not slow down, and the minority may even effectively disappear.

Serbs in Bosnia-Hercegovina

The Serbs in Bosnia-Hercegovina make up over 30% of the population of the republic. They constitute an absolute majority of all of eastern Bosnia-Hercegovina (Bileca, Gacko, Ljubinje, Nevesinje and Trebinje). They also constitute majorities or relative majorities in parts of western Bosnia in the opstinas of Bosanska Grahovo (85.7%), Titov Drvar (88.4%), Bosanski Petrovac (68%), Banja Luka (50.9%), Bosanska Dubica (66.3%), Bosanska Gradiska (56.5%), Bosanski Novi (59.6%), Celinac (86.3%), Glamoc (78.7%), Kljuc (51.9%), Laktasi (78.2%),

Mrkonjic-Grad (78.7%), Prnjavor (70.9%), Skender Vakuf (69.5%), Srbac (85.8%), and Sipovo (79.5%). These Serb-dominated areas are divided by the solidly Muslim opstinas of Velika Kladusa (88.4% Muslim), Bihac (61%), Cazin (97%), and Bosanska Krupa (67.7%).

In July 1990 the Serbian Democratic Party of Bosnia-Hercegovina (SDS-BH) was founded in Sarajevo with the objective of reviving Serbian political life in the republic. This party was an offshoot of the main rallying force for Serbs outside of Serbia – the Serbian Democratic Party in Croatia. Young Bosnia, a more radical group of Serbs with para-military overtones (named after the group which was responsible for the assassination of Archduke Ferdinand in 1914), was also in operation and had close ties with Vuk Draskovic's SPO but its numbers and influence were small.[11]

SDS-BH leader Radovan Karadzic in an interview with *NIN*, the Belgrade weekly, clearly outlined the Bosnian Serbs' grievances which had built up over some time. These were that the Serbs of Bosnia-Hercegovina were an integral part of the Serb nation and that the Serbs in particular had been forced to give up more than other national groups in post-war Yugoslavia. In Bosnia-Hercegovina this meant 'giving up their very substance, names, national culture, traditions, they [Serbs] have had to turn their backs on their Serbian Orthodox Church in ruins...This resulted in the exile of several hundreds of thousands of Serbs from Bosnia-Hercegovina.' He also alleged that Serbian regions had been deliberately partitioned to weaken them and gave the example of Ozren, 'a compact and well-defined Serbian region partitioned among five municipalities'.[12]

SDS-BH on 11 October announced the formation of a Serbian National Council to be held at an all-Serbian assembly in Banja Luka on 13 October. At the same time the SDS-BH voiced its concern at the inadequacies of social self-defence in the event of a future civil war.[13] In the elections of December 1990 the SDS-BH confirmed its leading role as the political expression of the Serbs in Bosnia-Hercegovina by winning 72 of the 85 seats won by Serbs out of the 240 seats to both chambers.[14]

Despite the ethnic voting in Bosnia-Hercegovina, and at times, the hard-line rhetoric there were signs of rapprochement between the leaders of the three groups immediately after the elections, and Muslim leaders Alija Izetbegovic and Muhamed Filpovic were both speakers at the founding SDS-BH meeting welcoming the new organization.[15] Such signs give some cause for encouragement in this area where there has been so much mutual bloodshed in the recent past. If Yugoslavia is to survive in any form at all then such mutual understanding in Bosnia-Hercegovina will be crucial. A less encouraging note was struck by reports of Serbs fleeing Hercegovina after alleged harassment in western regions by Croats[16] – such reports are hard to assess.

Serbs of Croatia

Serbs make up about 12% of the population of Croatia according to the 1981 census. They live in concentrated areas mostly bordering on Bosnia-Hercegovina to which they migrated mostly in the 17th Century to escape Ottoman pressure. Their Orthodox faith helped to keep them distinct from their Catholic Croat neighbours. As noted above, they have held a disproportionately high number of key posts in the republic, especially after the ending of the Croatian *Maspok*. As shown above, in 1981 Serbs were over- represented in the Communist Party by a factor of two. Other more recent figures indicate higher numbers. According to Franjo Tudjman, immediately prior to the elections in April 1990, Serbs made up 40% of the Croatian Communist Party, eight out of 12 senior editors in Radio Zagreb and 60% of the police'[17] and the Sarejevo daily, *Oslobodjenje*, of 11 August 1990, stated that 67% of Croatia's police force were Serbs.

When the political relaxation came to Croatia in late 1989 and early 1990, the Serbs saw themselves faced with resurgent Croatian nationalism which the Communist Party seemed powerless to combat, and quickly began to organize themselves. Serbs saw new Croatian parties formed and tended to see a 'purge' of Serbs at the top levels of the Croatian party.

Again Kosovo was used as a symbol of Serbianism. With the Croatian leadership becoming increasingly unwilling to support Serbia's repressive policies in Kosovo, 'letters of truth' – from the 'Kordun children' (Serb colonists who had moved from the Kordun region to the Vojvodina)- were circulated calling on ethnic Serbs from Kordun and Karlovac to gather in Karlovac bus station on 4 February 1990 so that they could be told 'the real truth about Kosovo'. A Serbian cultural society, *Zora*, was set up and plans for a similar one in Topusk to be called *Savl Mrkali* were made. At a meeting at Lika in Donji Lapac, attended by Zora's president, Jovan Opacic, and other Zora directors, the genesis of a new party was created.[18] The moving spirit behind it was the undoubted leader of the Serbs in Croatia, Sibenik psychiatrist Dr Jovan Raskovic, and in February 1990 the Serbian Democratic Party (SDS) was founded in Knin – a Serb stronghold with Raskovic as leader and Opacic as vice-president.

During the election campaign Tudjman pledged that Croatia's Serbs would have cultural autonomy but said that the HDZ would stop short of granting them political autonomy.[19] Following his election triumph, Tudjman, in a statesmanlike manner offered Raskovic the vice-presidency of the Croatian parliament. Raskovic dragged out negotiations and eventually refused[20] but the Serb Simo Rajic, a former communist functionary, was appointed instead.

However, this was not enough to allay Serb fears. Tudjman has so far significantly failed to be seen as president of Croatia as opposed to president of the Croatians and failed to visit Serb majority areas after the election. A new flag and other symbols helped stir already present Serb fears of a return to the Ustasha period. Many Serbs left the police force and their replacements, inevitably predominantly Croat, and new uniforms and names, further revived Serb memories of the war period.[21] Tension increased throughout the summer and finally exploded in Knin.

The unrest in Knin and beyond

Knin has for some years been a centre of tension between Serbs and Croats with a number of nationalist incidents between the different nationalities. The Serbs, especially in and around Knin, rely almost entirely on Belgrade media which, with the rise of Milosevic, has become more and more partial to the point of broadcasting outright lies. A central point in Belgrade's disinformation campaign was the allegation that Tudjman was an Ustasha and was planning genocide against Croatia's Serbs. Similarly the Croatian press tended to give a less extreme version, but often one-sided view, of the events which were very critical of Serbia and Serbs in Croatia.

In late July 1990 the Serbian National Council (SNC), an unofficial parliament of Serbs in Croatia, first declared autonomy for Croatia's Serbs. On 1 August Serb activists called for a referendum on Serbian autonomy to be held in Serb majority areas. On 3 August the Croatian authorities banned the referendum but the Serbs went ahead anyway. The Croatian authorities further antagonized Serb sensibilities by ordering the removal of Cyrillic signs.

A virtual insurrection followed. Armed Serb civilians patrolled the streets of the Knin-Benkovac areas on 16-18 August with some complicity by the Serb-dominated officer corps of the JNA but not as much as some initial reports indicated (reporting on events from Knin and other Serb areas in Croatia has often been highly suspect)[22]. For a short period control of these areas had passed to Serb irregular forces and civil war appeared to be beckoning. On the more radical wing of the SDS this was definitely envisaged. Dusan Zelenbaba, deputy for Knin, said at a meeting in Banja Luka in early August that Serbs in Croatia were already arming and would soon form a Serbian Dinaric Corps to topple the 'Ustasha' government.[23]

In the event major hostilities did not happen and the referendum was held from 19 August to 2 September with ballot slips distributed which merely stated 'For Serbian Autonomy: Yes or No. Despite the deliberately vague wording the organizers of the referendum described it as referring to cultural autonomy (providing Yugoslavia remained a federation) in the shape of Serbian schools using the Cyrillic script and teaching Serbian history, and a television station serving the Serb majority areas of Knin-Benkovac, Lika, Kordun, Banija and Slavonija. The organizers explicitly held that the referendum would also declare territorial autonomy if Yugoslavia became a confederation.[24]

The Croatian authorities rejected this referendum and ordered that arms of police reserve units in the Serb-dominated areas be reduced by 60%. This sparked off Serbian riots on 28 and 29 September involving several hundred people in Petrinja, Dvor na Uni and Donji Lapac near Knin. Quantities of arms were taken by the rioters and telephone lines were cut in Knin. On 29 September in Petrinja a crowd of Serbs went to the police barracks requesting JNA protection and the Croatian Interior Ministry reported that police had been shot at. Again the spectre of civil war loomed large with broadcasts by Radio Knin of the formation of a 'Council of National Resistance' which said, 'The Serbian nation has not risen against the Croatian nation, but will resist the Ustashas until the last drop of blood'.[25] Belgrade media again stirred up passions by announcing that 360 people ('innocent Serbs') had been arrested in the Sisak region but this was denied and the actual figure was 22, of whom 19 were immediately released.[26]

On 1 October at Srb the SNC announced the results of the referendum. In Croatia 567,317 people took part of whom 567,127 voted for and 144 against, with 46 invalid ballots. The SNC also announced that the referendum had been prevented by Croatian police in areas including Split, Sibenik and other areas so that over 150,000 Croatian Serbs were unable to participate. A statement signed by Milan Babic, Knin's mayor and SNC president, declared 'Serbian autonomy on the ethnic and historic territories populated by the Serbian people within the existing borders of the Republic of Croatia, as a federal unit of the SFRJ.'[27] On 12 December the presidium of municipalities in Croatia with a Serb majority approved the 'Outline of a Statute of the Community of Municipalities of Northern Dalmatia and Lika – a Serbian

Autonomous Region (Prefecture)'.[28] This move was speedily and predictably annulled by the Croatian Constitutional Court. Undeterred, Croatia's Serbs continued to assert their autonomy and on 4 January 1991 the 'Serbian Region of Krajina in Croatia' – unrecognized by the Croatian authorities – announced the formation of its own Internal Affairs Secretariat.[29] On 26 January, Raskovic announced a forthcoming Serbian Assembly to be founded in Croatia with one representative for every 5000 Serbs and representatives from the Serbian Orthodox Church.[30] How effective the January 1991 federal ban on armed groups outside the army has been in the Serb regions of Croatia is debatable.

Thus, the Serbs of Croatia have now claimed what Serbia has denied the far more numerous ethnic Albanians in Kosovo. A moot point is how close is the SDS to the Milosevic camp. Raskovic has given conflicting statements on this: at times he has denied that Serbia had anything to do with organizing the referendum and even disagreeing with Serbia's policies towards Croats in Serbia; while at other times he has praised Milosevic as the 'paradigm of all that is Serbian' and similar sentiments.[31]

The situation remains extremely tense. Milosevic confirmed that if Yugoslavia was to become a confederation, then the borders would have to be reconsidered. The inference is clear – a Greater Serbia including those areas of Bosnia-Hercegovina and Croatia where Serbs make a majority but where large numbers of Croats and Muslims also live.[32] The threat of outright civil war remains. An encouraging sign was the recent action by a group of Catholic and Orthodox priests in Prakac appealing for mutual understanding[33] – this in marked contrast to the hitherto position of the Serbian Orthodox Church which, similarly in Kosovo, has hysterically accused the Croats of violent persecution and oppression against Serbs.[34] However, with the resignation on 5 January of Simo Rajic – the remaining Serb in high office in the republic – complaining of Croatian domination[35], the outlook does not look promising.

3

THE CATHOLIC NORTH –
CROATS AND SLOVENES

The Croats

The Croats are the second largest national grouping in Yugoslavia. In 1981 they numbered 4,428,043 or just under 20% of the population. Croats live mainly in Croatia and Bosnia-Hercegovina. They make up 70% of the population of the republic of Croatia – Serbs make up 11% and 'Yugoslavs' make up some 8%. Croats also make up just over 18% of the population of Bosnia-Hercegovina.

Like the Serbs, the Croats settled in present-day Yugoslavia in the 7th Century but an independent Croat state lasted only until 1102. From then onwards Croatia belonged first to the Kingdom of Hungary and then to the Hapsburg Empire. The Croats are overwhelmingly Catholic and use the Latin alphabet, as opposed to the Serbs who are Orthodox and who use the Cyrillic alphabet. Both speak Serbo-Croat although it is sometimes claimed that Croatian is a separate language to Serbian.

Relations between Serbs and Croats were strained in the post-1918 state and the Ustasha, a Croatian separatist and pro-fascist underground movement, was founded in the early 1930s. During World War II, an 'Independent State of Croatia' (incorporating Bosnia-Hercegovina) was established under Axis protection. It was administered by the Ustasha, who, under Ante Pavelic, persecuted and killed Jews, Serbs, Romanies and Croatian opponents of the regime. Memories of this infamous period live on, compounded by reprisals against Croats by Serb partisan units.

Croatia, which includes most of the Dalmatian coast, the main tourist attraction, is responsible for some 50% of the country's foreign trade and the major foreign currency earner. This has been a source of constant tension with Croats resenting having to share this revenue with the other republics and a feeling that Croats are once more the victims of Serb domination. Some groups, especially in the large Croat

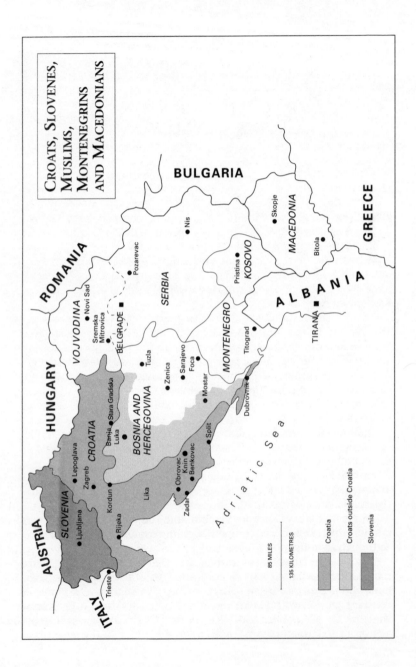

CROATS, SLOVENES,
MUSLIMS,
MONTENEGRINS
AND MACEDONIANS

BULGARIA

GREECE

MACEDONIA
Skopje
Bitola

ROMANIA

Nis

Pozarevac

SERBIA

KOSOVO
Pristina

ALBANIA
TIRANA

VOJVODINA
Novi Sad
Sremska
Mitrovica
BELGRADE

MONTENEGRO
Titograd

HUNGARY

Tuzla

Sarajevo
Zenica   Foca

BOSNIA AND
HERCEGOVINA

Banja Stara Gradiska
Luka

CROATIA

Mostar

Dubrovnik

Adriatic Sea

Lepoglava

Zagreb

Kordun

Lika

Obrovac
Knin Benkovac

Split

SLOVENIA
Ljubljana

Rijeka

Zadar

AUSTRIA

ITALY
Trieste

85 MILES

135 KILOMETRES

Croatia

Croats outside Croatia

Slovenia

30

diaspora, have consistently called for an independent Croatia and Croatian nationalism has always been viewed with official hostility.

However, the late 1960s saw the growth of an increasingly assertive nationalism in Croatia which was supported by both members and non-members of the Croatian League of Communists. This 'mass movement', as it became to be called, mushroomed dramatically with organizations like the ostensibly cultural *Matica Hrvatska* increasingly challenging party rule. The 'mass movement', known as *Maspok*, was abruptly curbed in December 1971 by the arrest of its leading members and a purge of the Croatian League of Communists initiated at the 21st session of the SKJ Presidium. Those purged included the leading 'triumvirate' of the Croatian party – Miko Tripalo, Savka Dapcevic-Kucar, and Pero Pirker. Many of those arrested (reportedly some 550 in Zagreb alone)[36] were soon released. Others were tried in 1972, charged with crimes 'against the people and state'. According to official statistics[37] 427 people in Croatia were convicted in 1972 of offenses 'against the people and state' with many sentenced to up to seven years' imprisonment including Vlado Gotovac, Dr. Franjo Tudjman and Dr. Marko Veselica.

All three were released by the end of 1977 but were later again imprisoned. The purging of the Croatian party was in turn followed by a purge of reformers in the Serbian party apparatus as the government tried to avoid the stigma of vendetta against any single national group as well as reaffirming control. Matica Hrvatska, seen by the authorities as nationalist and separatist in orientation, was abolished in 1971 and would remain so until December 1990. The result of the Croatian Maspok was the expulsion of many able reformers within the party and the new constitution of 1974.

Following the failure of the 'mass movement', any manifestation of Croat nationalism was liable to be severely punished with orders clearly emanating from the political leadership. The Yugoslav daily paper *Borba* reported on 13 February 1981 that the President of the Croatian Assembly, Jure Bilic, had 'mentioned the illegal activity of the well-known nationalists Gotovac, Veselica and Tudjman, and in this connection had announced the forthcoming trials of the latter two' (although investigation proceedings in the case of Dr. Marko Veselica had not even started at that time). On 12 February 1981 the Zagreb paper *Vjesnik* reported that Jure Bilic had declared: '...because of the situation in our country we must expose this group around Veselica, Gotovac and others, regardless of what they used to be, because by their actions objectively they are heading for fascism.' The inference was clear and to be repeated in countless political trials against Croats in the future – Croatian nationalism, because of the Ustasha wartime period, was, in official eyes, inextricably linked to fascism.

On 20 February 1981, Dr. Tudjman, a historian and retired partisan general, was sentenced to three years' imprisonment for interviews he gave to foreign journalists in which he expressed his view that the official figures for Serbian losses in World War II had been deliberately greatly exaggerated as a weapon against the Croats – the Ustasha regime being responsible for many of those deaths. (Conversely another retired partisan, the Serb, Terzic, who on the same topic gave a greatly exaggerated figure, according to official figures, for Serb losses, was not so prosecuted.) On 5 June, Vlado Gotovac was sentenced to two years' imprisonment and on 9 September, Dr. Marko Veselica, a former Communist Party official and economics don, was sentenced to 11 years' because of an interview he gave to a foreign journalist in which he claimed Croatia was unfairly disadvantaged within the Yugoslav federation, and because he was alleged to have sent abroad documents about human rights abuses in Yugoslavia. Along with these leading Croat nationalists, many other Croats were imprisoned for alleged nationalist activity in the 1980s. Such cases often involved migrant workers who had contact abroad with emigre Croat groups hostile to SFRJ.

In the 1980s Croatia continued to be closely ruled by the Croatian League of Communists which had an extremely high percentage of Serbs in its ranks in view of the population figures and a correspondingly low percentage of Croats. In 1981, in Zagreb 47.43% of the Serbian population were party members while the figure for Croats was only 11.43%.[38] These and other figures combined with the continuing clamp-down on any form of Croatian nationalism, helped fuel sentiment that the Yugoslav state was Serb dominated at Croatia's expense and merely a continuation of the old pre-war Yugoslavia.

Inevitably when the relaxation came in 1989/1990, Croatian nationalism again became a powerful force and those politicians who benefited most tended to be those who had proved their 'loyalty to the nation' in the dark years – often by long prison sentences. Marko Veselica became a leading figure of the Croatian Democratic Party, Vlado Gotovac was elected president of Matica Hrvatska when it was re-opened on 8 December 1990[39] but the real winner was Franjo Tudjman who formed the Croatian Democratic Community (HDZ) which quickly became a mass party. The ruling Communist Party, similarly to other republics, changed its name to League of Communists of Croatia-Party of Democratic Changes (LCC-SDP) and introduced a first-past-the-post system for the elections in April 1990, as it apparently reckoned that this system would help it maintain its supremacy.

In the election campaign Tudjman, playing unashamedly to Croatian nationalism, raised the notions of 'Greater Croatia' and its 'natural frontiers' (ie. Bosnia) and the HDZ staged parades through Serbian towns in Croatia. HDZ posters with the slogan 'God in the Heavens and Tudjman in the Homelands' rammed the message home.[40] Such appeals inflamed Serbs and at a rally on 4 March of some 50,000 Serbs at Mount Petrova Gora in Croatia there were slogans shouted for Tudjman's assassination. At the founding meeting of the HDZ branch in Benkovac on 18 March, there was an attempted assassination on him.[41] This helped fuel Croat fears of renewed 'Serbian domination' and cassettes of the assassination attempt, entitled 'Firing on Croatia', soon appeared in the markets.

At the election the HDZ was the main beneficiary of the voting system. Many voters abstained. In all three rounds of the elections the HDZ failed to get a majority of the votes, winning some 42% of votes cast, but won 67.5% of the seats to the Chamber of the Assembly of Croatia and 51.8% to the Chamber of Associated Labour. Tudjman became the republic's president but somewhat allayed fears by appointing a Serb as assembly vice-president. (In fact Tudjman had pledged the Croatian Serbs cultural autonomy during the election campaign and there is little basis for the Serbs' accusations of him being a Ustasha reincarnation.) The new authorities in Croatia, however, were quickly faced by serious challenge from the Serb minority in the east of the republic in Knin and elsewhere which threatened civil war (see CHAPTER 2). In these Serb-dominated areas the Croats are a minority and there were reports of discrimination against them.[42]

Events in Croatia tended to follow those in Slovenia with a natural alliance between the two Catholic former Hapsburg territories faced with Milosevic's Serbia. On 25 July the National Assembly (*Sabor*) adopted constitutional amendments declaring Croatia's sovereignty[43] and in November the leadership announced that it would be in charge of territorial defence – Croatia having had similar problems with the JNA (army) as Slovenia[44].

The HDZ also organized in Bosnia-Hercegovina – HDZ(BH) – and quickly became the main party for Croats there. However, there was some tension between the HDZ leadership in Zagreb and those in Sarajevo. Following a meeting in Zagreb on 7 September, HDZ(BH) President Davor Perinovic was expelled from the party with Tudjman reportedly revealing Perinovic's Orthodox Christian birth certificate. This dismissal was challenged by the HDZ(BH) on 9 September but remained in force and Stjepan Kljuic took over as acting leader of

HDZ(BH).[45] In the December elections the HDZ(BH) was confirmed as the political party of the Bosnian Croats when it won 44 of the 240 seats to the assembly. A total of 49 seats were won by Croats as opposed to 99 by Muslims and 85 by Serbs, reflecting the national structure of the republic.[46]

Croats make up just over 5% of the population of the Vojvodina and in the December elections in Serbia the Democratic Alliance of Croats in the Vojvodina won one seat in the 250 seat assembly to the whole republic.

There is no doubting the strength of Croat nationalism and the historic Serb-Croat tension which has so bedevilled Yugoslavia throughout its existence. The Croat experience when they negotiated with the powerful centre for rights, in the Hapsburg Empire of the second half of the 19th Century, was at odds with the Serb experience of independence, and the difference showed in the new Yugoslav state. Large sections of the Croat community both within and outside of Yugoslavia, have consistently been hostile to the whole notion of Yugoslavia. Often this opposition was heavily coloured with Catholic antagonism to the Orthodox Serbs (although ironically it was a Catholic prelate, Bishop Strossmayer, who was a leading personality in establishing the groundwork for the founding of Yugoslavia in the first place).

Tension between Croatia and the Serbi dominated JNA threatened to produce a major crisis in early 1991. The Federal Presidency ordered the disarming of all armed units outside the JNA in early January. Croatia claimed that this measure should be directed at the armed Serb-groups in Knin and elsewhere and not at its own territorial defence groups. On 21 January, the Croatian Defence Ministry called on JNA reserves not to obey a reported JNA call-up without confirmation from the relevant municiapal secretariat for national defence.[47]

This was followed by revelations of arms deals between Croatia and Hungary and accusations of involvement by Lieutenant General (retired) Martin Spegelj – Croatia's defence minister – in a supposed conspiracy against the Yugoslav state and organizing terrorist bands armed with illegal weapons. Hungary at first denied the arms trading allegations but then confirmed them. Croatia refused to hand Spegelj over to the JNA military prosecutor and the situation remained tense. It seems that the JNA stopped supplying arms to Croatian and Slovene security units after the victory for non-communist nationalists.

With Milosevic's triumph in Serbia the chances of reconciliation seem to have receded and Croatia is likely to follow Slovenia's path towards independence and a possible future Catholic union. Whether such a scenario is economically possible is debatable. However, Croatia does have most of Yugoslavia's spectacular coastline with its tourism potential. A by-product of the deterioration of Serb-Croat relations has been the boycott by Serbs of the Dalmatian coast to Croatia's temporary disadvantage. However, in purely national terms, independence for the relatively homogenous Slovenia is comparatively easy. Croatia with its large vocal Serb minority which has already shown itself willing to envisage armed struggle, and the problem of Bosnia-Hercegovina with the Croatian claims on the Muslims as well as the sizeable Croat minority there, make the future very unclear and very threatening.

The Slovenes

The Slovenes account for just under 8% of the population and live predominantly in the republic of Slovenia in the north-west of the country. Slovenia is the most homogenous of the republics with Slovenes accounting for some 90% of the population. Slovenia, along with Croatia, belonged to the Hapsburg Empire until 1918 and culturally the Slovenes look more to Western Europe than do many of their compatriots. The Slovene language, although Slavic, differs considerably from Serbo-Croat, and the Catholic Church is firmly entrenched.

Slovenia is the most developed region of Yugoslavia and has the highest per capita income. The economic gap between Slovenia and the more backward southern regions, especially Kosovo, Macedonia and Montenegro, continues to widen and Slovenia has come to rely on migrant labour from the poorer Yugoslav republics, which in recent years has on occasions resulted in ethnic tension between Slovenes and their 'guest-workers'. While the Yugoslav federation has proved a convenient market for Slovenian goods there is a current of feeling in Slovenia which resents Slovenia paying a relatively large amount into the federal budget to help develop the poorer southern regions.

Slovenia has for many years been by far the most liberal of the republics with a good human rights record which has contrasted greatly with other areas. The resurgent Serbian nationalism led by Slobodan Milosevic and the continuing economic and political crisis which grips the country have in the past year fuelled separatist tendencies. On 27 September 1989, the Slovene Assembly overwhelmingly endorsed amendments to the Republic's Constitution which explicitly allowed the republic to secede. This provoked Serbia and the Serb-dominated command of the army, the JNA, which has tended to see itself as the guardian of Yugoslavia's integrity, and since then relations between the two republics have deteriorated with Slovenia seemingly inexorably moving towards total independence.

There has also been widespread sympathy among Slovenian public opinion for the plight of ethnic Albanians in Kosovo. For example, the Slovene youth federation in November 1989 published a book in defence of Azem Vllasi, the ethnic Albanian Kosovo leader arrested on charges of counter-revolution.[48] Such moves, combined with the Slovene Assembly's decision on the possibility of secession, further antagonized Serbia, and in response the Serbs led by Milosevic planned to repeat the mass rallies held in 1988 in Vojvodina and Montenegro which helped unseat local politicians and replace them with those more sympathetic to Milosevic/Serbian sensibilities. Some 5000 Kosovo Serbs and Montenegrins announced their intention of travelling to Ljubljana for 'a rally of truth' on 1 December to put Serbia's side of the Kosovo events to the Slovene public. The Slovene authorities first banned the rally on 21 November by prohibiting gatherings of more than 30 people and closed the Slovenian borders to any buses, trains or cars carrying Serb demonstrators.[49] Milosevic responded by calling for an economic boycott of Slovenia and by the end of January when the boycott had reached its peak, 229 Serbian enterprises had suspended business relations with 207 Slovene enterprises.[50]

Such activity only helped to fuel Slovene nationalism both from within the ruling Communist Party and in the newly formed opposition party, the DEMOS, which at a press conference on 13 December 1989 presented its programme of economic sovereignty for Slovenia and the suspension of federal legislation which countered this. The DEMOS also suggested introducing a temporary Slovene money unit.[51] A walkout by the entire Slovenian delegation at the Extraordinary 14th LCY Congress SKJ Congress on 22 January was followed in February by the Slovene League of Communists formally leaving the SKJ and changing its name to the League of Communists of Slovenia-Party of Democratic Renewal (LCS-PDR). Slovenia also withdraw its police units from Kosovo.[52]

In the republic's elections in April 1990 the DEMOS won a majority of seats but LCS-PDR candidate Milan Kucan defeated the DEMOS leader Joze Pucnik in the presidential election. In terms of Slovene nationalism the result hardly mattered as both sides were resolutely defending Slovenia's interests against perceived Serbian hegemony. On 2 July by a vote of 187 to three, the three chambers of the Slovenian National Assembly adopted a 'declaration of sovereignty of the state of Slovenia'. While secession from Yugoslavia was not mentioned, Slovenian laws henceforth took precedence over federal laws and the republican authorities announced that they would control Yugoslav military units stationed in Slovenia and guard Slovenia's frontier posts.[53] This was further reinforced on 27 September by the Assembly adopting a relevant amendment to the Republican Constitution, and the refusal to accept amendments to the Federal Constitution because ethnic Albanian delegates of the dissolved Kosovo Assembly no longer took part in the Federal Assembly.[54]

Such moves inevitably antagonized the predominantly Serbian leadership of the JNA (army) and the JNA ordered the removal of territorial defence weapons from warehouses in Slovenia, and, despite a ruling of the republican assembly, did not return them by the stipulated date of 10 August. Nor did the JNA alter its rules to allow Slovene recruits to perform their military service in Slovenia. In retaliation on 6 September the Slovene government suspended territorial defence payments.[55] The dispute continued and on 4 October the JNA reasserted its control over the republic's defence headquarters in Ljubljana – a move which brought protests from the Slovenian Presidency and from the Slovenian public.[56]

Meanwhile the developments in Croatia meant that Slovenia was increasingly supported by Croatia in its struggle with Serbia. On 5 October the two Presidencies proposed restructuring Yugoslavia into an alliance of sovereign states, each with its own armed forces and separate diplomatic missions abroad. In this scenario the centre would be a 'consultative parliament, a council of ministers, an executive commission and a confederal court.'[57] The possibility of some kind of Catholic alliance of Slovenia and Croatia with Austria was increasingly mooted. On 6 November a Slovene mission was opened in Vienna and a number of Austrian-Slovene working groups in the spheres of economy, energy, culture and education were set up.[58]

Serbia continued to attempt to pressure Slovenia and on 23 October 1990 the Serbian Parliament passed an economic package placing import duties on goods from Slovenia and Croatia to protect Serbia from 'disloyal domestic and foreign competition', thus effectively ending Yugoslavia's fragile internal market.[59] Such measures were beginning to have some effect to the Slovenian economy which, prior to 1989, was relatively strong. Unemployment rose by almost 80% in 1980 to just over 50,000 in November 1990[60] and the economy was said to be in a state of collapse with a trade deficit of US$600 with hard-currency countries, a down-turn of 10.1% in the period January-November 1990 and almost 40% of the working population employed in loss-making enterprises.[61]

Against this backdrop the Slovene authorities announced a plebiscite to be held on 26 December 1990 as to whether Slovenia should be an independent and autonomous state. Ignoring threats from the JNA and Serbia, the plebiscite was held and 93.5% of the electorate voted. The vote in favour was 88.5% and Slovenia was formally announced to be an independent state.[62]

The Yugoslav Constitutional Court ruled that the articles of the plebiscite emppowering Slovene bodies to take over duties of the federal centre should be banned and in the crisis of the Croatian arms from Hungary, there were fears of the JNA intervening directly in Slovenia. However, despite talks at the federal level by all the republic leaders to try and possibly salvage Yugoslavia in one form or another, it seems certain that Slovenia is set on independence.

Perhaps the only factor delaying this is a wish by Slovenia not to leave Croatia in the lurch and abandon it. Croatian-Slovene defence and security agreements were signed in January 1991. Slovene Prime Minister Alojz Peterle stated that Slovenia had requested to join the European Community as an independent state but that the community had opposed its bid for secession.[63] If true this is a short-sighted view by the community which should not compel Slovenia to remain bound to the likes of Milosevic's Serbia. Either way, independence in 1991 looks probable.

It was not perhaps so surprising that Slovenia, the most homogenous and prosperous republic in the SFRJ with its borders with Austria and ties with central Europe, has led the drive towards republican independence. Slovenes of all shades of political opinion have shown themselves overwhelmingly in favour of independence. All the attempts by Milosevic and the JNA have only served to harden Slovenian attitudes. However, whether Slovenia is economically viable on its own – ideally it looks towards some form of union with Croatia and Austria – remains to be seen. What is perhaps certain is that any process of independence will be considerably easier for the Slovenes, due to the homogenous nature of Slovenia and the lack of problematic sizeable Slovene minorities elsewhere in Yugoslavia (there is a sizeable Slovene minority in Italy),[64] than for the other regions of Yugoslavia, if, as seems increasingly likely, the country does split up.

4

THE NEWEST NATIONS – MUSLIMS, MONTENEGRINS AND MACEDONIANS

The Muslims

The term 'Muslim' in Yugoslavia is used to describe descendants of Slavs who converted to Islam under the period of Ottoman rule. Since 1971, they have been officially recognized as a distinct 'Yugoslav Nation' who make up about 9% of the population, mostly in Bosnia-Hercegovina where they are the largest single group constituting 39% of the population. They also constitute some 13.4% of Montenegro's small population.

Although the overwhelming majority of Muslims speak Serbo-Croat there are some 40,000 or so Macedonian-speaking Muslims, often called Pomaks. These are descendants of Macedonians, as opposed to Serbs or Croats, who converted during the Ottoman period. Their inclusion in the term is something of an anomaly and they have been treated separately (see section on Muslim Macedonians). It should be stressed that the term 'Muslim' does not refer to the Albanian, largely Muslim, or Turkish, wholly Muslim, minorities.

After the collapse of the Ottoman Empire, the Muslim Slavs, faced by pressure from both Serbs and Croats, organized themselves into a political force, the National Muslim Organization, which sought to protect both the religious and cultural life of the community as well as the interests of the Bosnian elite which had been islamicized in the 15th and 16th Centuries and which were the driving force behind the organization. It was not persecuted by the Hapsburg authorities who controlled Bosnia-Hercegovina but fell after 1878.

After the creation of the new state in 1918, it tended to side with those who would help defend its rights, and avoided outright opposition to the authorities. Increasingly, it looked to the Croats.[65] After World War II and the communist victory, there was considerable emigration of Muslim Slavs from Bosnia and especially from the Sandzak region of southern Serbia which lasted until 1966.[66] This was in no small part due to the initially hostile attitude of the new authorities.

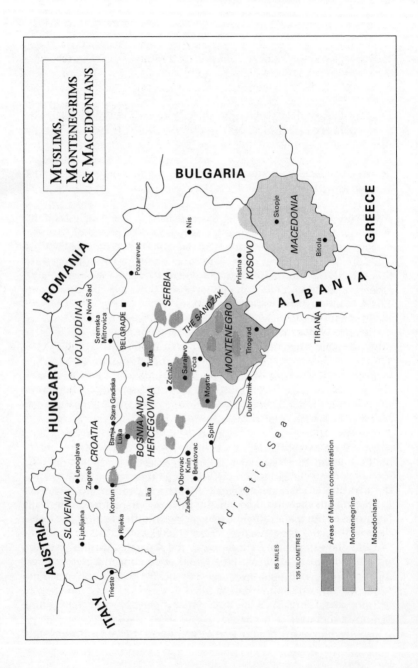

MUSLIMS,
MONTENEGRIMS
& MACEDONIANS

BULGARIA

GREECE

ROMANIA

MACEDONIA

Skopje

Nis

Bitola

Pozarevac

Pristina

KOSOVO

SERBIA

ALBANIA

VOJVODINA

Novi Sad

THE SANDŽAK

MONTENEGRO

Sremska
Mitrovica

BELGRADE

TIRANA

Titograd

HUNGARY

Tuzla

Zenica

Sarajevo

Foca

Dubrovnik

CROATIA

Zagreb

Lepoglava

Stara Gradiska

Banja
Luka

BOSNIA AND
HERCEGOVINA

Mostar

Split

Adriatic Sea

SLOVENIA

Ljubljana

Kordun

Lika

Obrovac
Knin
Benkovac

Zadar

Rijeka

AUSTRIA

ITALY

Trieste

85 MILES

135 KILOMETRES

Areas of Muslim concentration

Montenegrins

Macedonians

The Islamic community in Yugoslavia is divided into four administrative regions: the Sarajevo region, which ministers to the Muslims of Bosnia-Hercegovina and the small numbers of Muslims in Croatia and Slovenia; the Pristina Region; the Skopje Region; and the Titograd Region. The head of the Islamic community in Yugoslavia, the Reis-ul-ulema, is based in Sarajevo. Immediately after Tito's death, there were in the Sarajevo region over 1000 mosques, over 550 *mesdzids* (smaller places of worship), some 400 places of religious instruction, and two *madressahs* (religious schools).[67] The numbers of mosques has since grown considerably due to the large scale building programme undertaken by the Islamic community. There are a number of Islamic publications of which the most important is *Preporod*, a fortnightly newspaper published in Sarajevo in Serbo-Croat. However, unlike its Orthodox and Roman Catholic counterparts, *Pravoslavlje* and *Glas Koncila*, *Preporod* has avoided controversial social or political comment. The Muslims are overwhelmingly Sunni, although the Dervish order was introduced in Yugoslavia in 1974 and by 1986 numbered 50,000 followers. This order has so far proved to be more attractive to Muslim Albanians than Muslim Slavs with, in 1986, 53 of the 70 'monasteries' being in Kosovo, 10 in Macedonia and only seven in Bosnia.[68]

The area of Bosnia-Hercegovina was the scene of many of the worst atrocities committed during the civil war in World War II, and the ethnic mix of Orthodox Serbs, Catholic Croats and Muslim Slavs has historically been an explosive one with both Serbia and Croatia claiming the territory for their own. In addition, immediately after the war, an organization called 'Young Muslims' was set up, ostensibly to protect Muslims in Bosnia from alleged ill-treatment by the communist partisans. The Yugoslav authorities outlawed this group which they described as a terrorist one.

The republic of Bosnia-Hercegovina, which was created specifically to find some form of modus vivendi for the three main groups, well portrays the ethnic tangle in Yugoslavia as it is here that the three main religions meet head on. In the Balkans, religion has historically been one of the main differentiators between different peoples. In the light of this, and the tendency for both Serbs and Croats to claim the Muslim Slavs of Bosnia as their own, the separate 'Muslim' category was introduced. The ethnic tangle and competing rivalries resulted, until recently, in Bosnia being somewhat notorious in the matter of human rights, with individuals from all three ethnic groups persecuted for any manifestation of nationalism not sanctioned by the ruling Communist Party.

Despite religious freedom guaranteed under the constitution, religious practice, with its close correlation with a particular national standpoint, has often been viewed with official distrust (especially Roman Catholicism due to its centre of authority being outside the country). This has especially been so in Bosnia-Hercegovina and in Croatia. Also, any form of Islamic fundamentalism has, until the great changes in 1989-90, been severely treated as being a party to a conspiracy to make Bosnia-Hercegovina an 'ethnically pure Islamic Republic'.

The trial of 'the Sarajevo Muslims'

The most important example of this attitude by the communist authorities was the trial in mid-1983 of 13 Muslims accused of 'hostile and counter-revolutionary acts derived from Muslim nationalism'. The main defendant was Dr. Alija Izetbegovic, a lawyer and retired director of a building company, then aged 59. He was found guilty by the Sarajevo district court and sentenced to 14 years' imprisonment, reduced on appeal to 11 years. Four of the 13 on trial, Dr. Izetbegovic, Omer and Salih Behmen, and Ismet Kasumagic, had been convicted in the late 1940s for membership of the 'Young Muslims'. In the indictment Dr. Izetbegovic was accused of claiming that Muslims had suffered considerably at the hands of communists when the partisans entered their villages at the end of World War II and that the Young Muslims and other similar organizations were set up to counter this.

The main charge centred on a 50-page treatise written by Dr. Izetbegovic in 1970 entitled 'The Islamic Declaration.'[69] Parts of this treatise had been legally published in Yugoslavia some 10 years previously. The prosecution maintained that it indicated a desire to create an ethnically pure Muslim state out of Bosnia-Hercegovina, Kosovo and other Muslim areas, and was 'the modernized platform of the former terrorist organization, the Young Muslims'. Dr. Izetbegovic and Omer Behmen, however, stressed that the Islamic Declaration was concerned with the general emancipation of Muslims, not with Yugoslavia and Bosnia in particular, and that it was meant to apply to countries where the overwhelming majority of the population was Muslim. He also maintained that he had never uttered the phrase 'Islamic republic, ethnically pure Bosnia-Hercegovina' and pointed out that it did not feature in the declaration. He stated that he had given the declaration to Omer Behmen and some Arab students in order to get their opinion of it and that he had it translated because he felt that 'the Muslim world was turning into a third world power... the declaration offers the vision of a democratic and humanistic social order'. He denied that there was any link between the declaration and the programme of the

Young Muslims. Dr. Izetbegovic and Omer Behmen were accused also of having written articles which, according to the prosecution, contained falsehoods about the position of Muslims in Yugoslavia including the following:

> *'In the circumstances of the Second World War the partisans emerged.*
> *They were in effect armed detachments of the Yugoslav Communist*
> *Party which was imposing communist order in Yugoslavia step by step.*
> *While the physical survival of the Muslims was no longer in question,*
> *spiritual survival was now threatened. The Islamic Religious Commu-*
> *nity was placed under the control of the authorities. Supporters of the*
> *Communist Party and often even members of the Communist Party*
> *were appointed leaders of the community. The most severe losses were*
> *inflicted at the time by the Communists on the Muslims when military*
> *units entered villages. All potential opponents, mainly people of higher*
> *social standing and intellectuals known to be [Muslim] believers, were*
> *simply put to death without any judicial proceedings or investigation.'*[70]

Members of the group were also accused of having links with Iran, and one defendant, Melika Salihbegovic, was accused of having written a letter to Ayatollah Khomeini in Iran which included the following statement:

> *'For 37 years I have been living in a Christian milieu and in atheist*
> *Europe, where a handful of scared Muslims live in an atmosphere of*
> *falsehood and hypocrisy. It is no wonder therefore that my youth and*
> *that of thousands of my young compatriots was spent straying along*
> *paths of ignorance; it is no wonder that we are returning to Allah. If we*
> *are submissive, it is our despair...'*[71]

Although the percentage of religious believers in Bosnia-Hercegovina was not particularly high – at 17% it was lower than Kosovo's 44%, Croatia's 33%, Slovenia's 26% and Macedonia's 19% – in an opinion poll in 1985, the attitudes expressed by the 'Sarajevo Muslims' for which they were so heavily penalized, appears to have elicited strong support from the Muslim population in Bosnia-Herzegovina.

Alija Izetbegovic was released early in November 1988 and when the relaxation came to Bosnia-Hercegovina, as it came to other republics, he founded in May 1990 the Party of Democratic Action (SDA). Despite a split in the leadership of the SDA between Izetbegovic and Adil Zulfikarpasic (a former leading figure of the emigre Muslim community who returned to Yugoslavia but who fell out with Izetbegovic over what he saw as the latter's 'too rigid Islamic approach' and instead founded a rival party, the Muslim Bosniak Organization on 21 September 1990), the SDA triumphed in the elections held December 1990 and became the largest party with 86 of the 240 seats in both chambers of the assembly. The voting was along national lines with 72 seats for the Serbian Democratic Party and 44 for the Croatian Democratic Community. In all there were 99 Muslims, 85 Serbs, 49 Croats and seven declaring themselves as 'Yugoslavs' in the new assembly.[72] Alija Izetbegovic, similarly to Franjo Tudjman in Croatia, had progressed from being a political prisoner under the old regime to being president of the republic.

This republic, however, is still a long way from becoming 'an Islamic Republic', even if that is what Izetbegovic wants (which is debatable). Despite much paranoia among some politicians and members of other religious groups in Yugoslavia about the growth of Islam in the country, a leading sociologist specializing in the sociology of religion claims that statistical data disproves this common fear, and that in fact, in relation to the country's population, the percentage of Muslim believers in Yugoslavia is the same as it was in 1921.[73] The difference is in the growing politicization of Muslims, not only in Bosnia-Hercegovina but also in the Sandzak where they are in a majority and where there are growing demands for autonomy. Sulejman Ugljanin, President of the SDA for the Sandzak, in February 1991 accused the Serb and Montenegrin authorities of denying rights to Muslims and tension appears to be growing.[74]

The potential break-up of Yugoslavia poses great problems for Bosnia-Hercegovina, and the old question of 'who are the Bosnian Muslims?' appears to be as alive as ever. In 1989, a small Zagreb publishing house brought out a 'Bibliography of Croatian Writers of Bosnia-Hercegovina between the Two Wars' which included a number of Muslims as 'Croatian writers'. The Muslims were outraged and *Preporod* denounced the apparent Croatization of 38 Muslim writers.

In addition there is the age-old habit of Islam at times transcending national divisions. Slav Muslims in Montenegro joined in an electoral party with Albanians in the 1990 elections there and the SDA appears sympathetic to the aspirations of fellow Muslim Albanians in Kosovo. Similarly, in February 1990, Muslim nationalist leaflets supporting Kosovo's secession and attacking the Serb leader Slobodan Milosevic appeared in Novi Pazar in the Sandzak.[75] Further hostility between Slav Muslims and Serbs was evident at a rally held by Vuk Draskovic's Serbian Renewal Movement (SPO) in September 1990 in Novi Pazar, in the Sandjak, Serbia, when Muslims and SPO supporters had to be separated by militia with armoured cars, tear gas and shots after Draskovic accused Muslims of being closer to Tehran than to their Serb neighbours.[76] The SDA after the electoral victory in Bosnia-Hercegovina, announced that it would concentrate more activity in the Sandzak and in Macedonia where it aims to appeal to the Muslim Macedonians.

Despite this potential alliance between Slav Muslims, predominantly in Bosnia, and Kosovo Albanians, it is hard to see how the Muslims of Bosnia-Hercegovina would profit from the break-up of Yugoslavia with the inevitable claims of Serbia and Croatia on its territory. Izetbegovic has repeatedly stated that he considers it advisable for Yugoslavia to remain intact, and that the border at Bosnia-Hercegovina should not be changed. Despite the delicate ethnic mix of the region, politicians of all persuasions have shown ability in the past to compromise. However, it seems likely that in a choice between Serbia or Croatia, the Muslims of Bosnia-Hercegovina would choose Croatia if that was the only option. The worst scenario is a re-run of the mutual slaughter of 1941. Yugoslavia as a confederation would appear to suit them best. Either way, the Muslims of Yugoslavia are perhaps an anomaly in terms of modern nationalism, and still pose one of the countries' most perplexing problems.

The Montenegrins

The republic of Montenegro lies in the south of the country on the northern borders of Albania. It is extremely mountainous with a total population of only 584,310. The Montenegrins number 579,043 or some 2.6% of the Yugoslavian population. The majority live in Montenegro where they constitute 68% of the population with the remainder largely made up of Muslims (13.4%) and Albanians (6.5%). The Montenegrins speak Serbo-Croat, are Orthodox in religion and have been traditional allies of the Serbs. Some Montenegrins claim that they are, in fact, Serbs; a constant feature of Austro-Hungarian policy, which saw the emergent Serbian state as a rival for Bosnia in the late 19th Century, was to prevent the independent Serbian and Montenegrin states from uniting.

The area has been plagued by wars and raids and even during the Ottoman occupation parts of Montenegro were so inaccessible as to escape Ottoman control. Montenegrins have traditionally made good soldiers and their territory proved extremely suitable for the partisan struggle. A result of this is that Montenegrins have a far higher number in the army officer corps than their percentage in the population would suggest. The resurgent Serbian nationalism of the last two years has had profound effects in Montenegro with the replacement in 1988, after mass demonstrations, of the republic's leadership with those more in tune with the current Serbian leadership.

The elections in Montenegro in December saw other similarities with Serbia, with a resounding victory for the Montenegrin League of Communists who won 83 out of the 125 seats to the assembly. The Yugoslav party of Ante Markovic, the Alliance of Reformist Forces, came second with 17 seats. This communist victory further underlined Montenegro's similarity with Serbia, in contrast to other republics where nationalist parties defeated the communists in every case.

Conversely it must be remembered that Montenegro was an independent state, formally confirmed at the Congress of Berlin in 1878, with a heroic history of struggle in its mountain fastnesses prior to the founding of Yugoslavia in 1918. It has been a distinct political entity since the 15th Century and its mountainous terrain protected it form complete domination first by the Venetians and then in the 16th Century from the Ottomans.

With nationalism currently proving so strong throughout the whole country a rebirth of 'Montenegrinism' truely distinct from Serbianism is a possibility. With the often noted importance of religion in Balkan affairs, the August 1990 petition of about 1500 people, sent to the Montenegrin parliament demanding the restoration of the Independent Montenegro Orthodox Church (which was granted autocephalous status from the Serbian Orthodox Church in 1855 but lost it in 1920 after the incorporation of Montenegro into Yugoslavia), may be a significant sign. Despite this, however, all the indications are that Montenegro sees its future with Serbia, and with the disintegration of Yugoslavia a distinct possibility, it seems probable that Montenegro will, in such a scenario, opt for union or at least continued close cooperation with Serbia.

The Macedonians

Macedonia – the geographical area bounded to the north by the Skopska Crna Gora and the Shar Planina mountains; to the east by the Rila and Rhodope mountains; to the south by the Aegean coast around Salonika, Mount Olympus and the Pindus mountains; and to the west by the lakes of Ohrid and Prespa; and comprising approximately 67,000 sq. kms. – is currently divided between Yugoslavia, Greece and Bulgaria. Macedonia was one of the first areas in the Balkan peninsula to be conquered by the Ottoman Empire and was one of the last to be liberated during the Balkan Wars of 1912/13.

The population of the Socialist Republic (SR) of Macedonia was 1,912,257 according to the census of 1981 of which there were 1,281,195 Macedonians, 377,726 Albanians, 44,613 Serbs, 39,555 Moslems, 47,223 Gypsies, 86,691 Turks and 7190 Vlachs, the remainder consisting of a variety of other ethnic groups. There were also 1984 Bulgarians (as opposed to Macedonian) recorded.

History

The founding of the Exarchate church in 1870 had pitted Greek against Bulgarian in Macedonia and the short-lived 'Greater Bulgaria' of the San Stefano Treaty, annulled by the Treaty of Berlin, made the new Bulgarian state permanently revisionist and revanchist. Another aspect of the Treaty of Berlin was the administration of Bosnia-Hercegovina and the garrisoning of the Sanjak of Novibazar (the Sandzak), dividing Serbia and Montenegro, by Austro-Hungary, resulting in Serbia also looking towards Macedonia for future expansion as her 'natural' territories for expansion (ie. those territories with large Serbian populations) fell under Austro-Hungarian control.

After defeat by Bulgaria in 1885 Serbia actively pursued an expansionist policy in Macedonia, calling it South Serbia and claiming that Slav Macedonians were Serbs. The Society of Saint Sava was founded in 1886 to promote Serbian nationalism especially in Macedonia. By the mid-1890s Serbia claimed 100 Serbian schools in Macedonia to the Bulgarian's 600 to 700 schools mostly under the aegis of the Exarchate church. The Greeks also founded a society similar to the Serbs, the Ethnike Hetairia, which aimed to liberate all Greeks still within the Ottoman Empire beginning with those in Macedonia, including the Slav-speaking population who they called Slavophone Greeks. This society was supported by three-quarters of Greek army officers and had many wealthy patrons. By 1895 the Greeks claimed 1400 schools in Macedonia and were spending proportionally more on education in Macedonia, which was still within the Ottoman Empire, than in Greece itself. The Vlahs scattered in Western Macedonia, Epirus and Thessaly, who speak a form of Romanian, allowed the Romanians also to make a claim and by 1912 they also were subsidizing over 30 schools.

Within Macedonia itself the Internal Macedonian Revolutionary Organization (VMRO) was set up in 1893, opposing the partition of Macedonia and supporting the idea of a south Slav federation of Serbs, Macedonians and Bulgarians. This organization won wide support and made plans for an armed uprising. However, huge numbers of Macedonians had fled to Bulgaria following the failure of the San Stefano 'Greater Bulgaria' – by 1903 almost half the population of Sofia was comprised of Macedonian refugees or immigrants – and this mass of refugees, as well as destabilizing Bulgaria internally for many years, allowed a rival organization to VMRO, the External Organization or Supremacists, to be set up in Sofia in 1895 which aimed at the incorporation of Macedonia within Bulgaria, ie. the 'Greater Bulgaria'. Thus, almost from the outset, VMRO was fatally divided in its aims between those who wanted Macedonia for Bulgaria and those who wanted a separate Macedonian state either within some form of federation or independent.

The overall result of all these competing rivalries in Macedonia was disastrous for the resident population, which by most accounts was most sympathetic to one of the wings of VMRO, with the peasants being subjected to repeated visits by armed gangs from the VMRO factions, Serbs, Bulgarians and Greeks, as well as the Ottoman authorities until the Balkan Wars, when the Ottoman Empire was finally driven out of Macedonia.

Since then the portion now in Yugoslavia – known there as Vardar Macedonia – has, except during the two world wars when for a sizeable period most of it was occupied by Bulgaria, belonged firstly to Serbia and then to the Kingdom of Serbs, Croats and Slovenes, later known as Yugoslavia, which came into existence in December 1918. In line with Serbian claims that the Macedonians were in fact Southern Serbs, the church was put under the control of the Serbian Patriarchate and Serbian, the official language, became compulsory both in schools and public life. This policy alienated the population and spread pro-Bulgarian feeling.

During World War II, Bulgaria, allied to Nazi Germany, occupied most of Yugoslav Macedonia, and although Hitler did not allow Bulgaria to formally annex the territories they occupied both in Yugoslavia and Greece, the Bulgarian government acted as if they had. Bulgarian officials were sent in, teachers were replaced by Bulgarian ones, and the July 1942 law on citizenship resulted in the exodus of many Serbs to Serbia. However, despite being welcomed by many as liberators, the attitude of the Bulgarians (the Ministry of the Interior even had to warn that officials who treated Macedonia as a foreign country would be punished) quickly led to disillusionment by the population of Vardar Macedonia.

Pro-Bulgarian sentiment had meant that the Partisans, the Yugoslav communist resistance movement led by Tito, had initially made little headway in Macedonia but this situation changed after the visit to

Skopje of Tito's aide Vukmanovic-Tempo, and by the end of 1943 the Partisans were becoming increasingly popular resulting in Bulgarian reprisals which further alienated the population. In 1944 Bulgarian troops began to desert to the Partisans and in September 1944 Bulgaria changed sides and joined the allies. The Bulgarian occupation of 1941-44 had disillusioned many if not most Yugoslav Macedonians but there remained a residual pro-Bulgarian sentiment.

The Yugoslav Communist Party's attitude to the Macedonian question underwent successive changes. Up till 1934/5 the Comintern, the International Communist movement orchestrated from Moscow, was revisionist regarding the boundaries of Yugoslavia and called for a united Macedonia, similar to that of one of the factions of VMRO. In line with this, a 'United VMRO' was set up under communist aegis but this new organization did not prove a great success. Hitler's rise to power, with the result that Germany now became the leading revisionist power in Europe, heralded a change in the Comintern line to that of the Popular Fronts. During World War II, under Tito's leadership, the Partisans resolved to create a Macedonian republic within a new federal Yugoslavia. This republic was seen as providing a bridge between Yugoslavia and Bulgaria which would be united in a Balkan federation which might also include Albania which was also under communist control after the war, and Greece where there was a civil war between the communists and non-communists for control. The Bulgarian leader, Georgi Dimitrov, both of whose parents were from Macedonia, was receptive to Tito's plans of uniting Vardar Macedonia in Yugoslavia with Pirin Macedonia in Bulgaria but his death in July 1949, and the break between Tito and Stalin over Tito's ambitions, made the Yugoslav-Bulgarian cooperation a short-lived affair. Henceforth, relations between the new Macedonian republic and Bulgaria would be strained and this situation has lasted till the present.

Language and education

In Yugoslav Macedonia the new authorities quickly set about consolidating their position. The new nation needed a written language and initially the spoken dialect of northern Macedonia was chosen as the basis for the Macedonian language, but this was deemed as too close to Serbian and the dialects of Bitola-Veles became the norm.[77] These dialects were closer to the Bulgarian literary language but as the Bulgarian was based upon the eastern Bulgarian dialects it allowed enough differentiation for the Yugoslavs to claim that it was a language distinct from Bulgarian – a point which Bulgaria has bitterly disputed ever since.[78] In fact the differentiation between the Macedonian dialects and the Bulgarian ones becomes progressively less pronounced on an east-west basis. Whether Macedonian, which shares nearly all the same distinct characteristics which separate Bulgarian from other Slav languages – lack of cases; the post-positive definite article; the replacement of the infinitive form; and the preservation of the simple verbal forms for the past and imperfect tenses – is truly a different language from Bulgarian or merely a dialect of it, is a moot point.

The alphabet was accepted on 3 May 1945, the orthography on 7 June 1945 and the first primer in the new language appeared by 1946 which year also saw the founding of a Macedonian Department of the Faculty of Philosophy in Skopje. A grammar of the Macedonian Literary Language appeared in 1952 and the Institute for the Macedonian Language 'Krste P. Misirkov' was founded in 1953. Since World War II the new republic has used the full weight of the education system and the bureaucracy to make the new language common parlance; indeed, it is noticeable still that old people tend to speak a mixture of dialects which include obvious Serbianisms and Bulgarianisms while those young enough to have gone through the education system in its entirety speak a 'purer' Macedonian.

In addition to the new language the new republic needed a history and the new school textbooks quickly reflected this need by tracing the Macedonian nation back through history. Again this has caused bitter resentment from Bulgaria as the Macedonian historical figures are also claimed by Bulgaria as Bulgarian heroes eg. Gotse Delchev who was one of the leaders of, and died in, the abortive rising of 1903 in Macedonia – Macedonian textbooks even hint at Bulgarian complicity in his death at the hands of the Ottomans[79] – and the medieval emperor Samuil whose empire was centred around Lake Ohrid.

Religion

Religion was another important tool for the new authorities and the freeing of the Orthodox Church in Yugoslav Macedonia from Serbian control with the autocephalous Macedonian Orthodox Church, and the revival of the ancient archbishopric of Ohrid in 1958, was an important step along the path to nationhood – a rare occurrence of atheist state cooperation with organized religion. This move was resisted by the Serbian Orthodox Church as was the final declaration of the autocephalous status of the Macedonian Church on 18 July 1967. The Serbian Orthodox Church, along with the other Orthodox Churches, remains firm in its refusal to recognize the Macedonian Church.

There are reports of a faction within the Macedonian Orthodox Church which wishes that the church give up its claim to independence and rejoin the Serbian Orthodox Church. This faction apparently was based around Bishop Petar of Prespa and Bitolj. This was believed by some to be the real reason behind the 1990 ultimatum issued by 200 Macedonian Orthodox priests for his resignation, ostensibly on grounds of neglect and embezzlement.[80] On the other hand relations between the Macedonian Orthodox Church and the authorities in Yugoslav Macedonia have continued to be good, aided by a common front against the threat of Albanian nationalism and the attendant growth of Islam.

Official unease

Thus, the new authorities overcame the residual pro-Bulgarian feeling among much of the population and the split with Bulgaria in 1948, and apparently were successful in building a distinct national consciousness based on the available differences between Macedonia and Bulgaria proper. The change from the pre-war situation of unrecognized minority status and attempted assimilation by Serbia to the current one, where the Macedonians are the majority people in their own republic with considerable autonomy within Yugoslavia's federation/confederation, had obvious attractions. The authorities were also aided by the comparative lack of attraction for its population of Bulgaria, which remained within the Soviet bloc, in comparison to the new Yugoslavia.

However, the increasingly desperate economic, political and social situation in Yugoslavia developing throughout the 1980s, and the national question of the Albanians within Yugoslavia which threatens the new republic probably more than any of the other republics including Serbia, as well as Bulgaria's continuing ambitions, make the future still problematic for the Macedonian republic. The unease of the communist authorities was shown by the never-ending polemics with Bulgaria and the treatment of Albanian nationalism and the harsh attitude to emigre groups deemed hostile to the republic. An example of this was the kidnapping from Paris and the 13-year prison sentence imposed by Skopje district court in 1979 on Dragan Bogdanovski, a Macedonian emigre, for leading an organization calling for a united independent Macedonian state which would incorporate not only the Yugoslav republic of Macedonia, but also the Macedonian territories in Greece and Bulgaria – ironically, a similar aim to that of Gotse Delchev who is lionized by the authorities.[81]

Political relaxation and nationalist expression in 1989 and 1990

In mid-1989, in line with developments elsewhere in Yugoslavia and the recent momentous changes in Eastern Europe, the ruling League of Communists of Macedonia committed itself to the introduction of a multi-party system in Macedonia.[82] However, as noted above, the Macedonians have probably as much if not more to lose in terms of their very existence if Yugoslavia breaks up. One reaction to this was to assert Macedonian nationalism more aggressively to hide potential weakness. In 1989 the constitution was reworded so that Socialist Republic (SR) of Macedonia was redefined as 'a nation-state of Macedonian people' in place of the previous 'a state of the Macedonian people and the Albanian and Turkish minorities'.

In October 1989 slogans stating 'Solun [Thessalonika] is ours', 'Prohor Pcinjski [a monastery near the border with SR Macedonia which since 1953 has been part of Serbia] is Macedonian', 'Cento' (a Macedonian nationalist leader tried by the communists after the war), and 'We fight for a united Macedonia' began to be chanted by football supporters of Vardar, the main Skopje football team.[83] Similar slogans soon appeared on the walls of Skopje, with the authorities apparently not pursuing such erstwhile 'hostile' activity.[84]

More serious manifestations soon emerged. On 4 February, the founding assembly of the Movement for All-Macedonian Action (MAAK) was set up mainly by the Macedonian intelligentsia with the head of the Writers Union, the poet Ante Popovski as its initial leader.[85] MAAK stated that it had no territorial ambitions on Macedonia's neighbours but has expressed criticism of Bulgaria and Greece and in July local MAAK leaders from Strumica met with delegates from the Ilinden movement in Bulgaria to discuss cooperation.[86] In the same month, on 20 February, a large demonstration of Macedonians (estimates vary from 30,000 to 120,000 people) took place in Skopje to assert their identity and protest at perceived oppression of Macedonians in Bulgaria, Greece and Albania. The rally was apparently timed to coincide with the visit of the Greek Prime Minister, Constantine Mitsotakis, to Belgrade.[87]

A more radical nationalist party than MAAK emerged in June 1990 with the founding congress in Skopje on 17 June of the Internal Macedonian Revolutionary Organization-Democratic Party of Macedonian National Unity (VMRO-DPMNE) with delegates from the Macedonian diaspora. The name choice was significant and VMRO-DPMNE, led by Ljupco Georgijevski, pledged to carry on the principles of the Ilinden uprising of 1903 and work for 'the ideal of all free Macedonians united' in a Macedonian state.[88] VMRO-DPMNE also expressed the desire for improvements in relations with Slovenia and Croatia and for the return of some territories currently in Serbia. On 2 August, to mark the Ilinden uprising, it held a demonstration of over 100 members at Prohor Pcinjski Monastery which Serbian police had to forcibly disperse.[89]

Meanwhile an organization for Bulgarians in SR Macedonia had begun to be active and on 4 August the Society of Bulgarians in Vardar Macedonia published an appeal 'to the Bulgarian people' in which the whole concept of a Macedonian nation was denied and the Bulgarian nature of all Macedonians in Yugoslavia and Greece as well as Bulgaria was stressed. The letter appealed to the 'new democratic Bulgaria to intercede on their [Bulgarians outside of Bulgaria] behalf....that millions of Bulgarians live outside their native land but part of them for decades have been denied by all possible means their rights to self-determination as a nation and people'.[90]

Such actions prompted the communist authorities in SR Macedonia to suspect VMRO-DPMNE of provoking national intolerance vis-a-vis the Serbian people and favouring 'the Bulgarian nation'.[91] This latter charge of being pro-Bulgarian seems unfounded but similarly to the turn of the century VMRO there have been apparent splits in VMRO-DPMNE with in one case a member sentenced to death by a kangaroo court of fellow members.[92]

The growing Serbian nationalism also worked to revive fears of Serbian claims on Macedonia. Laws passed by Milosevic's government on 'returns', whereby Serb emigrants from Kosovo who were allegedly forced out received compensation, could in theory be applied to Serbs forced out of SR Macedonia after the war when the territory changed from being 'South Serbia'. On 2 June 1990, Petar Gosev, president of the Macedonian Communist Party, now called the League of Communists of Macedonia-Party for Democratic Renewal (SKM-PDP), while indulging in the routine castigation of Bulgaria and Greece for failing to recognize Macedonian rights in the respective countries, also criticized Serbian nationalism and said that Serbia also, like Bulgaria and Greece, had designs on Macedonia.[93]

Such designs were explicitly formulated by Vuk Draskovic, leader of Serbia's main opposition party and Milosevic's main rival, when on 3 November he told a Bulgarian newspaper that a new Balkan alliance of Orthodox countries including Serbia, Bulgaria and Greece was needed to resist advancing Islam, and that Macedonia would cease to be a republic and be reabsorbed by Serbia if Yugoslavia became a confederation.[94] At about the same time Draskovic also called for the partition of SR Macedonia between Serbia and Bulgaria.[95]

Yugoslav Macedonia once again appeared under threat from out-side. In January, Yugoslavia accused Dimitar Popov and Constantine Mitsotakis, Prime Ministers of Bulgaria and Greece, respectively, of making a joint statement denying the existence of the Macedonian nation.[96] Further Macedonian protests took place at the announcement that the Pan-Serbian Council for National Salvation was to hold a meeting in Kumanovo – a blatant provocation.[97] The alleged meeting – denied by President Tudjman – between Dimitar Gotsev, leader of the IMRO in Bulgaria which calls for unification of Yugoslav Macedonia with Bulgaria, and Tudjman in Zagreb, further raised Macedonian fears[98] of Bulgarian aims – this fear shown in the conviction and fine of a Bulgarian citizen on 21 January, for alleging in private conversation that there are Bulgarians living in Yugoslav Macedonia.[99]

In November 1990, MAAK and VMRO-DPMNE made an alliance, the Front of Macedonian National Unity, for the forthcoming elections, specifically to combat the SKM-PDP communists who were expected to perform well. After apparent failure in the first round when the Front won no seats, the Front complained of many irregularities and announced that it would boycott the second round to be held on 25 November.[100] However, they rescinded this decision and VMRO-DPMNE in particular achieved great success so that after the third and final round they were the leading party with 37 seats out of 120 in the assembly, with the SKM-PDP second with 31 seats and the mainly ethnic Albanian PDP third with 25.

The political situation in Macedonia following these inconclusive elections is at present unclear. VMRO-DPMNE expressed its support for the Slovene plebiscite on Slovenia's possible secession from Yugoslavia.[101] In January 1991, VMRO-DPMNE split into two factions after Vladimir Golubovski challenged Georgijevski for leadership. However, the dreams of a united Macedonia as espoused by both factions of VMRO-DPMNE seem as far away as ever, given Bulgaria's intransigence and Greece's policies and a possible break-up of Yugoslavia may even prove fatal for the whole concept of a separate Macedonian nation. What seems incontestable is that there are many Slavs in Yugoslavia (and for that matter in Bulgaria and Greece and Albania) who live in the geographic area of Macedonia and who see themselves as Macedonian in identity. Conversely, there are many in the same areas who see themselves as Bulgarians and many in Greece who have become unquestionably Hellenicized.

Incorporation of the territory into a united Europe, whether as a separate unit or as part of existing countries, but in either case with allowance for people to express different national identities, appears to the outsider to be perhaps the best solution but one which does not take into account the passions and fears of those involved. The 'Macedonian Question' is as alive and problematic as ever.

The Muslim Macedonians – Torbeshes, Pomaks and Poturs

This apparent confusion over identity of the different Muslim groups shows again, that in the Balkans religion has often been of paramount importance in ethnic differentiation. This is further illustrated by the Muslim Macedonians, known as Torbeshes, Pomaks, or Poturs. Similarly to the Pomaks in Bulgaria, these Muslims often showed in the past greater identification with fellow Muslims, especially Turks, although, the authorities have been worried at the penetration of Albanian nationalism into this community by way of, among other things, Albanian-speaking hodzhas.

The numbers of these Slav Muslims has fluctuated greatly in past censuses – 1591 in 1953; 3002 in 1961; 1248 in 1971; and a dramatic rise to 39,555 in 1981. This last figure presumably includes many who previously declared themselves as Turks.

These Slav Muslims formed themselves into an association and held their first historical, cultural meeting in 1970 at the monastery of Saint Jovan Bigorski in Western Macedonia. This association claims that over 70,000 of their numbers have been assimilated by other Muslim groups since the war, especially the Albanians.[102] If this has been the case, then the rise in their numbers as reflected in the 1981 census shows that the founding of the association has been very successful.

Despite this apparent success, there remain contrary signs indicating that the Slav Muslim Macedonians remain susceptible to assimilation into the Muslim (Albanian) majority in the republic – again showing that in the Balkan context Islam is often a more unifying factor than ethnicity. On 13 August, Dr. Riza Memedovski, chairman of the republican community for cultural and scientific events of Macedonian Muslims, sent an open letter to the Chairman of the Party for Democratic Prosperity of Macedonia (PDP) – a predominantly ethnic Albanian party based in Tetovo – on the subject of this 'quiet assimilation', accusing the PDP of abusing religion for political ends by attempting 'Kosovozation and Albanianization of western Macedonia'.[103] The same concern was voiced by the Council of Elders of the Islamic Community of Macedonia on 6 November.[104]

This tendency for Macedonian Muslims to lean towards the ethnic Albanians was underlined by apparent support from Slav Muslims for the PDP, the predominantly ethnic Albanian political party. In the second round of elections in Macedonia on 25 November 1990, the PDP complained that in Slav Muslim villages in western Macedonia, inhabitants were prevented from voting for the PDP by members of the nationalist parties in the Front for Macedonian National Unity, the militia organs, and even by members of the electoral commissions.[105]

5

THE LARGEST NATIONALITY I
– ALBANIANS OF KOSOVO

The background

The largest 'Nationality of Yugoslavia' is the Albanian one with just over 1.7 million or 7.7% of the total population in 1981, but now almost certainly well over two million in number. The Albanians, who claim descent from the ancient Illyrians, live mainly in Kosovo, where they now constitute over 85% of the population, and in compact communities in Western Macedonia bordering on Albania where they constitute some 19.8% of the population.

Kosovo, which for centuries has been inhabited by a mixed population, occupies a major place in the national consciousness of both the Serbs and the Albanians. It has become the focus of competing claims and ethnic conflict. For the Serbs it is the heartland of the medieval Serbian kingdom where many of the greatest monuments of the (Christian) Serbian Orthodox Church are located. For the majority ethnic Albanian population (predominantly Muslim but with some Roman Catholics) it was in Kosovo that the Albanian national revival began with the founding of the League of Prizren in 1878.

The Albanian national revival, however, was a late arrival on the Balkan stage. As the majority of Albanians in the Ottoman territories were Muslims and as such faced no obstacle to advancement – many Albanians succeeded in reaching high positions in the Ottoman Empire – the impetus for the creation of an Albanian national state was not as strong as for neighbouring nationalities, especially as these tended to have Great Power support for a combination of ostensibly ideological (Christian) reasons and, more often, reasons of their own self-interest. It can be argued that the Albanian national revival was in many ways a reaction to Serb and Greek claims on the decaying Ottoman Empire; if the Albanians did not organize, then there was a real chance that they would lose out completely in territorial stakes and the Albanian-inhabited territories might be divided between Ser-

ALBANIANS

SERBIA

BULGARIA

MONTENEGRO

Mitrovica   Podujevo
        Pristina
Pec   Gnjilane
Titograd   KOSOVO
        Prizren   Kumanovo
            Skopje

Adriatic Sea

MACEDONIA

ALBANIA

Gostivar
Debar
Ohrid

85 MILES

135 KILOMETRES

GREECE

Albanians in Kosovo

Albanians outside Kosovo

bia to the north and Greece to the south.

In the event, during the final break-up of the Ottoman Empire in the Balkans, the modern Albanian state was created in 1912 due to the insistence of the Great Powers, notably Austria-Hungary who viewed the expansion of the new Balkan states, especially Serbia, with great alarm. However the 'late arrival' of the Albanians resulted in a somewhat truncated state with large Albanian minorities in neighbouring border areas where they constituted local majorities. The largest of these was in Kosovo.

After the chaos of the years of World War I, the new Yugoslav state attempted to re-colonize the territory with Serb settlers, especially war veterans. The appalling hardships of the war years, especially the fighting of the winter of 1915 between local Albanian tribesmen and the retreating Serbian army making its way over the Albanian mountains to Corfu, left deep scars and there were many acts of vengeance by the eventually victorious Serbs. The *Chetniks*, irregular Serbian troops, were created to insure Serb domination in the newly acquired territories. Serb-Croat was compulsory in schools and for all official purposes. Instability in Albania itself added to the continuation of the border dispute which was settled in 1926.

In the inter-war period an estimated 40,000 Orthodox Slav peasants (mostly Serbs and Montenegrins) moved into Kosovo while over half a million ethnic Albanians were forced to emigrate. The new settlers received good land and benefits from the authorities resulting in two separate communities in Kosovo: a small, relatively prosperous Serb/Montenegrin settler community, and a mass of less well-to-do Albanians.[106]

Unsurprisingly, given this situation in this most backward part of the new state, the Albanians viewed the Serb-dominated state as an oppressive one. This allowed local support for the Italian puppet Kingdom of Albania, after Yugoslavia's disintegration in World War II, to incorporate many of the Albanian-inhabited territories of the former Yugoslav state. These territories, however, once more reverted to the new post-war Yugoslavia.

The post-war period saw major improvements in the official status of ethnic Albanians in Yugoslavia, although a large number, declaring themselves to be Turks, emigrated to Turkey, taking advantage of emigration agreements. For the first time Albanians were recognized as a distinct national group; their language was recognized as one of Yugoslavia's official languages and Albanians gained the right to education in the vernacular. These gains were, however, undermined by repressive policies for which Alexander Rankovic, a Serb and head of the state security police, has been held responsible. Dissatisfaction and organized Albanian resistance continued in Kosovo with arrests of Albanians for nationalist activity. Among those arrested was the young writer Adem Demaqi who was arrested for the first time in 1958 and sentenced to five years' imprisonment.

After the downfall of Rankovic in 1966, Serbs and Montenegrins lost their dominance in the Kosovo political and administrative apparatus and Albanian dissatisfaction was allowed to be freely aired with large-scale demonstrations in November 1968 calling for Kosovo to be granted republican status. To grant such a republic was (and still is) officially seen as being merely the first stage towards the unification of Kosovo province, and other regions inhabited by ethnic Albanians especially in Macedonia, with neighbouring Albania, an aim explicitly formulated by a minority of Albanian nationalists.

Constitutional amendments in 1968 granted the regions of Kosovo and the Vojvodina some republican prerogatives and Kosovo was also allowed to fly the Albanian flag. This compromise was confirmed in the constitution of 1974. Kosovo was an Autonomous Province within the Serbian Republic with, *de facto* if not *de jure*, many of the powers of a republic within the Yugoslav federation. At the same time Kosovo experienced significant demographic changes due to the extremely high natural birth rate among the Albanians, combined with the emigration of Serbs and Montenegrins with over 30,000 leaving the province between 1971 and 1981.[107]

Though naturally rich in resources, Kosovo is economically one of the most backward regions in Yugoslavia and economic problems have exacerbated growing nationalist unrest. The setting up of an Albanian university in Pristina, the capital of Kosovo, in 1968 and the huge number of Albanian students who enrol there, in part due to the acute unemployment problem in Kosovo, helped create a large Albanian intelligentsia with little outlet in terms of job opportunities for them; in 1984 unemployment in Kosovo was 29.1% compared to 12.7% national average and only 1.8% in Slovenia. In addition in Kosovo, 70% of those unemployed were aged 25 years or under.[108]

Nationalist discontent continued with further arrests and imprisonments in 1975 and 1976. In February 1976, Adem Demaqi was imprisoned for the third time along with 18 other Albanians. They were tried in Pristina and charged with 'organizing against the people and the state', 'hostile propaganda' and 'crimes endangering the territorial integrity and independence of Yugoslavia'. Demaqi was accused of forming the 'National Liberation Movement of Kosovo', whose goal was alleged to be the unification of Kosovo with Albania. They were also accused of distributing publicity material attacking the policy of the Communist Party and the Yugoslav leadership in the student quarters of Pristina university and other places in Kosovo and Macedonia. Demaqi was sentenced to 15 years' imprisonment.[109]

Unsurprisingly Pristina university became a breeding ground for nationalists. Figures for the number of students at Pristina university vary – original figures for academic year 1981/2 gave some 45,000 but this figure was changed to 20,434 regular students, with 8174 enroled in other institutions of higher education in the province.[110] Whatever the actual figure it was a far higher percentage than for other areas in the country. Renewed nationalist unrest began again in Kosovo in late 1979, when numerous arrests were reported following the appearance of anti-government pamphlets and slogans printed on walls. Some 19 people were later tried.

The riots of 1981 and continuing unrest

The situation exploded in 1981 when there was further nationalist unrest in Kosovo in March and April. According to official Yugoslav sources, it was sparked off on 11 March by students at Pristina university protesting about their living conditions. Later in March and early April, demonstrations took place in Pristina and many other parts of Kosovo; the demonstrators' main demand was for Kosovo to be accorded republican status. Some also called for union with Albania. The demonstrations appear to have begun peacefully but, according to various official sources, nine or 11 people died and several hundred were wounded in violent clashes following intervention by security forces. Unofficial sources estimated far higher casualty figures, and the Central Committee of the League of Communists of Serbia was reportedly told that over 300 were killed.[111]

A State of Emergency was declared and heavy security force reinforcements and army units were brought into the province. At least 2000 people were arrested. In June 1981 the authorities announced that 506 demonstrators had been summarily sentenced under the Code for Petty Offenses (which allowed for imprisonment for up to 60 days or fines). By 31 August a further 245 people had been reportedly sentenced under federal law to sentences from one to 15 years' imprisonment[112] and over 60 people were tried and convicted in September.

The official figures for the number of convictions of ethnic Albanians in Kosovo between the large-scale nationalist demonstrations of March till April 1981 and the end of 1983 were 658 convictions for 'irredentist' activity and 'about 2000 punished for violations' – that is sentenced to up to 60 days' imprisonment or a fine[113]. Unofficial figures gave far higher figures. On 10 March 1984, *Tanjug* announced that 72 'illegal organizations' with 'about 1000 members' were uncovered in the province during the same period. These figures give some indication of the complexity of different groups in Kosovo at this time.

There appears, however, to have been five major groups: the Movement for the National Liberation of Kosovo (MNLK), whose leaders in exile, Jusuf and Bardhosh Gervalla, were shot in West Germany, probably by Yugoslav agents, which called for the unification of all Albanian-inhabited territories of Yugoslavia with Albania; the Group of Marxist-Leninists of Kosovo (GMLK), whose leader Kadri Zeka was shot with the Gervalla brothers, had aims similar to MNLK – these two organizations appeared to be planning to unite when their leaders were assassinated; the Red Front, which also aimed at unification with Albania; the Communist Party Marxist-Leninist of Yugoslavia – *Partia Komuniste Marksiste-Leniniste ne Jugosllavi* (PKMLSHJ) which aimed at republican status for Kosovo within Yugoslavia, and appears to have been based in Kosovo and comprised mainly of Communist Party members; and the Movement for an Albanian Republic in Yugoslavia – *Levizje per Republiken Shqiptare ne Jugosllavi* (LRSHJ), newspaper *Zeri i Kosoves* ('The Voice of Kosovo') published in Switzerland, one of whose founders, Nuhi Berisha, was killed in a shoot-out with police in January 1984 in Pristina. This last organization, the LRSHJ, appears to have been formed in early 1982 by a unification of the MNLK, GMLK and PKMLSHJ.

Mass arrests and trials continued. Most of those convicted were young teachers or high-school and university students – products of Pristina university – and were under 25 years old. A typical case was that of Nazmi Hoxha, a 33-year-old teacher, and 15 co-defendants most of whom were fellow-teachers or students. They were tried on 10 and 11 July 1982 by Gnjilane districts court and accused of belonging to the GMLK. According to *Tanjug*,[114] the GMLK was founded in 1976 in Pristina by Hydajet Hyseni, who was sentenced to 15 years' imprisonment on 17 November 1982 for nationalist activity. The group in Gnjilane, a branch of this organization, was apparently founded in 1978 by Nazmi Hoxha (who had known Hydajet Hyseni since 1975), and Bejtulla Tahiri, a 30-year-old teacher. Members of this group allegedly used pseudonyms, paid membership fees to subsidize the group's travel and printing expenses, and took an oath to defend the 'freedom and rights of Albanians in Yugoslavia and the Balkans'.

The statute of the GMLK, set out in the group's newspaper Paroja

('Vanguard') reportedly recommended the recruitment of educated people as they were considered better able to persuade others of the need to achieve republican status for Kosovo. The defendants were accused of having written and produced leaflets calling on Albanians to take part in boycotts and strikes and which were 'hostile' to the Yugoslavian state. They were said to have distributed these in Kosovo as well as in towns with large Albanian communities in the neighbouring republic of Macedonia. Some of the defendants were charged also with possessing and distributing 'hostile' literature (originating either in Albania or Albanian emigre circles) and with writing in various places the 'hostile' slogans 'Kosovo – Republic', 'Long live the socialist republic of Kosovo!', 'Down with traitors', 'There is no brotherhood and unity with chauvinists' and 'It cannot be held by terror'. The accused said that their organization was based on the tenets of Marxism-Leninism and Stalinism and that nationalist irredentist activity could not be attributed to them. They did not deny, however, that their organization aimed to achieve republican status for Kosovo and hoped that it would eventually be united with Albania. The Tanjug reports noted that despite the group's claim to have a strictly Marxist-Leninist-Stalinist basis, its members were unable to quote from any of Marx's works and appeared to be interested only in the works of the leaders of Albania. It was reported that no works by Marx or Lenin had been found among the group's possessions. Nazmi Hoxha was sentenced to 15 years' imprisonment while his co-defendants received sentences of up to 13 years.

This case was typical of many and illustrates many of the main features of the Albanian nationalist organizations in Kosovo in the early 1980s. These were underground groups, predominantly made up of young teachers and students, with branches throughout the province and with an ostensibly left-wing idealogy which in practice appeared to be mainly based on Albanian nationalism rather than the usually claimed Marxist-Leninism. Republican status for Kosovo and other Albanian inhabited regions of Yugoslavia like western Macedonia was the initial aim, to be followed by probable unification with Albania. The methods were initially essentially peaceful propaganda – most usually the writing of the slogan 'Kosovo Republic' which was seen by the authorities as an offence meriting lengthy prison sentences – and there seems little doubt that most of the Albanian majority in Kosovo supported this demand.

The severity of the prison sentences – many of six years or more for writing slogans like 'Kosovo Republic' – was somewhat ameliorated by the appeal courts. The President of the Supreme Court of Kosovo, Riza

Fazlija, in 1983 when referring to sentences passed in political trials in Kosovo after 1981, said that 60% of the verdicts of the courts of first instance (ie. the district courts) had been reduced on appeal by the Supreme Court of Kosovo. Young people in particular who had been 'led astray and who had expressed sincere repentance' had their sentences reduced. Fazlija commented:

> *'It is correct that some sentences of the lower courts were too severe. Perhaps the courts of the first instance had reason to impose these sentences in the situation that prevailed three years ago as a general preventive measure. But when these cases reached us the situation was different. Later courts of first instance themselves began to change their criteria and to adapt them to the social danger represented by the offenders. For this reason we have now fewer changes of sentence on appeal. As far as organized activity is concerned, sentences are still relatively severe, when imposed both by courts of first instance and by the Supreme Court of Kosovo'.*[115]

This meant that many young Albanians charged with 'hostile propaganda' under Article 133 of the federal criminal code, had their sentences reduced. However, those taking part in 'organized activity' (ie. members of underground groups) did not. Since October 1980 female prisoners from Kosovo have served their sentences in a women's prison in Lipljan, Kosovo. In the case of male prisoners, because of the lack of a 'penal reformatory institution' – *Kazneno-popravni domovi* (KPD) where sentences of over six months (in some republics, a year) are served – in Kosovo, male ethnic Albanian prisoners from Kosovo were sent to KPDs in other republics, often being continually moved and hundreds of kilometres from their homes and relatives.

There were many complaints of ill-treatment of ethnic Albanian political prisoners, and relatives visiting them were often forbidden to speak in Albanian.[116] In 1979 the Governor of Idrizovo prison (in Macedonia) and six guards were sentenced after two prisoners had died. They were apparently found guilty because 'while carrying out their superiors' orders they had become overzealous in discharging their duties and overstepped the bounds of their authority' after beating to death two ethnic Albanian prisoners who refused to go into solitary confinement.[117]

In 1983 emigre sources published a complaint by a group of Albanian political prisoners from Kosovo sent to the Secretariat of Justice of Croatia in which they described the ill-treatment they claimed to have received while being transported from Pristina district prison to Gospic prison in Croatia and while detained in Gospic. They stated, among other things, that on arrival at Gospic prison on 15 November 1981 they were forced to undress, then assaulted by guards who hit them on the face and body. Two prisoners claimed to have been hit on the genitals by guards who taunted them saying they would never produce children. The corridor was reportedly stained with blood. A group of some 20 more prisoners from Kosovo who arrived at Gospic on 26 December 1981 were said to have received similar treatment. Two prisoners who complained to the Prison Governor about ill-treatment were allegedly beaten unconscious in reprisal on 12 December 1981.[118]

However, as time wore on, and the aim of republican status seemed to be as far away as ever, some groups began to turn to violence, including firing at members of the security forces; or in the case of one group, of having hijacked a police vehicle containing arms. In May 1984 six ethnic Albanians were accused of having smuggled arms, ammunition and explosives into Yugoslavia for use in Kosovo. Another group was arrested in March 1984 and accused of having caused nine explosions in Pristina between October 1982 and March 1984. Other groups were accused of issuing statements threatening armed uprisings if Kosovo were not accorded the status of a republic by peaceful means. Such groups, using or advocating violence, were, however, a minority.

In addition to the mass imprisonment of ethnic Albanian nationalists, there was the policy of 'differentiation' among the Albanian party cadres and especially at Pristina university. This policy essentially meant that all those who did not actively disown the calls for Kosovo to become a seventh republic were purged, and the newspapers and media were full of cases of those who were expelled from their positions. In 1983 an emigre group in USA published an open letter to the UN Secretary-General in which they listed 57 leading academic staff associated with Pristina university who had either been arrested or expelled and publicly reprimanded.[119] In addition, many other Albanian intellectuals were removed from prominent positions and hundreds of elementary and secondary teachers were dismissed, while the intake of students to Pristina university was reduced.[120]

The repression has continued and since 1981 over 7000 Albanians, mostly young men (students, teachers and even school children), have been arrested and imprisoned in Kosovo for nationalist activity with many receiving prison sentences of six years or more.[121]

However, it is important to realize that, in the early 1980s, culturally the Albanians in Kosovo were not particularly disadvantaged. The Albanian language was in officially use. There was Albanian television, radio and newspapers. The leadership of the League of Communists of Kosovo were ethnic Albanians. The police and courts were also staffed by ethnic Albanians, and those imprisoned were tried by Albanians in the Albanian language. These 'official' Albanians (often referred to by demonstrators as 'traitors' of whom, perhaps, Rahman Morina, the Kosovo League of Communist Party leader who died in 1990, was the most renowned) were defending the status quo – ie. the communist system and the 1974 Constitution. The aim of the demonstrators was to extend the 1974 constitutional arrangements for Kosovo and to gain republican status.

Relations with the People's Socialist Republic of Albania

The authorities also blamed the influence of Albanian language text-books used in Kosovo originating from the neighbouring Albanian state and began to accuse Albania of meddling in Yugoslavia's internal affairs. In fact Albania, under the leadership of Enver Hoxha, despite denouncing the draconian repression in Kosovo post-1981, did not actively pursue the Kosovo issue. Hoxha's successor, Ramiz Alia, in line with the gradual relaxation of Albania from Hoxha's extreme isola-tionist policies, has taken up the Kosovo situation more than his pre-decessor. On 2 February 1990, Reis Malile, Albania's Foreign Minister, appealed to the UN over the situation in Kosovo[122] and in December 1990, Ramiz Alia even went as far as meeting Professor Zekeria Cana, Secretary of the Council for the Protection of Human Rights and Free-doms in Kosovo, and express Albania's solidarity with the Albanians of Kosovo[123].

It is likely that Albania will increasingly become involved in the Kosovo issue. The leader of the Democratic Party of Albania, the first main opposition party in Albania since the communist take-over after World War II, Sali Berisha, in an interview with a Yugoslav paper in December 1990, stated that his party recognized 'Kosovo as a republic and the right of all Albanians living in other parts of Yugoslavia to self-determination.' While he recognized the 'republic of Kosovo' within a Yugoslav federation, he added that he could see the unifica-tion of the Albanian nation within the framework of a future united Europe.[124]

The Serb counter-attack

These continuing events further soured ethnic relations. Since 1981 Serbs and Montenegrins have continued to emigrate in large numbers, complaining of physical attacks and intimidation by ethnic Albanians who are now also beginning to dominate demographically in some southern areas of Serbia proper. These reports of ethnic attacks are hard to assess, and while in the steadily deteriorating situation it is likely that rising ethnic tension has led in cases to outrages against local Serbs, official statistics do not support Serb allegations of 'genocide'. However, beginning in late 1985 the situation of the Serbs in Kosovo began to feature more and more in the mainstream of Serbian public opinion with the January 1986 petition by some 200 prominent Belgrade intellectuals to the Yugoslav and Serbian national assemblies being crucial. By 1987 Serb nationalism was well and truly on the rise and Kosovo was the touchstone with 60,000 Kosovo Serbs signing a petition, again alleging 'genocide' against Serbs in Kosovo.

The Serb Communist Party leadership was also changing and the rise of Slobodan Milosevic, riding the upsurge of aggrieved Serb nationalism, saw a fundamental change in policy in Kosovo, vis-a-vis the Albanians. The new line was that autonomy for Kosovo (and the Vojvodina) as allowed under the 1974 constitution worked to Serbia's disadvantage as it allowed for *de facto* republics within the republic of Serbia. The new leadership set about changing this by reducing autonomy in the two provinces.

While the ethnic Albanian Communist Party leadership in Kosovo had apparently been willing to defend the status quo, they would not for the most part be party to its destruction at the expense of the ethnic Albanian majority. Thus they had to go. In November 1988, due to pressure from Serbia, former Tito protege Azem Vllasi, an ethnic Albanian and former Kosovo party leader, resigned from the Kosovo politburo. This sparked off mass demonstrations by ethnic Albanians and a general strike in Kosovo in protest at this, and at the constitutional changes limiting the province's autonomy which the Serbian leadership was pushing through.

In February 1989 troops were sent into Kosovo and when the changes were passed in March there were clashes between Albanian demonstrators and troops in which at least 24 people were killed and hundreds arrested and detained. Following these disturbances up to 2000 Albanian workers were jailed for up to 60 days or fined, sacked or disciplined for taking industrial action, and some 200 others had their passports withdrawn. Journalists, teachers and Communist Party members were purged and an unknown number of school pupils who took part in the demonstrations were expelled from schools.[125]

Azem Vllasi was arrested in March 1989 and charged along with 14 other leading ethnic Albanians with 'counter-revolutionary endangering of the social order', a charge which could carry the death penalty. The trial began on 30 October in Titova Mitrovica and was preceded on 27 October by an underground sit-in strike by some 60 ethnic Albanian miners in Stari Trg mine nearby in protest at the trial. The mine was immediately sealed off by security forces and on 30 October police entered and arrested the organizers. Further demonstrations against the trial took place in Pristina, Urosevac and Podujevo and were dispersed by armoured cars and tear-gas.

Deterioration in 1990

Further waves of demonstrations and violent clashes with police began again in Kosovo on 23 January. At least eight people died by the end of the month and press reports gave figures as high as 22. The demonstrators' demands were for free elections, the release of political prisoners and an end to the partial State of Emergency in the province. Tension between Kosovo Serbs and Albanians reached new heights with students in Belgrade demanding weapons to go and protect fellow Serbs in Kosovo. By the end of February the death toll – all ethnic Albanians – had risen to at least 32. Federal troops were sent in and a curfew declared.[126]

Circles within the Serbian Communist Party and in the Serbian opposition began to raise the possibility of expelling 'disloyal' Albanians 'back' to Albania. The huge figure of 300,000 was given for emigres from PRS Albania who were accused of being subversives, and in some cases ethnic Albanians, some of whom had lived in Yugoslavia since 1948, were given 30 days to leave the country. The figure was later revised to 732 persons whose refugee status had not been recognized.[127]

The situation further deteriorated with a outbreak of poisoning in March which affected only Albanian schoolchildren. These still unexplained poisonings continued as late as September 1990.[128] Albanians attacked local Serbs accusing them of mass-poisoning and, as a result, Serbia took over direct control of policing in Kosovo, suspending over 200 members of the mainly Albanian provincial police force and drafting 2500 Serb policemen into the province.[129] This provoked the resignation of first the Kosovo police chief and then the Kosovo prime minister and six other ministers. A Serb deputy prime minister was 'stationed' in Kosovo.

Increasingly Serbia was taking direct control of the key instruments of power away from local (Albanian) officials. The essentially Serbian character of these moves is illustrated by the withdrawal of Slovene and Croatian contingents from the federal ministry's militia units in Kosovo on 4 February and 4 April, respectively,[130] and even the demand for withdrawal of Macedonian militia from Kosovo.[131] This Macedonian demand was reiterated by the Macedonian Secretary for Internatal Affairs, Jovan Trpenovski, in early 1991.[132] In a rare (for this period) move of apparent appeasement, it was announced on 18 April that Serbia had agreed to the Yugoslav Presidency's proposal to lift emergency measures in Kosovo and many political prisoners (predominantly Albanians) were released.[133] Azem Vllasi and his 14 co-defendants were also released on 24 April as was Adem Demaqi who had spent a total of 28 years in prison for Albanian nationalist activity and who still had five more months of his sentence to serve.

Such moves, however, were against the overwhelming trend. By the end of May 1990 all ethnic Albanian members of Kosovo's government had resigned in protest at Serbian interference, and the Kosovo Assembly reached stalemate with Serb and Montenegrin deputies routinely walking-out when out-voted by ethnic Albanians. In all areas of public life, the economy and education etc., the two communities confronted each other and the government, increasingly supported only by the Serb/Montenegrin minorities, appeared powerless.[134]

On 20 June, 61 ethnic Albanian delegates from the Kosovo Assembly tried to block the new Serbian constitution, which aimed to abolish what was left of the province's autonomy, and proposed instead a new provincial constitution making Kosovo independent of Serbia (ie. a Kosovo Republic). The assembly's president, Djordje Bozovic (a Serb), adjourned the assembly and promised to reconvene on 2 July. However he postponed this until 5 July so as not to conflict with the referendum on Serbia's constitution which was taking place on 1 and 2 July. He ordered the assembly to be locked but on 2 July, 114 out of 123 ethnic Albanian members (111 deputies constitute a quorum), of the 183-seat assembly, gathered outside the locked-up assembly building and adopted this declaration of self-determination for Kosovo.[135] The Serbian authorities replied by dissolving the Kosovo Assembly and government on 5 July. In protest the Kosovo Presidency resigned, and the Serbian Assembly introduced a 'special measures' law and took over the government.

By September over 15,000 ethnic Albanian functionaries had been dismissed since the closure of the Kosovo Assembly on 2 July, and Pristina university was being stacked with Serb students despite the shortfalls at other universities[136] and some, including a Serb lecturer in international public law at Pristina university, even went as far as calling for the complete closure of Pristina university.[137] In February 1991,

Vukasin Jokanovic, Vice- President of the Serbian Assembly, stated that the teaching of Albanian in schools in Kosovo-Metohija was to be dramatically reduced so that the number of Albanians allowed to attend secondary schools would be equal to the number of Serbs and Montenegrins.[138]

The 'Kacanak constitution'

On 7 September a two-thirds majority of Kosovo deputies met in secret at Kacanak in the south of the province near Macedonia and again declared Kosovo to be a republic. At this meeting a constitution was adopted which stated that: 'the Republic of Kosovo is a democratic state of the Albanian people and of members of other nations and national minorities who are its citizens: Serbs, Muslims, Montenegrins, Croats, Turks, Romanies and others living in Kosovo.'[139] The Serbian authorities quickly condemned this move and the Pristina public prosecutor declared it 'a criminal act' and moved to bring charges against those participating.[140] Many of the participants fled Kosovo and Serbia to other republics where they were free from prosecution. By late September four had been detained and others, including the former president of the Executive council, Jusuf Zejnulahu, and former head of the Kosovo militia, Jusuf Karakusi, remained wanted.[141] Even reportage of the event was seen as criminal and Zenon Celaj, a leading *Rilindja* journalist and Secretary of the Pristina-based Committee for the Protection of Human Rights, was kept in detention for a month merely for being present and reporting the incident.[142]

In tandem with the political confrontation, the Albanian language media was initially pressured and then closed. Thirty journalists from *Rilindja*, the main Albanian language newspaper published in Pristina, were suspended for reporting a political strike in Stari Trg by ethnic Albanians in February 1989 and in little more than a year *Rilindja* had five editors.[143] Albanian-language broadcasting on Pristina TV and radio was stopped and in August *Rilindja* was banned altogether until further notice. Some 1500 ethnic Albanian policemen were sacked and thousands of other ethnic Albanians who refused to recognize Serbia'a authority were likewise dismissed and replaced by Serbs. In September the new Serbian constitution was passed and the autonomy of the two provinces of Kosovo and the Vojvodina effectively ended – Kosovo was also renamed Kosovo-Metohija.

The old 'illegal' underground groups with their attempted semi-Leninist organizations had been replaced by mass organizations: the Democratic Alliance of Kosovo, the Social Democratic Party of Kosovo, the Peasant Democratic Party of Kosovo, the Youth Parliament of Kosovo, and the Committee for the Truth about Kosovo. Another group set up in February was the Pec Initiative Council, set up for the return of Albanian emigres from Kosovo to counter Serb demands for a Serbian re-colonization of Kosovo. This organization set up branches all over Kosovo as well as in Salzburg, New York, Norway and Sweden, and claimed that in Turkey alone, over 35,000 ethnic Albanians declared themselves prepared to return to Kosovo.[144] In late 1990 the Albanian Democratic Christian Party was reportedly set up, which claimed 70,000 members and offices in Pristina, Zagreb and which also claimed to have offices in Shkoder and Tirane in Albania. How successful such a party based on Roman Catholicism will be, remains to be seen.

The most important of these groups was the Democratic Alliance of Kosovo (KDA) led by the dissident ethnic Albanian writer Ibrahim Rugova. The KDA succeeded in transforming local branches of the Socialist Alliance of Working People of Kosovo into its own branches and became unquestionably the mass party of ethnic Albanians in Kosovo with a membership of hundreds of thousands. A further sign of Albanian solidarity were the agreements on 14 March and 1 May by tens of thousands of ethnic Albanians in Kosovo to end the traditional blood-feuds among hostile families which had been a marked feature of Albanian life.[145]

The KDA and other ethnic Albanian opposition groups refused to take part in the referendum held in Serbia at the beginning of July on the government proposal to delay free elections until the new constitution, which severely curtailed Kosovo and the Vojvodina's autonomy, was adopted. Turnout in Kosovo was only about 25% with the vast majority of ethnic Albanians boycotting the referendum. The success of the referendum meant that in the forthcoming elections Kosovo would be treated merely as a part of Serbia and the Albanians in Kosovo finally cease to be a majority with political clout in the federal structure and merely become an emasculated minority in Serbia. The KDA and other groups inevitably boycotted the elections held in Serbia in December which saw Slobodan Milosevic triumph.

Religion

The Albanians of Kosovo are Muslim by majority with some 50,000 Roman Catholics especially in Binac in Vitina Opstina and around Prizren. Some observers have held that Islam is not held in high esteem among the Albanians of Yugoslavia and that most *hodzhas* opposed the growth of Albanian nationalism. Official reports stated that: 'not a single Imam, teacher or student at the *medrece* [religious school] participated in the 1981 demonstrations but contributed to attempts to resolve the 'complicated situation'.[146] This would not appear to be the case in Macedonia where the authorities have attempted to protect (Slav) Muslims from what they see as encroaching Albanian nationalism through Islam.

However, the continuing repression in Kosovo has prompted the Islamic community leadership to raise the Kosovo issue. In March the leadership of the Islamic community in Yugoslavia pointed out that all people killed by the militia in Kosovo were Muslims and complaints regarding the State of Emergency in Kosovo were forwarded to the Federal Government and the Presidency of Yugoslavia.[147] It appears that, similarly to the political change in Kosovo where the opposition has expanded from illegal underground groups to embrace virtually all aspects of society, the Islamic community has also begun to be drawn into the Kosovo problem on the ethnic Albanian side.

As noted above, Kosovo has the highest percentage of religious believers in Yugoslavia and, while there are no formal links between the SDA, the main (Slav) Muslim organization in Bosnia-Hercegovina, and the KDA, there does appear to be some sympathy[148] while in Montenegro the ethnic Albanians and (Slav) Muslims fought the elections in December 1990 on a joint ticket. As so often in the Balkans, religion remains a crucial factor and future close cooperation between the predominantly Muslim ethnic Albanians of Yugoslavia, and not only the large numbers of Muslim Slavs in Bosnia-Hercegovina but also in the Sandzak in southern Serbia proper and Macedonia, may well be an important factor in the future.

There are also some 65,000 Roman Catholics in Kosovo of whom 10,000 are Croats in the three parishes of Janjevo, Letnica, and Vrnavo Kolo.[149] The remainder are Albanian Catholics. The Serb authorities and media have accused the Catholic Church of supporting the demand for a Greater Albania and of actively converting Albanians so as to help achieve this aim. For example, the Belgrade fortnightly *'Duga'* of 28 September-12 October 1990 accused the Vatican of having plotted with the Americans and CIA to incorporate Kosovo into an enlarged Albania and to reduce Serbia to a small Orthodox state dependent on mainly Catholic Europe.[150]

These attacks appear to be a continuation of age-old hostility between Orthodox Serbs and Catholic Croats with the Serbs seeing an anti-Serb alliance of Catholic Croats (and Slovenes) with Albanians to break up Yugoslavia at the Serbs expense. The culmination of these allegations was the armed raids by Serb militia on 4 August 1990 on a Catholic Church in Urosevac and a Catholic convent in Binac in Kosovo in which a quantity of medicines for which the convent had a licence was confiscated. The raid was followed by accusations in the Serb media that the recent mysterious mass-poisoning of Albanian schoolchildren was the work of the Catholic Church.[151]

The break-down of Tito's policy vis-a-vis the Albanians and the 1974 arrangement was complete. Whereas in the initial post-1981 period the opposition was predominantly underground groups, claiming to be Marxist-Leninist (although almost certainly with majority backing for their central demand of republican status for Kosovo) who were heavily repressed by the Albanian-dominated local authority, now it was undeniably the entire Albanian former majority in Kosovo and now a minority in Serbia who were in opposition and the province was nakedly under Serb military occupation.

Ironically, this ethnic clamp-down by the Serbs against the ethnic Albanians, which necessitated tactics akin to an army of occupation with many deaths, the systematic silencing of Albanian media, and the replacement of all key areas of the executive, was taking place at the same time as the rest of Yugoslavia was experiencing the rebirth of free elections and free political activity. Tragically, it appears that the main opposition to Milosevic in Serbia proper is at least as nationalistic and chauvinistic on the ethnic Albanian issue as the Milosevic camp. However, Serbia cannot rule Kosovo by force forever. The Albanian issue will not go away.

In addition to the Albanians of Kosovo who, until the recent changes in the political balance between Kosovo and Serbia proper, constituted a majority in that part of the federal structure, there are substantial Albanian minorities in Serbia proper, Montenegro and Macedonia. The most important of these, due in no small part to the controversial nature of the whole idea of a Macedonian nation, but also due to their size, are the ethnic Albanians of the SR Macedonia.

6

THE LARGEST NATIONALITY II
– ALBANIANS OUTSIDE KOSOVO

Albanians in Montenegro and south Serbia

The 40,000 Albanians in Montenegro make up 6.5% of the republic's population, living mostly on the borders with Albania and Kosovo. As in other republics there are Albanian language schools and media outlets. In 1983 in Ulcinj, Tuzi and Plav – the main Albanian dominated areas – some 5000 Albanians attended elementary schools and 1230 attended secondary schools. Radio Titograd broadcasts a programme in Albanian and there were plans for an Albanian language TV programme. In 1978 an Albanian language magazine *Koha* ('*Time*') began publishing in Titograd with almost half its 2000 copy print run sold in Ulcinj, and there are many cultural artistic societies.[152]

However, the events in Kosovo also had repercussions in Montenegro and in 1981 a number of educational workers in Ulcinj were expelled from the local League of Communists and dismissed from schools, due to Albanian nationalist activity following a seminar held in Ulcinj in September 1981, which apparently turned into an attack by ethnic Albanians on the then educational policies for the Albanians.[153]

The authorities were also worried by the proximity of Albania and the possible influence of propaganda through TV and radio from the neighbouring country. 'Irredentist' activity also took place in Plav, again the schools providing the arena[154] and, similarly to the events in Kosovo and Macedonia, the authorities claimed that the textbooks used in the schools were vehicles for Albanian nationalism. The Albanian activists in Kosovo and Macedonia often include the Albanian-inhabited areas of Montenegro in a proposed 'Kosovo' republic (or incorporation into Albania), and the events in Kosovo are watched carefully by Montenegro's Albanian minority. However, they are not numerous enough in the republic to take the lead in such matters.

They have, however, united with the more numerous Muslims who comprise 13.4% of Montenegro's population. In the elections held in Montenegro in December 1990 the Democratic Coalition of Muslims and Albanians won 13 out of the total 125 seats and came third behind the communists who, similarly to Serbia, won a convincing majority (83 seats) and Ante Markovic's Yugoslav party – the Alliance of Reformist Forces – which won 17 seats.[155] Thus once again, as so often in the Balkans, religion appears to be a crucial factor.

Ethnic Albanians also live in sizeable numbers in the south of Serbia proper, mainly in the *opstinas* of Bujanovac, Medvedja, and Presevo. Of the approximately half a million people who live in south Serbia, in 1982 80% were Serb and 10% Albanian. However, the Albanians made up 53% of Bujanovac opstina, 30% of Medvedja and 85% of Presevo *opstina*.[156]

Similarly to Kosovo, Serbs living in these areas have claimed that the Albanians have exerted pressure on them by desecration of graves, attempted rapes, threats and physical attacks, resulting in an emigration of Serbs and other groups (notably Roma) and allowing the creation of ethnically pure Albanian areas akin to the situation in Kosovo. Again with parallels to Kosovo, the Serbs claim that the Albanians also operate an unfair policy of house buying which works to their disadvantage.[157] Similarly to Kosovo it is hard to assess these claims. The emigration of Serbs out of these areas and the growth of the Albanian population is a fact, but economic motives, as opposed to nationalist pressure, and the high birth-rate of the ethnic Albanian population are also important factors.

The Albanians of Macedonia

The ethnic Albanians, by far the largest minority in the Socialist Republic of Macedonia, live in compact settlements in the west of the republic bordering on Albania, the north-west bordering on the predominantly Albanian province of Kosovo, and in Skopje where they make up over 14% of the population. They constitute a majority of the population in many western areas, notably the districts of: Tetovo – about 113,000 Albanians to 38,000 Macedonians; Gostivar – 63,000 to 18,000; Kicevo – 23,000 to 21,000; and Debar – 10,000 to 2500. In the towns the difference is not so marked, for example there are some 22,000 Albanians, 18,000 Macedonians and 2000 Turks in Tetovo itself.[158]

There were 377,726 Albanians according to the census of 1981, comprising 19.8% of the population which shows an increase of slightly more than 36% over the figures in the previous census of 1971 when there were 279,871 Albanians (17% of the population). Thus, the Albanians have a considerably higher birth-rate than the Macedonians and a delegate from Tetovo reported to the Macedonian League of Communists on 26 April 1988 that the birthrate in Tetovo, an area of high Albanian concentration, was three times the national average. The situation regarding the position of the Albanians vis-a-vis the Macedonians is reminiscent of that of the ethnic Turks vis-a-vis the Bulgarians in Bulgaria – a sizeable minority with a far higher growth rate, speaking a different language, living in concentrated areas especially in the countryside, Islamic as opposed to the Orthodox majority, and whose geographical position gives rise to a possible irredenta.

Education and culture

The post-war Yugoslav authorities pledged to solve the country's seemingly intractable national problems under the slogan of 'Brotherhood and Unity' and, as noted above, the Macedonians were recognized for the first time as a separate nation. The Albanians are recognized as a nationality of Yugoslavia, not as a nation as the Albanian national 'home' is outside of Yugoslavia, and as such have a number of education and cultural rights.

By 1951, there were over 200 Albanian schools in Macedonia employing over 600 teachers and catering for over 26,000 pupils and by 1973 this had been expanded to 248 schools employing 2150 teachers and over 60,000 pupils.[159] In 1981, *Tanjug*, the official Yugoslav news agency, reported on 9 July 1981 that there were 287 Albanian language elementary schools employing about 3000 teachers with over 74,000 pupils in Macedonia with a further 8200 in secondary schools attending classes in the Albanian language – figures which have changed little according to the Bosnian newspaper Oslobodjenje of 6 January 1989. There were also in 1980, 2365 students of Albanian nationality enroled at university-level institutions. Additionally there is an Albanian newspaper Flaka e Vellazerimit, Albanian television and radio programmes, and many Albanian cultural associations, theatre groups, sports clubs etc. However, in reality, the picture was not as harmonious as the above indicates.

The growth of Albanian nationalism and the authorities' reaction

In the republic of Macedonia all the ethnic minorities with the exception of the Serbs have a smaller proportion of membership in the

League of Communists (LC) than their proportion in the population. For example, the membership of the Skopje League of Communists compared with the population figures in 1981 was[160]:

Ethnic group	% of population	% of membership	% of group in LC
Macedonians	67.00	82.95	20.95
Albanians	14.36	5.43	6.39
Serbs	4.88	5.59	19.39
Gypsies	3.59	0.63	2.95
Turks	3.42	1.13	5.57
Muslims (Pomaks)	3.42	0.90	4.44

Thus the Macedonians had a considerably higher representation in the LC membership than in the population while the representation of the ethnic minorities, excepting the Serbs, was far below their share in the ethnic composition of the population and this situation was typical of the situation in the republic as a whole. The minorities of Macedonia were not keen to join the ruling LC and it appears that the Socialist Republic of Macedonia is a state effectively run by Macedonians more than their position in the population figures merits.

The fall of Rankovic in 1966 allowed Albanian dissatisfaction in Kosovo to come out into the open and there were large-scale demonstrations there in November 1968 calling for Kosovo to be granted republican status followed by a similar demonstration in Tetovo with the demand for the Albanian areas of Macedonia to join Kosovo in a seventh republic. To grant such a republic is seen, probably correctly, by many Yugoslavs as being merely the first stage in an Albanian plot to eventually separate these areas and to join them with neighbouring Albania. The events in Kosovo in 1981 and beyond were mirrored by similar, if smaller scale, nationalist manifestations by Albanians in Macedonia and the authorities became increasingly worried at them and reacted with, if anything, even greater severity in terms of penal sentencing than the authorities in Kosovo. Should such a proposed seventh republic comprising the Albanian-dominated areas of Western Macedonia occur, this would severely truncate the Macedonian republic and almost certainly revive Bulgarian (and even Serbian and Greek) claims to the remaining rump. Thus, the growth of Albanian nationalism in Macedonia could prove fatal not only to the territorial integrity of the republic but even to the very existence of the Macedonian nation.

In July 1981 the Macedonian Assembly's Commission for Intra-National Relations backed the demand by the Assembly's Socio-Political Chamber for a revision of syllabuses and textbooks to attempt to stem the rising nationalist tide among Albanians. The Commission called for the number of hours devoted to teaching Macedonian in Albanian language schools to be increased and measures taken to prevent schools from not teaching Macedonian at all. In August 1981 the Macedonian Republican Pedagogical Council in Skopje noted 'weaknesses in the teaching syllabuses, programmes, textbooks and reference works used by the Albanian nationality in Macedonia' and it was stated that 'publishers had been insufficiently vigilant in preventing the penetration of Albanian nationalistic, irredentist and counter-revolutionary tendencies through printed textbooks and other literature'.[161]

On 7 May 1984 the Macedonian Secretary for Internal Affairs reporting on 'activity by the internal enemy from positions of Albanian nationalism and irredentism' had become more pronounced and that 'in 1983 alone, three illegal groups with 11 members, six organizers of leaflet circulation and 15 authors of leaflets with contents from positions of Albanian nationalism and irredentism, were detected in the republic'. A further 'total of 160 persons had been detected making hostile verbal comments.'[162]

On 10 December 1986, Borba, the LCY organ published in Belgrade, reported on the increasingly frequent party punishments for 'unvigilant' participations in weddings and other celebrations in the Tetovo area by Albanian officials following a wedding in Strimnica village attended by senior officials at which supposed 'expressions of nationalist euphoria' were present. The same article reported on the findings of Muamer Visko, editor-in-chief of the Albanian-language service broadcast by Radio Skopje. He had apparently listened to the entire record library of Albanian popular tunes and folksongs and from just over 1000 records had found 260 which had 'nationalistic or national-romantic' content – many from the People's Socialist Republic of Albania and some even recorded by 'Balkanton' in Sofia, Bulgaria. The article went on to point to the dangers of unregistered Albanian artistic societies using unapproved repertoire of nationalist content, especially on local radio stations broadcasting in the Albanian language in Kumanovo, Tetovo, Kicevo, Gostivar, Struga and Resen.

The Macedonian authorities, again with parallels to the Bulgarian authorities' name-changing campaign, also turned their attention to Albanian names. On 17 December 1986, Tanjug reported that a registrar in Tetovo commune was expelled from the LC for registering names 'which stimulated nationalist sentiment and adherence to the

People's Socialist Republic of Albania' to newborn Albanian children of 'nationalist inspired parents'. The offending names quoted were Alban, Albana, Shqipe, Fljamur (Albanian flag); Kustrim (call); Ljiridu- am (we want freedom); and one meaning 'Red Eagle'. Additionally, it was reported that for the names of cities and towns, the Macedonian forms, not the Albanian ones, must be used. The banning of Albanian names and Albanian folksongs prompted protests from Albanian writ- ers in Kosovo.

The high birthrate of the Albanian population has also worried the Macedonian authorities and the spectre of expanding 'ethnically pure' Albanian areas akin to the situation developing in Kosovo has appar- ently prompted them to contemplate punitive administrative mea- sures against those with large families. On 28 January 1988 ATA, the official news agency of the People's Socialist Republic of Albania, using extracts from the Yugoslav newspapers Rilindja of Pristina, Kosovo, and Vecerne Novosti of Belgrade, accused the Macedonian authorities of 'neo-Malthusian' policies after it was reported that in Tetovo com- mune a 'package of administrative measures' would be introduced at the beginning of 1988 to restrain births. Among the measures are that families should pay for medical services of any children more than the ideal two in number and that there would be no child allowance, for such extra children and even a possible financial penalty. ATA report- ed that these measures are also to be introduced in the communes of Gostivar, Debar, Kicevo and Struga.

The campaign against Albanian nationalism, called 'differentiation', escalated. On 25 October 1987, Flaka e Vellazerimit, published in Alba- nian in Skopje, reported the decision by the President of the Tetovo LC Municipal Committee to apparently dismiss a further 100 Albanian officials from the state administration and subject them to 'ideological differentiation', and the same paper reported on 30 October of mea- sures taken by the Republican Secretariat for People's Defence against 34 Albanian officers in Tetovo commune, most of whom apparently were discharged for attending Albanian weddings at which 'national- ist' songs were sung. Many cultural clubs have also been disbanded.

These and other measures, which went even further than the corre- sponding anti-Albanian nationalism policies of 'differentiation' taking place at the same time in Kosovo, provoked opposition from within the LC, especially from the Albanian members in Kosovo, which in turn angered the Macedonian members. The delegates at the Macedo- nian Assembly session in February 1988 reacted sharply to criticism of Macedonian policies by Azem Vllazi – then President of the Kosovo LC Provincial Committee. The Assembly agreed that the legal measures –

'above all, the provisions concerning personal names, the ban on the sale of property in the western part of the republic [to prevent Albanians buying out Macedonians and creating 'ethnically pure territories'], the amendment to the law on religious teaching [to prohibit the attendance of organized religious instruction by young people up to the age of 15], and the resolution on population policy, whose purpose is to stop aggressive demographic expansion' – was 'to prevent the activities of Albanian nationalists and separatists'.[163]

For the Albanian population in Macedonia it was perhaps events in the field of education and language rights which provoked the most opposition. In 1983, teachers in Tetovo were disciplined and some dismissed from the LC for not observing regulations regarding the use of Macedonian in official matters, and Tanjug on 5 October 1983 reported that 'a large number of pupils of Albanian nationality also followed their teachers' example by boycotting and belittling the Macedonian language.' A law on secondary school education of 1985 in Macedonia stipulated that classes with Albanian as the language of instruction can only be created if over 30 Albanian pupils enrol for the class and there are enough qualified teachers. This law has become progressively more strictly enforced resulting in the closure of classes with an insufficient intake of Albanian pupils and compelling Albanians to attend mixed classes with the instruction in Macedonian. The impact of the enforcement of this law is that while in 1981 there were 8200 pupils attending classes in secondary schools in Albanian, by the end of 1988 the newspaper Oslobodjenje published in Sarajevo reported on 6 January 1989 that the figure was down to 4221.

Although some of the 'missing' pupils can be explained by the impact on secondary schools of the growing numbers of Albanian children who are failing to attend primary school – on 8 October 1987 Tanjug reported that in 1986 criminal proceedings were initiated in 3802 cases in the municipalities of Gostivar, Tetovo, Skopje, Struga, Kichevo, Titov Veles and Kumanovo, almost always against Albanians – the compulsory schooling in Macedonian for some Albanian pupils has caused great resentment and boycotts, such as the boycott by 60 Albanian pupils in September 1987 at the Nace Budjoni centre for vocational training in Kumanovo. The problems involved were highlighted by the fact that according to a Tanjug report of 10 September 1987 some of the pupils did not know Macedonian, and therefore, were unable to follow mixed classes in it. Albanian teachers also protested at the measures and at the Nace Budjoni and Pero Nakov centres in Kumanovo nine teachers and 26 pupils were expelled. Similar events took place in Gostivar.

The situation boiled over in 1988 with demonstrations by young Albanians in Kumanovo in August and Gostivar in October holding banners and shouting slogans against the measures and claiming their rights as guaranteed in the 1974 Constitution. In Kumanovo at least 128 Albanians were detained for up to 60 days and the authorities responded by arresting in both instances the organizers, 20 of whom were subsequently imprisoned. For example, in January in the district court of Skopje, three men aged 32, 29 and 19 were sentenced to between six and 11 years' imprisonment and four minors aged 16 or 17, two of whom were girls, and all of whom were pupils at the Pance Popovski school in Gostivar, received sentences of between four and six years' imprisonment for their part in the Gostivar demonstration.

Religion

The Albanians of Macedonia are overwhelmingly Muslim with a few orthodox villages around Lake Ohrid and a small number of Roman Catholics in Skopje, most of whom have moved from the Prizren area in the neighbouring province of Kosovo. Some observers have held that Islam is not held in high esteem among the Albanians of Yugoslavia and that most hodzhas oppose the growth of Albanian nationalism. However, in Macedonia the authorities see Islam as a tool of Albanian nationalism and as a way for the Albanians to assimilate other smaller Islamic minority groups like the Turks and Pomaks and Muslim Gypsies.

This was detailed in a 23-page instalment published by the Skopje daily Vecer between 25 September and 21 October 1980, entitled 'Islamism in Macedonia'. An article in Nova Makedonija published in Skopje on 19 June 1981, whilst reporting on the rejection by the Macedonian Islamic community of Albanian nationalism, noted that in some villages where Muslim Macedonians live hodzhas who preach in Albanian had been appointed. On 21 December 1986, NIN, a magazine published in Belgrade, commented on the large number of Albanians from Macedonia undergoing religious instruction in Arab countries and the same article stated that in the preceding 10 years there had been 210 mosques renovated or built in Western Macedonia.

There have been a number of subsequent articles and reports about 'too extensive' Islamic religious instruction in Macedonia and how the Islamic community in Macedonia is overstepping the legal regulations, especially regarding instruction to under-age girls. This last point is highlighted by the problem of the Teteks clothing factory in Pirok, just outside Tetovo, in recruiting women employees despite some 20,000 unemployed Albanian women in and around Tetovo, thereby necessitating the commuting of over 200 workers daily from Skopje.[164] Local Albanians, however, see such 'busing-in' of non-Albanian labour as another example of the authorities' anti-Albanian policies. The authorities blame Islamic indoctrination of women and traditional Albanian attitudes to women, and have been loathe to cooperate in allowing new mosques to be opened. For example, in 1983 authorization was sought for the erection of a minaret, financed privately by the Albanian inhabitants, in the village of Donja Arnakija, but was refused. The villagers went ahead with the construction but in December 1986 the minaret was dynamited by the authorities.[165]

As noted above the authorities have also amended the law on religious teaching to prohibit the attendance of organized religious instruction by young people up to the age of 15, specifically to counter the growing influence of Islam. Conversely, the authorities, as noted above, have good relations with the Macedonian Orthodox Church which is seen as a standard bearer of the Macedonian nation in the ethnically mixed areas of Western Macedonia.

Communities apart

The reality of the situation in Macedonia is that there is very little mixing between ethnic groups. A study published in 1974 by the sociologist Dr. Ilija Josifovski[166] on the Macedonian, Albanian and Turkish populations in the villages of Polog which includes the areas around Tetovo and Gostivar, showed that 95% of the Albanian and Macedonian and 84% of the Turkish heads of individual households would not let their sons marry a girl of different nationality, while for daughters the figures were even higher. For Albanians, this is shown by the numbers of Albanian students at Skopje university whose sisters attend Pristina university in Kosovo which is almost entirely Albanian in intake and where they will meet only Albanian men. Mixed marriages between Macedonians on one hand and Albanians and Turks on the other were found not to exist in the study. Religion was again seen as being of paramount importance and that 'a religious isolation stands behind the deceptive impression of national, ethnic cleavages.'

The drift from village to town among the Macedonian population is shown by 42% decline in agricultural population over the period 1963-1971 while for the same period the Albanian agricultural population declined only 11%, again similar to the differences between Slavs and ethnic Turks in Bulgaria, so that many Macedonian villages are now populated almost entirely by the old, despite the authorities offering financial inducements for young Macedonians either to stay in the villages or return to them. These declining communities and the new villages of 'Weekendicas' – holiday homes for the Macedonian well-to-do which are empty in the week – contrast greatly with the Albanian and Gypsy (and Muslim Macedonian) villages, with their numbers of youths and children readily visible on the streets.

Thus, despite the aim of 'Brotherhood and Unity' as espoused by the communist authorities, the picture was one of mistrust and increasing alienation between the Macedonians and the rapidly expanding Albanian population of Macedonia mirrored in everyday relations by chauvinist attitudes from both sides.

In 1989, the Macedonian authorities amended the republic's constitution so that the Socialist Republic of Macedonia was defined as a 'nation-state of Macedonian people' instead of the previous formulation which defined it as 'a state of the Macedonian people and the Albanian and Turkish minorities.' This change reflected the growing unease of the Macedonian authorities in the face of Albanian nationalism and the possible break-up of Yugoslavia which has manifested itself in a more aggressive Macedonian nationalism.

Events in 1990

During 1990, the situation in Kosovo, always closely watched by all Albanians in Macedonia and often an important pointer to future action in Macedonia, deteriorated. On 1 February, some 2000 ethnic Albanians, demanding that the Albanian dominated areas of western Macedonia be granted independence, attempted to block the centre of Tetovo. The demonstrators, chanting 'We want a Greater Albania', were quickly dispersed by police.[167] However, the situation in Macedonia remained relatively quiet throughout most of 1990 as Kosovo took centre stage.

The language issue in and out of schools remained. On 19 June, over 11,000 ethnic Albanians from Struga signed a petition to the SFRJ Assembly, the Macedonian Assembly and the Struga Municipal Assembly, calling for 'pure' parallel tuition in Albanian to be opened in the Niko Nestor secondary school centre in Struga.[168] The authorities, however, remained unmoved by such appeals. On 28 August, the Macedonian government rejected a petition from several Albanian alternative groups and civic leaders calling for the use of Albanian in teaching and school administration, the revision of the curriculum, and the reinstatement of ethnic Albanian teachers suspended on political pretexts. The government justified its rejection by reference to the newly worded constitution by saying that the demands 'deviated from existing legal regulations and the constitution, which states that Macedonia is a state of the Macedonian nation.'[169] On 16 August, a Tetovo Albanian, Remzi Redzepi, was sentenced to a month's imprisonment and a fine for 'causing anxiety and feeling of insecurity among the citizens' after he 'warned' the speaker of the Tetovo municipal assembly, Trpko Nikolovski (a Slav Macedonian), that he wanted documents in Albanian not Macedonian.[170]

One reason for the lack of major inter-ethnic incidents was that the political relaxation allowed the ethnic Albanians to organize openly. The main ethnic Albanian party quickly became the Party for Democratic Prosperity of Macedonia (PDP) founded by Nevzat Halili, an English teacher from Tetovo, who was elected chairman on 25 August 1990. Despite its non-ethnic name, the PDP is accused of being essentially an ethnic Albanian party and this was underlined at the August session when the majority of participants reportedly boycotted Macedonian and Turkish.[171] Other reports, however, indicate that the PDP is not an ethnocentric party and that Muslims from other national groups have gravitated towards it.[172]

The PDP has frequently been accused by the authorities and rival Macedonian political parties of being merely an appendage of the mainly ethnic Albanian Democratic Alliance of Kosovo led by Ibrahim Rugova and of aiming for a break up of Macedonia and ultimately Yugoslavia. Halili has expressly denied this and has categorically recognized the territorial integrity and sovereignty of Macedonia and Yugoslavia and the inviolability of Yugoslavia's borders and commitment to its federal arrangement.[173] Such statements have to be seen in the light of the situation of the ethnic Albanians in Macedonia, an oppressed minority for the first time operating openly and faced by authorities dominated by a hostile majority nationality which itself views the future with some alarm.

Jovan Trpenovski, the secretary of internal affairs for the Macedonian republic, stated that the PDP was formed by Halili probably 'under the influence of separatists from Kosovo' and that while the PDP does not have a separatist programme, at its meetings its members frequently voice irredentist demands.[174] This last claim has been often repeated and 'hostile Albanian emigres' are also seen as financial support to the PDP.[175] Not so convincingly, Trpenovski also claimed that the *Sigurimi* – the secret police of Albania – have been active in Macedonia especially in Tetovo, implying that if ethnic Albanian parties took power in Kosovo and western Macedonia through the ballot box, then this would facilitate the establishment of a Greater Albania. As such, Trpenovski sees irredentism in almost every ethnic Albanian action, including the campaign organized by Albanians in Tretovo, Gostivar, Kumanovo and Struga to end the traditional blood feuds between ethnic Albanian families as had already happened in Kosovo.[176]

The first round of elections in Macedonia were held on 11 November and only 11 of the total 120 seats were decided. Of these, the PDP in alliance with the small People's Democratic Party, another predominantly ethnic Albanian party from Tetovo led by Jusuf Redzepi, won six seats – the remainder went to the communist and socialist parties with Ante Markovic's party gaining one but with the Macedonian nationalist parties apparently nowhere in sight. In a number of predominantly Albanian constituencies including Gostivar, Debar, Kumanovo, Struga, Tetovo and four in Skopje, there were apparent irregularities[177] with Macedonian claims that some ethnic Albanians had voted in more than one constituency and that insufficient screening of newly arrived emigres had taken place to see who was eligible to vote and who wasn't.

The second round of voting took place on 25 November and the PDP claimed that it had been blatantly hindered. After the third and final round of voting, the PDP and People's Democratic Party alliance finished with 25 seats to 37 for the Macedonian nationalist party, VMRO-DPMNE and 31 for the Communist Party. No real winner had emerged.

Splits soon appeared in both the VMRO-DPMNE, and the ethnic Albanian alliance of PDP and People's Democratic Party. With the continuing uncertainty over the future of Macedonia as a separate entity and the corresponding assertive nationalism of VMRO-DPMNE supported in the elections, the hopes for rapprochement with the ethnic Albanians in Macedonia look slim. As before, events in Kosovo will be crucial.

7

OTHER NATIONALITIES AND ETHNIC GROUPS – ROMA, TURKS, HUNGARIANS, VLAHS AND OTHERS

Roma

The Roma originated from India. From the 5th Century onwards Roma filtered into the Persian and, later, Arab empires of the Middle East, early groups of them reaching Byzantium in the 10th Century. Their attachment to established religions, whether Hindu, Muslim or Christian, appears to have been a matter of convenience rather than conviction. In the Balkans where Ottoman rule lasted longest in Europe, especially Bulgaria, they are Muslim by majority while in areas which historically have been under Christian control they are Christian by persuasion.

Traditionally independent and the product of migration and adaption, the Roma have, in all countries, remained predominantly outside the various systems in operation, be they feudal, capitalist or even socialist, by becoming horse-dealers, smiths, musicians and, more recently, scavengers. The Roma have historically been persecuted and discriminated against in all countries of Eastern Europe and have suffered from racism, at least in part due to their colour. During World War II when Eastern Europe fell under the dominion of the Nazis, genocide was used against the Roma and some half a million are believed to have died.

Yugoslavia has the largest Roma population in Europe which also has important links with emigrant Rom groups in France, Germany, the United States, Australia and elsewhere. Since 1981, the 850,000 Roma in Yugoslavia have had in theory, nationality status on an equal footing with other national minorities like the Albanians, Turks or Hungarians. However, there appears to still be some confusion over this status. *Politika*, the Belgrade daily on 4 December 1982 confirmed the official status of nationality; however, this was not uniformly applied by the republics. Roma pointed to the illogicality of the current arrangement and in 1989 a petition by Rajko Djuric, then

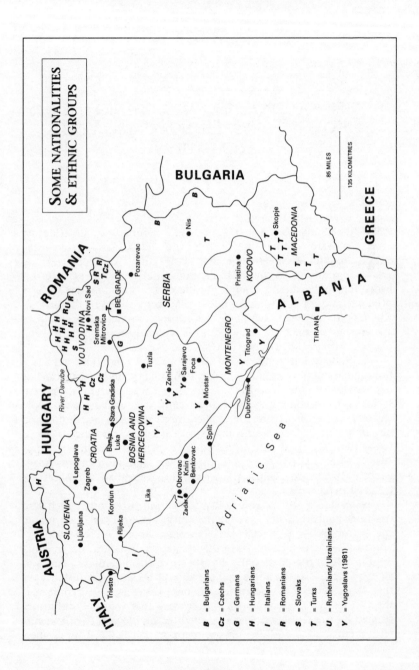

Secretary-General of the World Congress of Romanies, tabled before the SFRJ Assembly, proposed that a uniform status of nationality be agreed for the Roma in all republics and provinces, the constitutions of which – with the exception of Bosnia-Hercegovina and Montenegro – place Roma in the category of an ethnic group.[178]

Since 1983 Romanes has been used in state schools. At least 10 primary schools are using the Romani language as the teaching medium for the first four grades, and the number will rapidly rise once more Rom teachers can be trained. The break-through occurred in the Albanian populated region of Kosovo, where Muslim Roma have had a hard time making their voice heard in the past. Pristina television station in Kosovo now has a weekly programme in Romanes and Belgrade radio is broadcasting regularly in the language as are the smaller stations of Nis and Tetovo. Publications are still rare but there are several full length books which have been issued, and in May 1980 the Nasa Kniga publishing house of Skopje brought out the first Romani grammar to be entirely written in the Romani script and orthography.[179] A modified Roman alphabet was used for the 32-letter Romany alphabet so that it could be as widely understood as possible.[180] In January 1991 it was reported that Dobra Vjest, the publishing house of the Association of Baptist Churches of Yugoslavia had published the first translation of the Bible into Romanes.[181]

The bigger communities in Belgrade, Nis, Suto Orizari (Skopje) and other towns have had their own cultural and social associations for many years. The Belgrade Drustva Rom was founded in 1930 and Skopje's Phralipe (Brotherhood) in 1948. Today there are some 60 such local associations, linked in Serbia by the Romani Union, presided over by Sait Balic who also president of the International Romani Union (IRU). An annual festival has been held for the past 15 years, and several national and international events have also been held. In 1986 the IRU co-sponsored the International Symposium on the Romani Language and History in Sarajevo.

Perhaps the most significant feature is the Romani town of Suto Orizari outside Skopje, comprising some 35,000 inhabitants, with its own elected council and MP. This town enjoys a higher standard of living than many Macedonian villages, although whether such tactics of almost segregation are advisable, given the general everyday chauvinism and racism shown by the general population is debatable.

Recognition of the actual existence of Roma and willingness for Roma to self-identify are still the important first steps in some areas. In November 1980 *Tanjug* announced that the Committees for Intranational Relations of the Croatian SAWP Republican Conferences and the Croat Assembly held a joint meeting with Roma representatives from the Zagreb area and a delegation of the Federation of Rom Societies from Serbia to discuss the position of Croatia's Roma. At that time official data gave only 4150 Roma in seven municipalities for the whole republic. On 22 July 1990 the Romani Party of Croatia was founded to seek recognition of the Roma nationality and rights, and to appeal to the Croatian national assembly for primary and secondary level classes and textbooks in Romanes for the now estimated 150,000 Roma in Croatia.[182]

Although as indicated above the granting of nationality status is still somewhat problematic, there was in 1981 a significant increase in the number of Roma declaring themselves as such. In Macedonia, for example, their numbers in the census remained more or less static until the last census of 1981 when they rose dramatically from 24,505 to 43,223, reflecting their greater official status and a decline in stigma attached to being a Rom in Yugoslavia.

The authorities in Macedonia have for some time alleged that the Roma, especially the Muslim Roma, have been subjected to Albanianization. This claim was again made on 1 August 1990 by the presidium of the republican committee for nurturing the ethnic and cultural traditions of Roma in Macedonia which accused the ethnic Albanian Tetovo-based Party for Democratic Prosperity in Macedonia (PDPM), of persistently manipulating Roma on a religious Muslim basis. On 1 September the Macedonian Romani community called on all Roma to stop declaring themselves to be Albanians simply due to the shared religion and decided to mark 11 October – already a Macedonian public day – with the first republican festival of the cultural achievements of Roma in Macedonia.[183]

Despite these advances, the majority continue to live well below the economic average and there is discrimination in the work place and in the streets. Only a few hundred Roma have benefited from university education and entered the professions. Half the wage- earners are industrial workers and 20% are farmers – many owning their land. The rest are self-employed artisans and small traders. Nomadism has dwindled although is still seen.

Discrimination continues in many forms. In Bosnia in 1986 the Muslim inhabitants of the village of Nova Kasaba opposed the burial of Muslim Roma in 'their' cemetery and the police had to intervene.[184] In Slovenia the Romani Union protested that during elections in April 1990 officials barred Roma from voting.[185] In the village of Hydej in Slovenia, the local inhabitants refused to share voting booths with Roma and set up separate ones for them.[186]

Other allegations go further. In Pristina, Kosovo, a young Roma woman was allegedly beaten up in the streets because of her origin and petrol sprinkled on her hair and set alight with no one attempting to help her, and in Kursumlija in Serbia several Roma reportedly died in mid-1990 under suspicious circumstances with the police apparently unwilling to investigate as it would do no harm if 'even more of them burned'.[187]

Roma as Egyptians

Given the racism faced by Roma and the ethnic uncertainty of many Muslim citizens (a carry over from the Ottoman times when religion was the main factor of differentiation rather than ethnicity), especially in areas dominated by highly organized and nationalistic Muslim Albanians, it is not perhaps so surprising that unusual national claims from time to time appear. In 1990 the 'Egipcani' Association of Citizens in Ohrid – in the Macedonia bordering on Albania – was set up under the leadership of Nazim Arifi. This association was initially set up by approximately 4000 inhabitants of Ohrid and neighbouring Struga who renounced being Roma in favour of being 'Egyptian'.[188]

The association soon attracted sympathizers in Kosovo and the Association of Egyptians from Kosovo and Metohija was set up with its founding assembly held in Pristina on 21 October 1990. Its primary stated object was to preserve the national identity of 'Egyptians' from the process of Albanianization and it was stated that a number of 'Egyptians' from Kosovo and Metohija still consider themselves to be Roma.[189] Some 6000 people in Kosovo had joined by September 1990 and the association claimed 100,000 'descendants of the Pharoahs' in Kosovo with between 20,000 and 30,000 in Macedonia. The associations have petitioned the Federal Assembly and the Serbian and Macedonian national assemblies to include the separate category of 'Egyptian' in the 1991 population census[190] and this has been agreed in the case of Macedonia. It seems unlikely that these associations will become mass ones and more likely that such apparently irrational claims are merely a symptom of the acute national crisis in Yugoslavia today.

The Turks

The Turks, remnants from the long Ottoman occupation, numbered 101,291 in the 1981 census of which the majority, 86,691, lived in Macedonia where they constituted 4% of the population. Assessing the number of minorities like the Turks and others in Macedonia is some-what problematic. The census of 1948 gave 95,940 Turks while that of 1953 recorded 203,938, yet by the next census seven years later the number was only 131,481.

Immediately after World War II the Turks had been seen as suspect because of the friendship between Turkey and the West, and in January 1948, 17 Macedonian Turks were tried as members of 'Judzel' – ostensibly a terrorist/espionage organization. The trial was given great publicity within Macedonia so as to intimidate the Turkish minority and as a result many Turks declared themselves to be Albanians in the 1948 census. However, by 1953, following the break by Yugoslavia with the Cominform, the Albanians were now seen as being suspect and so now many Albanians declared themselves to be Turks – of the 203,938 in the 1953 census, 32,392 gave Macedonian as their native tongue and 27,086 gave Albanian, and the number of declared Albanians fell from 179,389 in 1948 to 165,524 in 1953.

The period following 1953 saw extensive emigration to Turkey of large numbers of Yugoslavia's Turkish minority – some 80,000 according to figures from Yugoslavia's statistical yearbooks, or over 150,000 according to some Turkish sources. However, some of these emigrants were unable to speak any Turkish and were in fact Muslim Albanians who, fearing for their position in post-war communist Yugoslavia, claimed to be Turks so as to take advantage of the permitted emigration.[191]

In the 1971 census there were 108,552 Turks and by the census of 1981 their numbers had apparently dropped to 86,690. Such a decline is more surprising given the high birth- rate of the Turks in Yugoslavia which would have been expected to result in an increase of some 20,000 in the period 1971-1981 instead of a decrease of over 20,000. It appears that many who previously declared themselves to be Turks now call themselves Muslims while others now declare themselves to be Albanians or Roma (Gypsies).

A further complicating factor in assessing numbers of the smaller minority groups in Macedonia is the rise from 3652 to 14,240 between 1971 and 1981 of those declaring themselves to be Yugoslavs rather than as belonging to a particular ethnic group, although the percentage of those declaring themselves as such was still low in comparison to other republics in Yugoslavia.

The Macedonian authorities, worried at the rise of Albanian nationalism, assert that many Turks have been Albanianized under pressure. According to the director of the Macedonian Republic Bureau of Statistics in Skopje[192], this was especially pronounced in the Tetovo, Gostivar, Struga and Kicevo regions, and the Macedonian LC Central Committee Presidium in September 1987 gave the expansion of Albanian nationalism as one of the main reasons for the emigration of Turkish families from Gostivar municipality.[193] The Albanians apparently claim, in a manner strikingly similar to the Bulgarians vis-a-vis ethnic Turks in Bulgaria, that 'these are not Turks' but actually 'Illyrians (believed to be the forerunners of the Albanians) turned into Turks' who are now 'returning to their flock.'[194]

Similarly to the Albanians, the Turks, a recognized nationality of Yugoslavia, have been allowed educational and cultural rights from the outset – in the first academic year of the new republic, 1944/5, there were 60 primary schools with 3334 pupils using Turkish as the language of instruction. In 1950/51 there were over 100 schools with over 12,000 pupils and 267 teachers. By 1958/9, due to the emigration to Turkey the numbers had dropped to 27 schools (26 primary and one secondary) with just over 6000 pupils and 219 teachers, and while the number of primary schools had increased to 53 by the end of 1988, the number of pupils has remained more or less static.[195] Again, like the Albanians, there are television and radio programmes and a newspaper, *Birlik*, as well as various cultural organizations. The main political movement for Turks in Macedonia was the Democratic Alliance of Turks in Macedonia.

The Hungarians, Slovaks, Romanians, and Ruthenians/Ukrainians of the Vojvodina

The **Hungarians**, a residue from the Austro-Hungarian Empire, numbered 426,867 in 1981 and live predominantly in the Vojvodina, generally in the vicinity of the border with Hungary, where they constitute just under 19% of the population. Their numbers have been dropping in successive censuses however.

Because of its diversified ethnic make-up, the Vojvodina was made into an Autonomous Province within the Serbian republic, similarly to Kosovo (see above). Serbs make up the majority in the Vojvodina (54.4%) and the other minorities are Croats (5.4%), and the majority of Yugoslavia's small populations of **Slovaks** (80,334 in Yugoslavia – 69,549 in the Vojvodina), **Romanians** (54,955 – 47,289), and **Ruthenians/Ukrainians** (23,286 – 19,305). To satisfy the various national traditions there are five official languages in the province: Serbo-Croat; Hungarian; Slovak; Romanian; and Ruthenian.

Hungarians have about 200 elementary schools, a daily newspaper, Magyar Szo and the provincial radio station broadcasts regularly in

Hungarian. There were few apparent signs of Hungarian dissatisfaction, and it appeared superficially that until recently the province, unlike Kosovo, acted as a successful bridge between Yugoslavia and her neighbours.

However, as noted above, in 1988 resurgent Serbian nationalism led to a downfall of the Vojvodina party leadership opposed to Serb aspirations and greater control over the province by Serbia, formally entrenched in the new Serbian Constitution, and this led to dissatisfaction in the province. Part of this increased control was the replacing of Zoltan Csorba, the editor-in-chief of the main Hungarian language daily, Magyar Szo, by a decision of the provincial Executive Council. This decision was annulled by the Vojvodina Supreme Court on 17 October 1990 which ruled that the Executive Council had no legal basis for replacing the chief editor.[196] However, after his reinstatement, he was again dismissed for being anti-Serbian and this time the Vojvodina Supreme Court upheld his dismissal.[197] Additionally the new political climate allowed Hungarian dissatisfaction, hitherto not overtly apparent, to be more easily voiced.

The major political party of the Vojvodina Hungarians, the Democratic Community of Vojvodina Hungarians (VMDK), was founded on 14 February 1990 in Novi Sad and in its initial programme it aimed at equal participation in the political process as well as adequate representation in administrative and judicial organizations, and the use of Hungarian in education.[198] At its first congress held in Ada on 29 September 1990, the 400 delegates representing the 20,000 or so VDMK members decided to seek cultural autonomy in the Vojvodina. This was almost certainly in response to Serbia's new constitution which virtually eliminated provincial self-government. VDMK President Andras Agostan, commentating about Yugoslavia's future, said that he believed that a confederation would offer the Hungarians of the Vojvodina the only possibility of remaining in Europe. A break-up of Yugoslavia would be disastrous for them he concluded.[199]

Inevitably the main arena for this dissatisfaction will be the education system. In 1975 the education system was reformed. In the following years, supposedly because of the absence of qualified teachers, Hungarian secondary schools began to be closed down. From 1976 onwards a separate Education Law operated in the Vojvodina for the four main minorities there – Hungarians, Slovaks, Romanians and Ruthenians. However, the number of ethnic Hungarian students dropped by more than 4000 in the period from 1977 to 1988.

A new education law passed by Serbia in January 1990 rescinded the 1976 law. How this new law, which aims at a uniform education system throughout the whole republic of Serbia in line with the new Serbian constitution promulgated in 1989, will affect minority education remains to be seen, although it is likely that enrolment in minority schools will continue to decline.

It is apparent that the Hungarians and other minorities view the new law with alarm as shown by petitions from them to the Serbian Parliament[200] and the VDMK demands. Unlike the Kosovo Albanians who boycotted the December 1990 elections in protest at the removal of autonomy for the two provinces, the VDMK did take part in the elections and won eight seats out of the 250 total – thereby coming equal third behind the Milosevic's SPS, with 194, and Draskovic's SPO with 19. The VDMK also requested the Serbian Assembly to establish a nationality ministry due to the presence of three million non-Serbs out of the republic's nine million population but this request was rejected.[201]

On 12 May 1990 the Yugoslav Alliance of Ruthenians and Ukrainians was founded in Novi Sad. This organization disclaimed any political agenda and declared its purpose to be to preserve the national identity of the Ruthenians and Ukrainians.[202] In March 1990, the Magyar People's Party of Croatia was formed to protect the interests of the small Hungarian minority in Croatia.[203] In November 1990 near Vrsac, the founding of the community of Romanians in Yugoslavia took place with Pavel Gataianu, a journalist from Novi Sad Radio elected president.[204]

The Vlahs

There is very little information on the situation regarding this ethnic group which speaks a form of Romanian and traditionally were pastoral people. They live primarily in Greece but also in Albania and Yugoslavia. Assessing their numbers is difficult and compounded by a lack of separatist current among Vlahs, also known as Koutsovlahs, Aromani and Cincari in Yugoslavia, which has resulted in their apparent peaceful assimilation into majority ethnic groups. In this shared religious faith, Orthodoxy, has been an important factor.

The Vlahs in Yugoslavia live in Serbia and, especially, in Macedonia. In Serbia in and around Bor there are sizeable Vlah communities but an interesting fact was that while they made up 10.29% of Bor's population according to the 1981 census, there was not a single Vlah in the League of Communists in Bor.[205]

The Vlahs in Macedonia live especially in and around Bitola, Resen and Krusevo, and also in the Osgovo mountains and the Kriva valley in the west. There are Vlah societies in Bitola and Skopje and these societies have pointed to the lack of language rights for Vlahs in schools and in religious matters eg. the appeal in February 1988 by the Pitu Guli Cultural association in Skopje to the Foreign Ministers of Yugoslavia, Albania, Bulgaria, Greece, Romania and Turkey who were meeting in Belgrade, although with little apparent effect. Successive censuses has shown a gradual decline in their numbers in Macedonia from 8669 in 1953 to 6392 in 1981, and it appears that they are becoming assimilated by the majority Macedonian population.

Studies in the 1930s recorded 3000 to 4000 Vlahs in Bitola, 2000 to 3000 in Skopje and 1500 in Krusevo which was predominantly Vlah at the time. However, recent studies, especially those by Jovan Trifonoski, show a pattern of gradual assimilation. Using the Ovce Polje area in the east of the republic as a case study[206] he showed how the Vlahs in this area originated from Gramos on the border between Greece and Albania but emigrated to Macedonia at the end of the 18th Century to escape the tyranny of the Ali-Pasha of Janjina. They were nomadic cattle breeders and maintained an extended family under a dominant headman, summering in the mountains of Osgovo, Pljackovica and Ograzden, and wintering in the plains of Strumica, Kocan, Ovce Polje and as far as Thessaloniki.

After World War I new boundaries and new economics induced a shift from nomadic flocks to farming, with the disintegration of the old Turkish estates and the narrowing down of pastures. This trend was amplified after World War II, as after 1948 the new economic system meant that it was not possible to own big flocks of sheep or horses. Most Vlahs abandoned their nomadic modes and settled in existing villages; they already were well acquainted with the areas from winter dwelling previously. Others from Ovce Polje settled in surrounding areas – Stip, Kocani and Titov Veles – but often moved back to the Ovce Polje area after 1948 when land became available due to the complete emigration of Turks in the area. A result of this was contact between the Vlah cultures on one hand and the indigenous Macedonian/Slavic culture of the other. Even in 1938 it was noted that nomadic Vlahs living in the Ograzden mountains could speak Slav well, including the women, and some children were attending schools.

In 1971 Trifunoski noted that the Vlahs of eastern Macedonia living in the mass of the Slavic population were fading away as a separate group, and the growth of industry in Titov Veles, Stip and Skopje, with the attendant mass emigration of the young from the villages, has further escalated this process.

Others, including those declaring themselves as 'Yugoslavs'

Among the remaining minorities in Yugoslavia's ethnic mosaic there are **Bulgarians** (as opposed to Macedonians) numbering 36,189, mostly in the republic of Serbia bordering on Bulgaria, and small numbers of **Czechs** (19,624) and **Italians** (15,132), mostly in Croatia.

Before World War II there were about 75,000 **Jews** living in Yugoslavia of whom about 16,000 survived the Nazi Holocaust. Emigration to Israel has diminished the number of Jews and today about 6000 remain, mostly in Zagreb (1300), Belgrade (1600) and Sarajevo (1000). There has been some anti-semitic incidents recently, especially in Croatia[206] following Serb press reports that the World Jewish Congress supported Serbia against Slovenia. The Society of Serbian-Jewish Friendship was set up in 1990 and has 3000 members while a similar organization was set up in Zagreb.

The Bulgarians of Serbia live mainly in the south Moravian area and have their own weekly, Bratstvo, published in Bulgarian in Nis. On 20 October 1990, the Democratic Federation of Bulgarians of Yugoslavia (DSBJ) was founded in Nis with Bratstvo journalist, Kiril Georgijev, elected Chairman and Professor Prokopi Popov of Belgrade, Vice-Chairman.[207] Professor Popov has expressed satisfaction with the situation of Bulgarians in Serbia and supports the Serbian side in the Kosovo question as well as over Serb minority rights in Croatia. He also pointed to future activity in Macedonia by stating: 'As a great number of Bulgarians live in Macedonia, we will fight for our compatriots there being granted the same rights the Bulgarian minority in Serbia has'.[208] It is possible that this small organization may well play an important role if and when the seemingly eternal 'Macedonian question' becomes acute again.

The Italian minority live mostly in Istria and around Rijeka although many emigrated to Italy in the period 1946 to 1954. In March 1990 the Italian Union for Istria and Rijeka was set up as a non-party social organization. Mario Quaranta, a member of the organization's presidium and president of the Pula-based Community of Italians, stated that the organization would not field candidates in the elections but would be involved in safeguarding the identity of Italian nationality in the region.[209] Demands for cultural autonomy for the Italians in the Istrian peninsula grew throughout 1990 fuelled by opposition to the Croatian governments plans to resettle over 20,000 Croats from Romania in Istria.[210]

Since the census of 1961 there has been a separate category for those who wish to classify themselves as **'Yugoslavs'** as opposed to other classifications (Serb, Croat etc.). The number of people doing so dramatically increased in the last census. In 1971 the figure fell to 273,077 from 317,124 in 1961, but in 1981 the figure was 1,219,024, or some 5.4% of the population, perhaps reflecting a turning away by a significant proportion of the population from the perennial national question which has become so tense in recent years, compounded by the present economic difficulties. The spread of these 'Yugoslavs', however, was not uniform and their numbers were significantly very small in Macedonia and Kosovo (0.2% and 0.7%, respectively) where the Albanian national question is most acute, and small in Slovenia (1.3%). The largest increases have come in Bosnia-Hercegovina (where the percentage in 1981 was 7.9%), Croatia (8.2%), Serbia proper (4.7%), and the Vojvodina (8.2%).

The developments in 1989/90 have shown a marked rise in overt nationalism and a fundamental doubting of the whole nature of Yugoslavia. As such it is likely that far smaller numbers of people will declare themselves as Yugoslavs in future. Such people would have been attracted by Prime Minister, Ante Markovic's attempt to counter the nationalist tide with the setting up of the Alliance of Reformist Forces, although a vote for Markovic's party does not signify lack of national allegiance. In the chaotic political scene of 1990 other non-national Yugoslav parties have included the Party of Yugoslavs, and a revamped hard-line communist party, the League of Communists-Movement for Yugoslavia, supported by the predominantly Serbian army high command. Whether this latter party was really a Yugoslav party or merely a front for hard-line centralism with a Serbian bias is debatable.

All these parties – with the possible exception of Markovic's party in Montenegro which came second with 17 of the 125 seats in the December election – have not proved successful compared to nationalist parties, or in Serbia and Montenegro, the communist/socialist parties riding Serb nationalism. 'Yugoslavism' as an ethnic concept appears to be declining along with the concept of Yugoslavia as a unified state.

8

PRESSURE POINTS
– THE ARMY AND THE EMIGRES

The Army (JNA)

Separate mention should perhaps be made of the Yugoslav army which in recent years has, correctly or not, widely been seen as one of the few, perhaps the only, all-Yugoslav institutions. As such, many commentators have pointed to the possibility of the JNA directly participating in the political arena in the form of 'restoring centralism' and protecting the integrity of the state by military action.

Military service is compulsory for all Yugoslav males over 18 and there is no provision for conscientious objection. In line with the view of the army being an all-Yugoslav body, conscripts were obliged to perform their military service outside of their republic or autonomous region so as to avoid the possibility of the army splitting along republican/ethnic lines as the Communist Party did.

Due to the high birth-rate of the Albanians in Yugoslavia, in recent years, JNA conscripts have increasingly been made up of larger numbers of ethnic Albanians – in 1990 they comprised some 14% of the total armed forces. 70% of the professional officer corps, however, has remained solidly Serb (or Montenegrin). This has caused growing tensions especially as the army, using wherever possible units without Albanians, has been used repeatedly in Kosovo to put down manifestations of Albanian nationalism.

Furthermore, the changes beginning in late 1989, especially in Slovenia and Croatia have seen a movement in these two republics to opt out as much as possible from the old arrangement whereby conscripts were sent to other republics. In both Croatia and Slovenia, increasingly the JNA is seen as a potential (Serbian) enemy and the new republican authorities are attempting to set up republican military structures.

This has brought warning signals from the JNA. In March 1990 the JNA attempted to bring criminal charges against Joze Pucnik, the

Slovene DEMOS presidential candidate who was also president of the ruling DEMOS, because he had 'grossly insulted' the JNA by individually autographing campaign posters used by the DEMOS.[211] Federal Secretary of Defence General Veljko Kadijevic in December 1990 warned that the JNA might have to intervene to prevent Yugoslavia breaking up, especially in view of the plebiscite which was held in Slovenia on 23 December. Predictably both the Slovene and Croatian republican authorities reacted sharply to this overt threat.

It is clear that the JNA, which launched the new all-Yugoslav Communist Party (see above) and disbanded the old communist JNA organiztaions and merged them with the new party, is openly hostile to the democratically elected governments of Croatia and Slovenia. General Kadijevic, a child of a Serb-Croat marriage from Dalmatia, has openly supported the reinstatement of centralized communist rule and has refused to meet the Slovene premier and defence minister to negotiate Slovene requests on JNA reorganization. Just how serious the threat of JNA intervention against eg. Slovenian secession is debatable. The large numbers of armed Albanian, (and Slovene and Croatian) conscripts who bear no loyalty to their supposed Serb superiors, make the use of the JNA in such a manner a very risky venture.

Slovene defence minister Janez Jansa – an authority on defence matters – believes that ethnic Albanians, who are pro-Slovenia, outnumber Serbs in JNA forces stationed in Slovenia. The Local Republican Territorial Defence Forces are 95% Slovenian and have high morale.[212] In such circumstances it is unlikely that the JNA will intervene in a major way in Slovenia. Some JNA officers did, however, intervene in the Serbian revolt in Knin in August 1990 when JNA MiGS threatened Croatian police helicopters. Furthermore, during the escalating tension in early 1991 over the Croatian arms from Hungary affair and the attempted disarming of all armed groups outside the JNA, it was reported that Slovenian and Croatian units from the Fifth Military District (Slovenia and Croatia) were transferred and replaced by more reliable units. Additionally, all-Serb paratroop units were reported to be formed.[213]

The nature of the Serb-Albanian problem in the JNA is shown by the regularity with which the authorities publish figures for 'underground groups' in the JNA. The Federal Secretariat of National Defence announced in April 1990 that in 1989: 'some 39 underground groups with 199 members were exposed in the JNA of which 35 groups with 179 members operated from positions of Albanian nationalism and separatism.' Furthermore: '550 nationalistic actions were registered in the army in 1989, the most numerous being from positions of Albanian nationalism.'[214] Some of these incidents within the JNA have been highly publicized incidents of inter-ethnic violence, often involving loss of life. Albanians have claimed that they have been subject to intense pressure and discrimination in the JNA resulting in large numbers of suicides of Albanian conscripts.[215]

Such allegations have been denied by the JNA which published statistics for the total numbers of fatalities in the JNA from 1982 to 1990. In this eight year period there were 496 fatalities, with an ethnic breakdown as follows: 202 Serbs; 77 Croats; 32 Slovenians; 29 Macedonians; 16 Montenegrins; 86 ethnic Muslims; 32 Albanians; 14 who identified themselves as Yugoslavs; and eight others. In the three year period from 1987 to 1990, the ethnic breakdown of fatalities was: Serb 49.66%; Croats 14.23%; ethnic Muslims 11.25%; Macedonians 7.61%; Slovenians 5.62%; Albanians 2.31%; and others 1.32%. For suicides in the same period the figures were: Serbs 47.50%; Croats 15.83%; ethnic Muslims 10.83%; Albanians 6.66%; Macedonians 6.66%; Slovenians 5.83%; Yugoslavs 2.50%; and others 1.66%.216 These figures would indicate that the Albanian claims of discrimination leading to fatalities are unfounded.

Yugoslav emigres

Separate mention should also be made of Yugoslav emigre groups as many have, by their opposition to the communist authorities, played an important role in domestic nationalist politics. With the relaxation of 1989/90, many have been able to openly return to Yugoslavia and take part in the developing situation there. The exact number of Yugoslav emigres is very hard to calculate. Official figures in given in the Pristina paper Jedinstvo in November, 1979 stated that there were 400,000 Yugoslav emigrants in Turkey, over 300,000 in Australia, a similar number in Canada, and about 200,000 in South America, although other sources give far higher numbers. Many have retained their national identity and cultural separateness.

The Yugoslav emigre scene is extremely complicated. In 1976 official Yugoslav sources stated that there were 230 emigre organizations hostile to the government, of which 127 were Croat ones; 78 Serb; 11 Slovene; 9 Albanian; 6 Macedonian; and 6 Muslim.[217] The largest emigre national group are the Croats and the largest emigre organization, the Croatian National Council (HNV), claims to represent a potential of three million Croats in the diaspora. There are also large numbers of migrant workers from all over Yugoslavia in western Europe, especially in Germany, although this number has declined from a high of over one million in the 1970s, due to the economic situation and the rise in unemployment in western Europe. There are a large number of emigre organizations which are overwhelmingly based on national (Serb, Croat, Albanian etc.) lines.

The largest and perhaps the most consistently hostile of the emigre groups to the communist authorities were the Croats, although Albanian groups since the clamp-down in 1981 have lately become as, if not more, hostile. There have been a number of terrorist attacks on Yugoslav representatives abroad. The HNV was founded in Toronto, Canada in the early 1970s and is an umbrella organization similar to the pre-war Croatian Peasant Party with a moderate wing and more radical factions. It aims at an independent Croatia through pacific and legalistic means. The Yugoslav authorities brand it as a terrorist organization with strong links to the Ustasha fascist period. While there are offshoots of Ustasha in the HNV, mostly in Argentina but also in Germany, the acts of terrorism in the past 20 years have been performed by smaller, more militant Croat groups in France, Germany, USA, Sweden, UK, Canada, Paraguay, Venezuela and Australia.

Additionally, there are claims that the Yugoslav secret service (SDS) has been responsible for some terrorist acts, especially the assassination of known Yugoslav opposition activists, Croats and Albanians, abroad. Over 20 assassinations of emigre nationalist activists have taken place since the early 1970s. These include the Croatian emigres Bruno Busic (a former political prisoner murdered in Paris in October 1978), Nikola Milicevic (murdered in Frankfurt in February 1980 after the West German government had refused the Yugoslav government's request for his extradition), the Serbian emigre Dusan Sedlar (murdered in Dusseldorf in April 1980), the Kosovo Albanian emigres Jusuf and Bardhosh Gervalla and Kadri Zeka (murdered in Stuttgart in January 1983) and the Croat Stjepan Djurekovic (murdered near Munich in July 1983). Allegations of SDS involvement in such outrages has been supported by evidence presented in foreign courts.[218]

In July 1984, the Frankfurt district court, after a trial that lasted for two and a half years, sentenced Zorica Aleksic and Iso Dautovski to seven and a half and 13 years' imprisonment respectively for the attempted murder of a Kosovo Albanian emigre, Rasim Zenelaj, in May 1981. The court reportedly implicated the SDS and 'at least some consular officials' in the attempted murder. The presiding judge, in reply to a question after the trial as to whether he thought that his statements in court might deter such killings in future, commented: 'No, I am afraid that a secret service using murder to achieve its goals will not be deterred by us.'[219]

Also in July 1984, the trial of Josip Majerski by Munich district court ended. He had been charged with intelligence activities, and during the trial he admitted he had been a long-time employee of the SDS. He gave detailed information about SDS actions against Yugoslav emigres in West Germany and named prominent members of the Yugoslav diplomatic corps he claimed had been involved. He also stated that he had been supplied with money and weapons and assigned the task of infiltrating various emigre organizations in order, as an agent provocateur, to encourage the use of violence. For this he said he was paid 2000 Deutschemark a month. He further stated that he had been ordered by the SDS to kill emigre Bruno Busic in Paris but had refused to do so.[220]

Both Croat and the Albanian emigre groups have actively pursued attempts to set up contacts within Yugoslavia and the communist authorities inevitably responded harshly. In the past, extreme Croat groups have attempted violent action within Yugoslavia although such actions have apparently decreased in recent years. However, the continuing tension in Kosovo and the apparent failure by Albanians there to achieve republican status for Kosovo by peaceful means, has led to a more aggressive stance from the emigres.

The Albanian opposition groups tended to be either 'Marxist-Leninist' in ideology, often looking to Albania as a model, or 'monarchist' looking to the anti-communist resistance in Albania during World War II, the Balli Kombetar, and the former royal family of Albania. The 'Marxist-Leninist' groups mirrored those operating within Kosovo in the late 1970s and early 1980s, and many of the leaders were those who were forced to move the centre of their operations outside of Kosovo due to clamp-downs by the authorities. It seems likely that the supposed Marxist-Leninist ideological component of such groups will, similarly to the evolution of Albanian political groups within Kosovo, decline.

The monarchists are strong in Turkey where many Muslim Albanians emigrated from Yugoslavia (or what was to become Yugoslavia) between 1912 and 1966. Over half a million emigrated from Kosovo alone in the inter-war period. Some Kosovo demographers estimate that about two million people of Albanian origin live in Turkey at the present while the Initiative Council in Pec put the figure at an almost certainly inflated three and a half million.[221] A large Albanian emigrant community also lives in the USA although many of these are from Albania proper.

According to official Yugoslav sources, the most prominent of these Yugoslav Albanian emigre groups are: The Prizren League (founded in

1961 in New York with national committees in Canada, USA, Belgium, France, Germany, Italy, Austria and Turkey); the *Balli Kombetar* (the successors to the 1939 non-communist war-time resistance movement); *Legalitet* (founded in 1949 with branches in USA, Australia, Canada, Belgium, France, UK, Sweden, and Germany and supporting the Zogu Albanian monarchy); and the League of Kosovars (founded in Rome in 1949).[222] There has been, and continues to be, much interplay between these organizations, all of which aim for the eventual unification of Albania with the predominantly Albanian territories of Yugoslavia (Kosovo, western Macedonia, and parts of Serbia and Montenegro) in a new Albanian state, whether that state be monarchic or socialist or whatever.

Similarly to the Zogists, many of the Serbian opposition emigre groups are royalists with loyalties to the pre-war Yugoslav/Serbian monarchy and the *Chetniks*, the Serbian-based anti-communist resistance movement in World War II. There is a community of interest between emigre Croats and emigre Albanians as both are hostile to what they deem 'Great Serb chauvinism' and neither claim territory belonging to each other.

There are large Macedonian emigre communities, especially in Australia. A minority calls for a united independent Macedonia including parts of present-day Bulgaria and Greece. The majority, however, were not at odds with the Yugoslav communist authorities, a reflection of the fact that while frustrated nationalism is the main driving force behind the actions of many other Yugoslav emigre groups, the Macedonians have for the first time in recent history been granted some say in their own affairs by the Yugoslav government. The setting up of the autocephalous Macedonian Church in 1967 has been especially significant, with the corresponding founding of churches among the Macedonian emigre communities.

There is a small 'Free Slovenia' movement based in Argentina and a very small number of Montenegrins who hope for the return of the Montenegrin royalty. Montenegrins were also numerous in the ranks of 'the Cominformists' – those who supported the Comintern (Soviet) line in 1948 at the time of the Tito-Stalin break – and some remain active in exile. There are also some active Muslim emigres whose main political organization is the 'Bosnia-Hercegovina Muslims Association' which calls for Yugoslavia to be a 'confederation of free and independent countries'. Finally there are many emigre groups which are seen as friendly by the Yugoslav authorities and have been set up under their aegis to serve both guest workers and emigres

9

BULGARIA AND ITS MINORITIES

Bulgaria in outline

The People's Republic of Bulgaria has an area of 110,912 sq. kms. and lies in south-east Europe. It shares borders with four countries: Greece, Romania, Turkey and Yugoslavia and is bounded to the east by the Black Sea.

The modern Bulgarian state was formed from territories of the Ottoman Empire in 1878 during the Russo-Turkish war of 1875-78 and mostly comprised the northern half of present-day Bulgaria north of the Stara Planina (the Balkan Mountains). The southern part, formerly called Eastern Rumelia, was added in 1885 and the country declared itself fully independent in 1908.

During World War II, Bulgaria was an ally of Nazi Germany but without ever declaring war against the USSR. However, in September 1944, the USSR declared war on Bulgaria and on 9 September 1944 the Fatherland Front, a coalition of opposition political parties including the Bulgarian Communist Party (BCP), took power. In September 1946 Bulgaria was proclaimed a People's Republic and by 1948 the BCP completely controlled the country.

The BCP remained in complete control until late 1989 when similarly to other East European countries, widespread political changes began with the ousting of Todor Zhivkov who had led the BCP since 1954 and was also Chairman of the State Council – the titular head of state.

Bulgaria had a population of 8,917,200 at the end of 1984, of whom 66.2% lived in towns and 33.8% in rural settlements. Due to large scale emigration in 1989/90, the total population fell to about 8,600,000. The capital is Sofia which had 1,182,868 inhabitants in 1984.[223] There are a number of minorities living in Bulgaria of which the most numerous are the ethnic Turks, estimated to number before the mass exodus of 1989 at least 900,000 and maybe as many as one and a half million, and the Gypsies, estimated to number 550,000.

Before World War II Bulgaria was primarily an agricultural producer

MINORITIES
IN BULGARIA

ROMANIA

River Danube

Vidin

Mihailovgrad

Silistra

Turks

Tolbuhin

Razgrad

Shumen

Varna

Lovech

Targovishte

Stara Planina

Yablanovo

Black
Sea

Sofia

BULGARIA

Rhodope

Plovdiv

Haskovo

Kardzhali

Blagoevgrad

Mountains

Smolyan

Edirne

Macedonians

Turks

TURKEY

Pomaks

GREECE

YUGOSLAVIA

———— International boundaries

- - - - - District boundaries in 1988
(the 28 districts were
replaced by 8 regions)

Mountainous areas

Areas where ethnic
minorities live

85 MILES

135 KILOMETRES

with a few important mineral resources, mainly lignite and some iron ore. However, since the war there has been rapid industrialization. Two-thirds of Bulgaria's exports now derive from engineering and the steel and petro-chemical industries have been developed. The main crops are wheat, maize, tobacco (Bulgaria is the largest European producer), fruit and vegetables. Agriculture was completely collectivized by 1958; however, the collective farmer was entitled to a private plot of between 20% and 50% of an acre per household. In 1980, 33.5% of the economically active population worked in agriculture.

Under BCP rule, Bulgaria was a centralized state. The BCP and the communist-controlled Agrarian Union were the only permitted political parties until late 1989. The supreme legislative body is the National Assembly, composed of 400 deputies elected for a five-year term on the basis of a single list of candidates. A Grand National Assembly empowered to rewrite the constitution as well as carry out the functions of the National Assembly was elected in June 1990. The National Assembly elects the Council of Ministers, the supreme executive authority whose chairman is the Prime Minister. The assembly meets three times a year and between sessions it delegates authority to the State Council (elected from among its own members) which is in permanent session. At the local level Bulgaria was until January 1988 divided into 28 districts, each administered by a People's Council, which is elected for a term of two and a half years. However, State Council Decree No. 2704 abolished the 28 districts (*okrags*) and replaced them with 8 regions (*oblasts*) again administered by a People's Council. Bulgaria joined the United Nations in 1955.

The Macedonians

'The Macedonian Question' has historically been one of the most contentious as well as one of the most complicated issues in the Balkans. The Macedonians (a Slavic people, not to be confused with the subjects of Phillip of Macedon in antiquity) live in the south- western regions of the country. Successive censuses have given conflicting figures for the numbers of Macedonians in Bulgaria.

The results of the 1946 Bulgarian census concerning the Macedonian population were never made public by the Bulgarian authorities. However, Yugoslav sources claim that 252,908 people declared themselves as Macedonians in that census.[224] The census of 1956 recorded 187,789 Macedonians, over 95% of whom lived in the Pirin region where they made up 63.8% of the population. However, in the 1965 census the number of people declaring themselves as Macedonian had dropped to only 8750 and in the district of Blagoevgrad which previously had the highest percentage of Macedonians it was less than 1%.[225]

Bulgaria has traditionally claimed that the Macedonians (including those living in Yugoslavia and Greece) are ethnic Bulgarians. However, immediately after World War II when Georgi Dimitrov, both of whose parents were from Macedonia, was leader, the BCP fully recognized a separate Macedonian nationality and allowed extensive contact between Pirin Macedonia and the newly formed Macedonian Republic in post-war Yugoslavia. Following his death and the break between Yugoslavia and the USSR, Bulgarian unease at this recognition became more apparent and the Bulgarians only admitted that the process of nationality for the Macedonians began in 1918. Later the date was changed to 1944 and at the April plenum of the BCP in 1956 when Todor Zhivkov cemented his power it appears that it was decided no longer to recognize a separate Macedonian nationality.[226] Throughout the early 1960s the Bulgarian authorities, when renewing the compulsory personal identity cards, allegedly issued cards stating that the holder was Bulgarian by ethnicity to those who had previously held cards stating that they were Macedonian.

From the early 1960s there have also reportedly been a number of political trials of people accused of activity based on Macedonian nationalism. For example, a group of inhabitants of Blagoevgrad were tried in 1962 by the District Court of Blagoevgrad on charges of creating a group whose aims were the secession of Pirin Macedonia from the People's Republic of Bulgaria and in 1964 four people from Blagoevgrad were reportedly tried for writing 'We are Macedonians' and 'Long live the Macedonian nation' on a restaurant wall.

Since the introduction of the latest Criminal Code in 1968, most of those accused of propagating such 'anti-democratic and nationalist ideology' have been charged under Articles 108 and 109 which deal, respectively, with 'anti-state agitation and propaganda' and with forming or leading and membership of an illegal group. Article 39 (1) of the People's Militia Law of 1976 (amended on 12 August 1983) also allows administrative punishment (that is without trial), which has reportedly been used to forcibly resettle members of the Macedonian ethnic minority in other areas of the country.[227] According to Yugoslav sources, whole families were forced to move from the Pirin region to other regions in the north because of their affirmation of a Macedonian ethnicity distinct from Bulgarian.[228] At the same time as this repression, the Bulgarian authorities have concentrated resources into the Pirin region, the health resort of Sandanski being a notable example, apparently so as to lessen any possible attraction from neighbouring Yugoslavia. [229]

In 1973 another group of Macedonian nationalists all from Petrich with the exception of one, Ivan Tipchev from Parvomay, six kilometres to the west, were arrested and tried reportedly for Macedonian nationalism. The leader, Sokrat Markilov, was sentenced to up to five years' imprisonment and the others, including Stoyan Georgiev, received similar sentences. Sokrat Markilov, a long time Macedonian activist, has spent a total of nine years in prison and several years in internal exile for his activity and his children were reportedly sent to live in other parts of Bulgaria.

In February 1990, all the spokesmen of the main Bulgarian political parties – BCP Supreme Council Chairman Aleksandar Lilov; Angel Dimitrov, secretary of the BZNS (the peasant party); Zhelyu Zhelev, Chairman of the Union of Democratic Forces (UDF); and Petar Dertliev, leader of the Bulgarian Social Democratic Party – all stressed that there was no 'Macedonian Question' and that Macedonians were Bulgarians[230].

However, developments from within Bulgaria pointed to the contrary. In March, a communique from an organization calling itself 'The Solidarity and Struggle Committee of Pirin Macedonians' appeared claiming to speak for 'the 250,000 Pirin Macedonians'. This communique stated that the Pirin Macedonians 'have decided to fight on the side of the Macedonian National Liberation Army' and called for an independent Macedonia uniting 'our Macedonian brethren struggling in Greece'. A more serious organization had emerged into the open immediately following Todor Zhivkov's downfall in November 1989. On 11 March, the Independent Macedonian Organization, Ilinden, which was formed in November 1989, organized a rally in Sofia with some hundred participants with demands for cultural and national autonomy of Macedonians in Bulgaria displaying slogans like: 'We are Macedonians and nothing else' and 'United Macedonia: a guarantee for peace'[231].

This organization changed its name to the United Macedonian Organization (UMO) Ilinden in April 1990 when it coalesced with several political clubs which had emerged in Petrich, Blagoevgrad and Sandanski[232]. It appears however that the Sofia organization lead by Georgi Angelov Solunski kept some degree of autonomy. On 22 April, UMO Ilinden held another rally at the Rozhen Monastery, the tomb of Yane Sandanski – a revolutionary claimed by both the Bulgarians and the Macedonians as a national hero. BTA claimed that Yugoslav citizens took part in this rally and mainstream Bulgarian public opinion saw such moves as a Yugoslav plot to try and dismember Bulgaria. UMO Ilinden also sent a declaration calling for an autonomous Macedonia to the UN, the Bulgarian National Assembly, the UDF, Bulgarian TV, the European Parliament, and the International Court in the Hague[233].

The authorities were quick to respond and on 15 May, the Sofia City Prosecutor served a written communication to Sofia chairman Georgi Solunski, warning that the organization should either register as a political party or disband within a month[234] and on 23 May, the prosecutor specified that the 15 May announcement meant that UMO Ilinden should 'terminate its activities immediately'[235]. On 27 May, BTA further reported that the organization intended to go underground under 'the direct guidance of organizations in the Yugoslav constituent Socialist Republic of Macedonia'. The inference was clear – UMO Ilinden was seen by the Bulgarians as a Yugoslav Trojan horse. On 6 June, Ilinden members participating in a hunger strike outside of Blagoevgrad district court in protest at the official pressures against the organization were forcibly removed and deposited some 20 kilometres from town.

In July, UMO Ilinden applied for registration at the district court of Blagoevgrad but was turned down as the 'targets of the organization and the means of its attainment are directed against this nation's [Bulgaria] unity, and are aiming at spurring a national and ethnic hostility'[236] and the Blagoevgrad prosecutor warned that the leaders faced prosecution under Article 162 of the penal code which allows for up to six years' imprisonment. Atanas Kiryakov, chief-coordinator of UMO Ilinden, refused to sign the notification of warning[237].

UMO Ilinden attempted to hold its first constituent congress in Oshtava village, Sofia Region but was prevented by the authorities and the leaders were fined[238]. The organization claimed that 103 members had been been prevented from taking part in this congress with the leaders being subjected to short-term arrest. August saw the anniversary of the Ilinden-Preobrazhenie Uprising against the Ottomans in 1903 (an event claimed by both Bulgarians and Macedonians as their own) and the major political parties including the new President of Bulgaria, former UDF leader Zhelyu Zhelev, again stressed that Macedonians were Bulgarians – a point which the Bulgarians tried to reinforce by publishing a letter from those claiming to be Bulgarians living in Yugoslav Macedonia[239].

The current (at the time of writing) leader of UMO Ilinden, Stoyan Georgiev, has reportedly suffered harassment and short-term arrest and in October 1990, the authorities reportedly removed his and

Sokrat Markilov's passports. This latter sanction has also been applied to others including a student studying in Skopje, Damyan Milenov Rizakov, whose passport was removed in 16 October. In late 1990/early 1991, police broke up an attempt (not ostensibly by Ilinden) to collect signatures in favour of Macedonian rights and it appears to be impossible to collect public petitions on the issue in the current climate.

It seems clear that there are a number of people in Pirin Macedonia who see themselves as distinct from Bulgarians in ethnicity (similarly in Yugoslav Macedonia there are those who see themselves as Bulgarians). The relaxation following the fall of Todor Zhivkov has allowed such people to become more open in their activities. Conversely, however, it also seems clear that all shades of mainstream political opinion in Bulgaria are hostile to such activity and see it as part of a Yugoslav (or even Serbian) plot against Bulgaria, and in this the UDF appears to be more nationalistic on this issue than their communist/socialist predecessors. The 'Macedonian Question' is destined to be as alive as ever in the future.

The Bulgarian Mohammedans (Pomaks)

The Bulgarian Mohammedans, usually called by the originally derogatory term 'Pomaks', are a religious minority. They are Slav Bulgarians who speak Bulgarian as their mother tongue but whose religion and customs are Islamic. They are estimated to number in excess of 250,000 (a figure of 268,971 was given by local authorities at the end of 1990) and live in compact settlements in the mountainous regions of the Rhodope mountains in south-western and southern Bulgaria and down the Mesta valley in the Pirin region.

Since 1948 the Bulgarian authorities have made repeated attempts to induce the Pomaks to change their names, renounce their faith and become integrated into the socialist Bulgarian state. Some Pomak activists and their families were resettled in 1952 to other areas, eg. the village of Hadzhiyska on the northern slopes of the Balkan mountains near Zlatoritsa. In the period 1971 to 1973 the authorities pursued a concerted campaign to force the Pomaks to change their names by obliging them to choose new ones from a list of 'official' Bulgarian names.[240] For example, a Pomak whose name previously was Mustapha Aliev could choose his new name to be Emil, but his surname would depend traditionally on that of his father so that his new surname depended on what his father chose. However, in practice, it was often the sons who would choose the new names – the name Emil Dimitrov,

111

a popular Bulgarian singer, was a frequent choice – so that the father would have to change his name accordingly, thus reversing the traditional manner by which people are named.

An eyewitness account relating to a town in the southern Rhodope mountains in this period states that in the town square, in front of the House of Culture, a long red table was set out with all the local state and Communist Party officials in attendance. Armed detachments with loaded weapons at the ready were also there to ensure order. The Pomaks were obliged to approach the table one by one over a long red carpet and hand in their old identity papers and receive new ones made out in new Bulgarian names and thank the officials publicly. Some Pomaks, mostly old people but some young ones as well, refused but from that day onwards the old identity papers were invalid for all inhabitants of the town and the official bureaucracy which pervades all aspects of life in Bulgaria refused to recognize them, so that for example no pensions, state salary or money from a bank account could be drawn unless the new cards were used.

There were a number of instances of violent resistance. For example, in 1971 there were riots in Pazardzhik in which two Communist Party functionaries were reportedly killed. The authorities reacted by arresting large numbers of people. Two Pomaks were condemned to death and two others sentenced to 15 years' imprisonment. A group of Pomaks travelled to Sofia and protested against these measures but were stopped near the town of Samakov by the militia, and in a violent clash two Pomaks were shot dead and 50 wounded. There were also reported violent clashes in Barutin and around Devin.[241]

According to an eyewitness now living in Turkey, in July 1971 in the village of Ribnovo in Blagoevgrad district, two Pomaks – Salih Mehemdov Hatibov and Nevzem Mustafova Issaeva – were publicly hanged in the village for resisting the name-changing and another, Yakub Halilov Mihrin, died in hospital as a result of injuries sustained during a beating by the security forces. From Ribnono alone in the early 1970s, 32 people were imprisoned in Belene prison camp for refusing their new names. According to Huseyin Memisoglu, a former history professor at Sofia University who fled Bulgaria in March 1988, intensive military operations were carried out in May 1972 in Blagoevgrad and surrounding districts against the Pomaks which resulted in the deaths of hundreds of Pomaks who resisted the forced assimilation.[242]

In March 1973 security forces supported by border guards again entered several villages in Blagoevgrad district and went from house to house with prepared lists of Bulgarian names from which the Pomak inhabitants were obliged to select new names. In the violent resistance which ensued at least eight people were reported to have died, including one army officer, and a number of people wounded. Large numbers of Pomaks were arrested, 20 from the village of Kornitsa alone, and sentenced to three to 15 years' imprisonment. About 100 Pomaks were also deported to other areas in Bulgaria.

In this operation, the village of Kornitsa was surrounded by mounted armed police who attacked the villagers assembled in protest against the compulsory name-changing in the village square and allegedly killed seven men. The others fled to their houses and the police went from house to house. One Pomak, Bayram Redzhepov Getov, was beaten by the police in his home, arrested and taken to Sofia investigation prison. He was subsequently sentenced to 12 years' imprisonment for 'membership of a group formed to commit offences against the State' and 'dissemination of false information with the aim of undermining the State'. It is reported that he spent the first two years in solitary confinement and that he was beaten and ill-treated in prison in order to extract a confession from him.

His wife and two daughters were deported to a village in the province of Vidin, where his wife and eldest daughter were compelled to do forced labour. His 16-year-old son was sent to a school to learn to be a tractor driver, and reportedly there he was pressured to denounce his father and change his name. When he refused and ran away from the school, he was beaten so savagely that he was subsequently exempt from military service, declared infirm and sent to a mental hospital. He has never fully recovered. Bayram Getov was eventually released from prison in 1980.[243]

In prison the Pomaks suffered particularly harsh treatment. If they failed to use or respond to the Bulgarian name assigned to them by the authorities they risked being deprived of their right to visits from their families. In 1975 Amnesty International was informed that about 500 Pomaks were serving prison sentences in Belene prison camp and in 1977 reported that there were 40 to 50 Pomaks held in Stara Zagora Prison, many kept in solitary confinement with reduced rations for periods longer than the maximum 14 days allowed by Bulgarian penal law. Former prisoners from Sara Zagora Prison have alleged that Pomaks have been put for as long as three days in a special concrete cell, 'one metre square', which has a curved floor often covered with water. In winter the water freezes, and prisoners have suffered from kidney diseases and pneumonia.[244]

Demonstrations by Pomaks began on 15 August 1989 in protest at the authorities apparent refusal to issue passports to people living in the predominantly Pomak area around Gotse Delchev – a new passport law had allowed over 300,000 ethnic Turks to emigrate in the summer of 1989. Protests were reportedly staged in over a dozen villages including Hvostyane, Kornitsa, Lazhnitsa, Breznitsa, Dabnitsa and Blatska. Security forces sealed off at least six villages. One hundred and two people were arrested, including Bayram Getov who was seen as one of the ring leaders, but despite some unconfirmed reports to the contrary, nobody was killed during the demonstrations. All those arrested were released in September.

In November, police reportedly banned Pomaks from the region from travelling to Sofia to join a mass rally organized by independent opposition groups. Similarly on 18 December, a police road-block at Gospodintsi at the northern end of the Mesta valley, effectively blocked off the whole area and again prevented Pomaks from joining the mass demonstrations on the name-issue being held in Sofia. However, from 20 December onwards, it was possible for Pomaks to freely obtain passports after the customary one month waiting period. However, Turkey has not been keen to take prospective Pomak emigres and at the Turkish embassy in Sofia, would be emigres are given a rudimentary language test to separate ethnic Turks from Pomaks. Additionally, despite the August 1989 demonstrations, there did not appear in mid-1990 to be the desired large scale emigration from the Gotse Delchev region. A demand from the Pomaks was for rehabilitation for those arrested, with property confiscated during the 1970s campaigns returned to the owners? Further demonstrations by Pomaks were held in Yakoruda in January 1990 in protest at the local authorities' apparent reluctance to implement the government's decision allowing the restoration of Muslim names, and in protest at the death of a young girl – Ayshe Mrishkova, who, contrary to some western reports which stated that she had been shot in the head, died after being punched by a fellow (non-Pomak Bulgarian) pupil at school – and a bomb attack in the local mosque. Despite the bomb attack, all the mosques in the region had been opened since November 1989 and all restrictions on Islamic religious practices lifted.

The villages around Gotse Delchev in the Mesta river valley like Breznitsa, Lazhnitsa and Kornitsa, are solidly Pomak – eg. some 2300 people live in Kornitsa of whom, at most 200 are Orthodox Christian with the remainder Muslims. As religion is the only factor that differentiates the Pomaks from other Slav Bulgarians, it is perhaps not surprising that they are more Islamic than the ethnic Turks. This is readily observable – in the middle of Lazhnitsa in early March 1990, there was a huge sign saying 'Happy holiday brother Muslims'.

114

The Pomaks do not feel themselves to be Bulgarians and have a closer affinity to the Turks due to the shared religion. They joined in large numbers the mass demonstration by ethnic Turks outside the National Assembly through the night of the 4 and 5 of March while the Assembly again discussed the procedure for returning Muslim names. Despite initial attempts during the negotiations (which lasted well into the night) to separate the ethnic Turks from the Pomaks by proposing an option whereby all those whose names were changed after 1984 (ie. ethnic Turks rather than Pomaks) could change their names administratively, it was agreed that all Muslims who had had their names changed could restore them by using a court procedure. From then onwards, the Pomak name-changing issue was the same as the ethnic Turk name-changing one, and in late 1990, a simplified procedure was introduced.

Fieldwork in 1990 in Hadzhiyska showed that 46.4% of the sample group chose definite Turkish/Islamic forms for their names in the new climate of 1990, while only 14.3% chose distinctive Bulgarian forms, with the remaining 39.2% exhibiting various types of Bulgarian-Turkish anthroponymic compromises – eg. choosing a name like 'Aldin' or 'Silvina' which would be acceptable to both ethnic Turkish and Slav Bulgarian groups.[245]

Many Pomaks initially supported the Independent Association for the Defence of Human Rights (IADHR) but, especially after the IADHR, and the democratic opposition in general, had shown itself to be somewhat equivocal on the national issue after the nationalist counter-demonstrations in January 1990. Pomaks had mostly moved their support to the Movement for Rights and Freedoms (DPS), the mainly ethnic Turkish organization led by Ahmed Dogan – Bayram Getov was DPS coordinator for the region of Gotse Delchev.

However, there appears to be less problems between Pomaks and Bulgarians than the case with Turks and Bulgarians. Similarly to the Slav Muslims of Yugoslavia, there appears to be an element of confusion and uncertainty in their self-identity. A frequent question from Pomaks was whether there was an outside Pomak country or state which might help them either materially or psychologically similar to the role which Turkey plays for ethnic Turks. However, despite their relatively small numbers, their strong religious beliefs and compact settlements in the south-west of the country should ensure their continued existence, especially as in these south-western regions, they are not surrounded by Muslim Turks who might prove more capable (than the neighbouring Orthodox Slavs to the west or Greeks to the south) of assimilating them through the shared religion.

The Roma (Gypsies), Albanians, Tatars, Vlahs and Sarakatsani

There is very little information available on the **Roma** minority in Bulgaria estimated to number over 550,000. A figure of 576,926 was given by local authorities at the end of 1990 but this is likely to be low due to the continuing stigma attached to being a Rom. Manush Romanov claims a figure of over one million for the Bulgarian Rom population. However, Manush Romanov's organization (see below), which claims some 50,000 members, has been, at the time of writing, denied permission to contest local or national elections due to the current ban on ethnically or religiously-based parties.

While Bulgaria has made a determined effort to raise the living standards and educational opportunities of the Roma minority, the authorities have been equally firm in denying them the right to preserve their own identity and culture through formation of socio-political organizations with only a few local music ensembles allowed. In the period of 1953/4 there was an operation to settle the nomadic Roma population, often in the northern plain below the Danube and, in the case of Muslim Roma – the majority – to change their names. A similar name-changing campaign to that concerning the Pomaks was reported to have taken place against Muslim Roma beginning in 1965 but few details are available. The restrictions on the practice of Islam which accompanied the crack-down against the Turkish minority in 1984/5 also adversely affected Muslim Roma. Despite the assimilation policy, the large settled Roma communities in Sliven, and the quarters in Sofia, Varna and Plovdiv remain strongholds of Roma social life and the assimilation policies appear to have had little impact. Small scale discrimination against Roma continues in everyday life. The literacy rate for Roma is only 13% and 80% of prisoners are Roma.[246]

The fall of Todor Zhivkov in November 1989 allowed the Roma to openly organize. At a rally held in Sliven on 7 January 1990, the Independent, Democratic Socialist Association of Gypsies in Bulgaria was set up which aimed at the improvement of Roma social and cultural standards.[247] This organization appeared to have been a socialist front type organization. More representative was the founding conference of the Roma Democratic Union in March 1990. At this conference it was stated that the assimilation against Roma in Bulgaria began in 1954 with renaming of Muslim Roma and speakers stressed the problematic aspects of Todor Zhivkov's rule – the closure of the Roma newspapers, the expropriation of Roma clubs, the prohibition of the use of Romanes, and the attempt to destroy Roma culture and customs. The conference elected Manush Romanov (formerly called Mustapha Ali) as chairman of the union.[248] Manush Romanov, the most influential Rom at this time, was also the leader of the Cultural, Educational Organization for Roma in Bulgaria, and is also a representative of the UDF.

Muslim Roma also had representatives in the Movement for Rights and Freedom (DPS), the predominantly ethnic Turkish organization led by Ahmed Dogan. During the June elections there were many reports of attempted intimidation of Roma to induce them to vote for the BSP.[249] A Roma official at a recent European forum stated that as an ethnic community the Roma in Bulgaria enjoyed the best material and cultural levels in comparison with Roma in neighbouring countries.[250] A sign of the changes was the holding in late October 1990 of a Miss 'Roma' – a Bulgarian competition to find 'the most beautiful Roma girl in the world'.[251] Despite the attitudes of much of the general population, the Roma have survived the attempts at assimilation and are now becoming increasingly organized and assertive. Their large numbers make it probable that they will play an increasingly important role in the future.

Ethnic **Albanians**, estimated to number some 5000 to 10,000 and remnants from the Ottoman trade route from Dubrovnik to Varna, also had their names changed at the same time as the 5000 or so **Muslim Tatars** in the north-east around Shumen.[252] Both groups still apparently succeed to some extent in keeping their identity separate from the majority Muslim population – the ethnic Turks. This does not appear to be the case for the **Cherkez** (Mongols), another Islamic group from the Ottoman period, who have become totally assimilated by the Turks. After the Crimean War of 1854/5, the Ottoman government settled some 150,000 Tatars and Circassians in Bulgarian territory and the 1876 Bulgarian uprising around Plovdiv, led by wealthy merchants, was in protest at raids on the local population by these Circassians. After 1878, all the Circassians are believed to have left with the retreating Ottoman armies, whereas some of the Tatars remained. They gradually became assimilated by the ethnic Turks.[253]

Similarly, little information is available on the **Vlahs**, also known in Bulgaria as the **Karakachani**. The Vlahs are a predominantly pastoral people living south of the Danube, primarily in Greece but also in Albania, Yugoslavia and Bulgaria, who speak a form of Romanian. A motion for a resolution to the European Parliament in November 1985 quotes 'recent specialists studies' as indicating that some 400,000 Vlahs live in compact areas in Northern Bulgaria[254] but this figure appears to be widely exaggerated. Vlahs tend to live in scattered communities in mountainous regions like the central Stara Planina range and the Struma valley although many live in the Dobrudzha region, where many Vlah emigres from Macedonia were settled by the Romanian government which controlled the area from the Second Balkan War until 1940, and the coastal areas around Varna.

Whatever the figure the Vlahs have been subjected to the same 'Bulgarization' process as the other minorities, excepting the Jews and Armenians, although the process antedates many later assimilation campaigns and there are reports of pressure on Vlahs in the early 1970s. It appears that the language will shortly die out. There is similarly little information on the small number of Greek-speaking **Sarakatsani** who are also transhumant shepherds, who share many customs and traits with the Vlahs, and still survive in the upland pastures.

Small Minorities

There are also small number of **Greeks** (8241 in 1965 living mainly in Sofia, Plovdiv, and Varna), some 10,000 **Russians** mostly descendants of 'White' Russians who fled to Bulgaria in the period 1918-1922, and some 20,000 **Armenians**. Unlike other minorities, the communist authorities recognized Armenians and **Jews**; they had their own organizations. The Armenians had their cultural-educational organization 'Erevan' of Armenians in Bulgaria with a youth organization (the Armenian Progressive Youth Organization), while the remaining Jewish population set up on 17 March 1990 a new organization, 'Shalom', under the chairmanship of Edi Shvartze, to replace the former 'Social, Cultural and Educational Organization of Jews'.[255] There are also very small numbers of **Serbs, Czechs, Hungarians** and **Germans**.[256]

Bulgaria also had, at the beginning of 1990, some 40,000 guest workers from Vietnam, Cuba, Ethiopia and Nicaragua. The majority (60%) of these were **Vietnamese**. Most of these guest workers were employed in menial jobs. There has been a spate of anti-Vietnamese incidents by ordinary Bulgarians, some of which has resulted in deaths, and on 29 March, the Council of Minister's Committee on Labour and Social Security announced that a number of major labour-exchange agreements with former socialist allies would not be renewed.[257] However, the head of the employment section at the Vietnamese Embassy in Sofia said the inter-governmental agreement was still in force although an agreement in May had been reached whereby present contracts were reduced and there would be no more new arrivals. All the 15,500 Vietnamese citizens, many of them now unemployed, would have left by 1992, he said.[258]

The largest minority – the ethnic Turks

The background

Ethnic Turks began to settle in Bulgaria towards the end of the 14th Century and have lived there ever since. They live mostly in compact communities in the south of the country in the Arda river basin and in the north-east in the Dobrudzha region. They also live in scattered communities in the central and eastern Stara Planina (the Balkan Mountains) and in the Rhodope Mountains.

Until the most recent campaign to assimilate them, the ethnic Turks were officially recognized as a 'national minority' along with certain other minorities including the Gypsies but excluding the Macedonians and the Pomaks. However, even this recognition was circumscribed by a general reservation about the very idea of minorities in Bulgaria and the 1971 Constitution, unlike the 1947 Constitution, makes no specific references to ethnic minorities but rather refers to 'citizens of non-Bulgarian origin' (Article 45). Between 1985 and 1990 the only recognized minorities in Bulgaria with their own minority organizations were the small number of Jews and the Armenians.

The 1965 census recorded 746,755 ethnic Turks, an increase of approximately 90,000 on the 1956 figure. Since then there have been no official figures for the total numbers of members of ethnic minorities in Bulgaria and in 1975 the section recording nationality on personal identity cards was reportedly removed.

Emigration

At various times since World War II, Bulgaria and Turkey have reached agreement over the emigration of Turks from Bulgaria to Turkey. The largest number of such emigrants left Bulgaria in the period 1949 to 1951. In August 1950 the Bulgarian government announced that a total of 250,000 Turks had applied to leave. The Turkish government, on the other hand, said it was unable to receive such a huge mass of people within such a short time and in November 1950 closed its border with Bulgaria because of 'illegal crossing of borders'. Two months later an agreement was reached by both governments that only those Turks who were in possession of a Turkish entry visa would be allowed to leave. Despite this agreement Bulgaria continued to evict Turks with the result that in November 1951 Turkey again closed its border. According to the Turkish authorities, Bulgaria had forged Turkish entry visas in order to rid itself of as many Turks as possible. However, some 155,000 left Bulgaria for Turkey in this period.

In 1968 a further agreement was reached which allowed the departure of close relatives of those who had left in the period 1944 to 1951. This agreement expired on 30 November 1978 and an announcement in the Sofia daily newspaper *Otechestven Front* of 2 August 1979 stated 'Since then between the two countries no agreement on emigration has existed.' The last official Bulgarian figure given for those who had emigrated under this agreement was 52,392 for the period up to August 1977 although Turkish sources state that some 130,000 left in total under the agreement.[259] From then until May 1989 emigration ceased except in a few individual cases of family reunification – such as when the Turkish authorities paid an estimated one million US dollars to the Bulgarian authorities to allow the emigration of the close relatives of the champion weight lifter Naim Suleymanoglu, who defected from Bulgaria in December 1986. Additionally, a number of children, 64 in the period January 1987 to April 1988, all of whom had both parents emigrated to Turkey, were allowed to join them although there remained still a number of such cases outstanding. Leading Bulgarian officials categorically denied that emigration would be restarted. For example, Stanko Todorov, then member of the BCP Central Committee, Politburo and Chairman of the National Assembly, stated in a speech of 28 March 1985: 'there is not and will not be any emigration to Turkey' and that 'no Bulgarian/Turkish talks will be held in this connection'.[260] However, the situation dramatically changed in May 1989.

Education and culture

In line with Marxist-Leninist theory, the first Constitution of the People's Republic of Bulgaria, adopted on 4 December 1947, contained provision for minority groups. For example, Article 71 stated that although the study of Bulgarian was obligatory in schools: 'National minorities have a right to be educated in their vernacular, and to develop their vernacular, and to develop their national culture.'

There was also set up a Turkish language department at Sofia university as well as a number of Turkish language publications and schooling in Turkish. In 1964, on the 10th anniversary of one such Turkish publication, *Yeni Hayat*, Todor Zhivkov himself stated:

> *'All possible opportunities have been created for the Turkish population to develop their culture and language freely . . . The children of the Turkish population must learn their mother tongue and perfect it. To*

this end, it is necessary that the teaching of the Turkish language be improved in schools. Now and in the future the Turkish population will speak their mother tongue; they will write their contemporary literary works [in Turkish]; they will sing their wonderfully beautiful songs [in Turkish] . . . Many more books must be published in this country in Turkish, including the best works of progressive writers in Turkey.'

However, after a plenum of the BCP Central Committee on 4 October 1958, Turkish language schools were merged with Bulgarian schools and by the early 1970s the teaching of Turkish in Bulgarian schools had ceased. The Department of Turkish at Sofia university which reportedly attracted large numbers of students, of whom 70% were estimated to be ethnic Turks, stopped admitting students. In 1974 the whole department was shut down and replaced by a department for Arabic studies with new staff and only a few students – mostly apparently children of diplomatic staff stationed in Arab countries. If the aim of this was to prevent the formation of a Turkish intelligentsia which might lead a movement in the future for minority rights, this may have been counter-productive as ethnic Turks were forced to pursue other subjects which had better job prospects than, for example, philology in the old Turkish department.

After 1951 the Bulgarian government and BCP made attempts to integrate Turks into the state and party apparatus and large numbers were admitted into the BCP. However, there was constant criticism in official publications about their lack of party discipline and socialist consciousness. In 1971, the BCP programme which is still in force, stated that: 'the citizens of our country of different national origins will come ever closer together'.[261] By the mid-1970s the use of the term 'unified Bulgarian socialist nation' became common parlance in official publications and speeches. In his speech of March 1985 (quoted above), Stanko Todorov categorically stated that Bulgaria was a 'one-nation state' and that in the 'Bulgarian nation there are no parts of any other peoples and nations'.

Ethnic Turks are reportedly unable to join the police force or make their career in the army and ethnic Turk conscripts serve in unarmed units engaged in national construction, for example building work after a couple of weeks rudimentary training with substitute weapons. The inference is that the Bulgarian authorities do not trust the ethnic Turks enough to train them properly in the army.

121

Population growth

The growth rate of the population in Bulgaria has been consistently decreasing in recent years. In 1980 the natural growth rate – that is the rate measured by the difference between the number of births and the number of deaths – was 3.6 per 1000, the lowest since records began. In 1981 it dropped to 2.8, in 1982 it dropped to 2.7 and in 1984 it was again down to 2.4. In 1989 it was as low as 0.6 while in 1990 it dropped to a negative figure of -0.35. There have been a number of articles on this decline in the official press in recent years. The growth rates for the minorities – especially the ethnic Turks, the Pomaks, and the Roma – has been considerably higher than that for the majority of the population. This can be illustrated by comparing the official figures for specific areas, for example Lovech, Mihailovgrad and Vidin, all areas with negligible minority populations, with those that have a high proportion of minority populations, for example Blagoevgrad (where there are large numbers of Macedonians) and Smolyan (Pomaks) and Kardzhali (where there are concentrations of ethnic Turks).

The figures in **Table 1** show that Lovech, Mihailovgrad and Vidin all have negative growth rates (that is the population is actually declining) and that this negative growth rate is increasing. The figures also highlight the continuous drift of the population from the countryside to the towns. The areas with large minorities, however, have higher than average growth rates, especially Kardzhali, and the drift to the towns is not so marked (and in the case of Kardzhali does not exist).

Table 1 Population growth per 1000 inhabitants

Year	Lovech	Mihailovgrad	Vidin	Blagoevgrad	Smolyan	Kardzhali
1979	-2.8	-1.6	-4.8	+9.6	+9.9	+17.9
Towns	+4.5	+8.6	+8.4	+13.1	+12.0	+17.7
Villages	-10.9	-11.8	17.9	+6.0	+7.7	+17.9
1981	-3.3	-3.3	-6.3	+9.3	+7.8	+15.9
Towns	+4.6	+5.9	+4.9	+10.9	+9.8	+12.7
Villages	-12.4	-13.3	-18.2	+7.4	+5.5	+17.3
1984	-4.6	-4.9	-7.2	+8.3	+7.7	+14.0
Towns	+3.6	+4.2	+4.4	+9.4	+9.5	+12.4
Villages	-14.9	-16.5	-21.1	+6.9	+5.5	+14.7

(Figures from *Statisticheski Godishnik na Narodno Republika Bulgaria*, 1980, 1982 and 1985)

This highlights a double concern for the authorities. Firstly, the minority population is rapidly increasing while that of the majority is actually declining and, given the high birth rate of ethnic Turks, the actual figure for their number may well be in excess of the estimated 900,000 and is probably nearer to 15% than the more conservative estimate of 10% of the total population. Additionally, ethnic Turks are estimated to be a larger proportion of the work force, some 15-20% due to the high birth rate.

Secondly, large areas of the countryside, especially the important agricultural areas in the south around Kardzhali – vital for Bulgaria's valuable tobacco exports – and the Dobrudzha – a major wheat-growing region – are becoming increasingly populated by the minorities; so much so that before the campaign in 1984/5 it was possible to travel through large areas of Bulgaria without hearing Bulgarian spoken at all. The authorities' concern is compounded in the case of the ethnic Turks living in the south near Smolyan and Kardzhali by the proximity of Turkey, so that while there was no apparent irredentist movement of any description before the name-changing campaign of 1984/5 such a movement arising in the future is not out of the question, and the example of the growth of the ethnic Albanian population in Kosovo in Yugoslavia and the attendant problems for the Yugoslav authorities must be a worrying one for the Bulgarian government.

Religion

Both the Pomaks and the ethnic Turks (with the exception of the Gagauz, estimated to number a few thousand, who profess the Eastern Orthodox Christian faith and live near Varna in the north) are Sunni Muslim, while the Gypsies are estimated to be 75% Muslim and 25% Eastern Orthodox in religious adherence. As religion was until the 20th century more important than language in differentiating between different groups, the Pomaks tended to feel greater affinity with the Turks than with Christian Bulgarians; similarly with the Muslim Roma (hence, the second part of the proverb mentioned in Introduction).

Ethnic Turks and Pomaks have often deliberately or otherwise been confused with each other and ethnic Turks were in many cases subjected to the same pressures as the Pomaks, especially where they inhabited the same village communities, to induce them to exchange their Muslim names for Bulgarian ones and, in effect, to renounce their religion and ethnic identity. This confusion between ethnic Turks and Pomaks has been deliberately used by the Bulgarian authorities which since the name-changing campaign of 1984/5 has consistently claimed that all ethnic Turks are Slav Bulgarians by descent who were forcibly Islamicized by the Ottoman authorities, ie. that they are all Pomaks.

Adherence to the Islamic faith was seen by the authorities as being a key factor inhibiting loyalty to the communist government. This was clearly set out in 1977 in an article in *Filosofska Misul* – an official publication published in Sofia. This article, which provides a valuable insight into the communist authorities' attitude to the Pomaks and to Muslims in general states:

'It was clear to the Bulgarian Communist Party that the Bulgarian Mohammedan problem was, above all, of social origin. That is why, following the 9 September 1944 victory of the socialist revolution, it set as its objective the elimination, above all, of the social roots of Islam in the Rhodope along with the age-old isolation and separation of Islamicized Bulgarians, to heal the wounds and traumas in their spirituality, to eliminate the division traced by the Turkish feudals, intensified by the Bulgarian bourgeoisie, to emancipate the Bulgarian awareness in them, dulled and concealed in the course of centuries, and to accelerate their joining the Bulgarian socialist nation.

However, in the Rhodope Islam has retained its strong positions in life and social mentality. Whereas it has already been 'expelled' in the realm of social relations and the collectives, and in the social system of rituals and ceremonies, it clings adamantly and reproduces itself in family relations, holidays, and traditions. It is precisely for this reason that the new stage in the course of the cultural revolution in the Rhodope requires a more active interference in the way of life and in 'expelling' Islam from the realm of family relations.

The struggle against Islamic fanaticism in the Rhodope and its derived tendency of alienation from what is Bulgarian is not a subjective requirement but an objective form of class and ideological struggle, and a reflection of the objective historical law of the consolidation of Islamicized Bulgarians within the Bulgarian socialist nation. The atheistic struggle in the Rhodope both presumes and encompasses the problem of breaking down the socio-political complex in the minds, behaviour, and way of life of a certain segment of the Bulgarian population and is interwoven with their class-party, patriotic, and internationalist education. A characteristic feature of the struggle for atheism in the Rhodope is that not only is it being deployed in the struggle against Islam but is also linked with the struggle for Bulgarian nationhood, and for the development of a new awareness, way of life, customs, and traditions. This presumes their cleansing from accumulated Islamic-Turkish influence.'

The uncompromising struggle against Islam and its adverse consequences to some Rhodope Bulgarians is an important task at the present stage and a necessary prerequisite for their consolidation within the Bulgarian socialist nation and more active inclusion in building a developed socialist society.'

The rise of Islamic fundamentalism, the influence of the Iranian revolution of 1979, and the example of Lebanon, relatively close to Bulgaria, hardened the attitudes set out in this article although there is no apparent indication that there has been as yet a growth of Islamic fun-

Table 2 Religious attitudes (%)

	Bulgarians	Ethnic Turks
Active believers	5.72	12.50
Passive believers	11.38	33.75
Uncertain	21.82	11.80
Passive atheists	23.94	16.08
Active atheists	23.94	10.23

(From S. Tahirov, *Sotsialisticheska obrechnost i duhovno edinstvo*, Sofia, 1984)

Table 3 Religious activity of ethnic Turks (%)

	Total	Workers	White-collar	Peasants
Mosque attendance	53.8	45.1	20.2	60.7
Weekly	11.4	5.1	3.6	14.8
Monthly	9.3	8.1	1.2	10.5
Festivals only	33.2	33.2	15.5	35.5
Non-attendance	45.9	54.6	79.8	39.9

(From M. Beytullov, '*Izmenie v religioznata praktika na Balgarskite Turtsi*' in *Ateistichna Tribuna*, Sofia, 1976)

damentalism within Bulgaria. However, there is little doubt that the ethnic Turks have stronger religious leanings than ethnic Bulgarians as is illustrated in Tables 2[262] and 3.[263]

The above figures show how religious attitudes have remained strong among the ethnic Turks, especially peasants, as compared to ethnic Bulgarians – a situation not to the liking of the authorities. An article in the daily newspaper *Rabotnichesko Delo* of 21 November 1984 spoke of 'the extreme aggressiveness of the ideological enemy, whose basic trump card is to play on the ethnic affiliations of part of the Rhodope population' and there have been a number of similar attacks against the penetration of Muslim influences into the country and against Islamic religious customs. For example, an article in the newspaper Nova Svetlina in June 1985 stated that fasting during the month of Ramadan was nothing but a 'destructive superstition' and an article in the newspaper Otechestven Front of 27 November 1984 referred to religious fanaticism still prevailing among 'Bulgarian Turks' and condemned those, especially in the Haskovo and Kardzhali districts, who raise families 'according to the dogmas of the Koran and the Muslim religion' without concluding civil marriages.

Modernization

Another factor in the assimilation campaign and one which is not prejudicial to the motives of the Bulgarian authorities is that of modernization. The BCP claimed to be possessor of an ideology, Marxist-Leninism, which aims at the rapid implementation of policies to turn Bulgaria into a modern industrial state. Progress along these lines since the BCP took power after World War II has been, up till recent years, fairly impressive. The existence of a large minority, living in concentrated areas, speaking a completely different language (Turkish is an Asiatic language whilst Bulgarian is an Indo-European one) and 'clinging' to a traditional way of life is, perhaps inevitably, to be seen as an obstacle to the modernization process. In a modern state such as the one the BCP claimed to be introducing it is essential for all citizens to speak a common language, in this case of course Bulgarian, and while Bulgarian has been compulsory in all schools many ethnic Turks, especially those living in areas where the majority of the population are ethnic Turks, learn only a basic Bulgarian and many older people speak it badly and some not at all.

Various Islamic customs such as fasting during the month of Ramadan were also seen by the authorities as being in contradiction to the precepts of modernization and articles in the official press attacked these customs as being outdated in the era of factory discipline, etc. Thus both language and customs can be seen as obstacles in the path of modernization and the authorities claimed that ethnic Turks, or 'Islamicized Bulgarians' as they were now officially referred to until late 1989, were offered the opportunity to become first-class citizens like the majority population. (All these aspects are reflected in the above mentioned article from Filosofska Misul.

1985 was the last year of the five-year period for replacing all identity cards and a national census was scheduled to be held in December 1985. This may have been one of the factors in the intensity and short duration of the campaign to change all the names of the ethnic Turks from Islamic forms to Bulgarian ones.

Fear of assimilation by Turkey and the examples of Greece and Yugoslavia

The five centuries of Ottoman control have indelibly left their mark on the Bulgarian national psyche. The title of the most famous book by Bulgaria's most famous author, Ivan Vazov, is Pod Igoto ('Under the Yoke') referring to this period and the symbolism of the yoke is universally used both officially and unofficially in this connection. The modern Bulgarian national awakening only occurred in the 19th century and was faced as much by the threat of Greek assimilation as Turkish. Throughout Eastern Europe fear of assimilation on the part of small nations is very real and examples like the Kashubs (a small Slavic people of northern Poland), who have effectively been assimilated over recent centuries, are a warning to other small nations like the Bulgarian which is not greatly enlarging its population, if at all. On its borders is the traditional enemy, Turkey, with a population of over 50 million and growing and within its own borders there is a large minority of Turks which are also growing at a rapid rate.

Compounding this situation are the examples of what has happened to the populations included in the San Stefano 'Greater Bulgaria' but which, apart from brief periods during the world wars, have been lost to Bulgaria. These are the Macedonians of Yugoslavia, Greece and Albania, and San Stefano Bulgaria is still seen by most Bulgarians as what should have been (and should be). The situation regarding the small number of Macedonians living in Albania is unclear due to the extreme secrecy of the Albanian authorities. The situations in Greece and Yugoslavia, however, are much clearer. In Greece the large Slav-speaking population in Aegean Macedonia has been successfully assimilated by a mixture of diluting the population with a massive influx of Greeks from Asia Minor after the population exchanges following the Greco-Turkish War of 1922, and an at times (especially under Metaxas in the late 1930s) severe discrimination similar to that now applied by the Bulgarian authorities to its own ethnic Turks.

In Yugoslavia since World War II the Yugoslav authorities have apparently successfully nurtured a Macedonian national consciousness separate from the Bulgarian one by using the regional differences between the populations of Vardar Macedonia in Yugoslavia and those in Bulgaria. These differences have been amplified by creating a literary Macedonian language as far removed from Bulgarian as is feasible, by retrospectively retracing the new nation back through history, and by using the full power of the state bureaucracy and education system to instill the new consciousness into the population.

10

BULGARIA'S ETHNIC TURKS – FORCED ASSIMILATION FROM 1984 TO 1989

Ethnic Turks and Pomaks have often, deliberately or otherwise, been confused with each other and where they cohabited in the same villages previous campaigns against the Pomaks to forcibly change their names have also included similar measures against ethnic Turks.

For example, during army manoeuvres in early 1984, the village of Dolni Voden near Asenovgrad in the district of Plovdiv was reportedly surrounded by troops and the inhabitants, all ethnic Turks and Pomaks, were forced to change their names. In 1976 there were reports of demonstrations of Turks and Pomaks in the Plovdiv area protesting at discrimination against Muslims in employment and at the closing of several mosques.

A number of ethnic Turks in this period were charged with espionage apparently because of their opposition to official policy vis-a-vis the ethnic Turks. An example is Yusuf Husnu, an ethnic Turk from Varna, born in 1937 who was an agrarian economist and a member of the BCP. He held strong views on discrimination against ethnic Turks, particularly in matters of religion and freedom of opinion. He also had relatives living in Turkey and had made attempts to leave Bulgaria with his family. He was arrested in 1976 on charges of espionage and sentenced to 12 years' imprisonment in 1977. The charges of espionage appear to have been related to his alleged connections with a Turkish lorry driver. In 1984 he was released and allowed to emigrate to Turkey.[264] Additionally, Turkish citizens, often former Bulgarian citizens who had emigrated to Turkey, were similarly imprisoned for espionage or for 'anti-state agitation and propaganda' while visiting relatives in Bulgaria.

The pressures on the population can be seen by the contents of an official document dated 3 August 1984, relating to the municipality and regions around Stambolovo, south of Haskovo. The document, widely publicized outside Bulgaria, forbade the wearing of *shalvari* –

traditional Turkish trousers – and the speaking of Turkish in the street, public places, and institutions. The order, signed by the mayor of Gledka stated that those wearing shalvari or speaking Turkish would be refused service in shops and that only Bulgarian would be allowed to be spoken in kindergartens. In the light of later official statements denying the existence of a Turkish minority in Bulgaria, it is significant that the order referred to 'the Turkish population'.

Thus, from the available information it appears that although there were certain instances of attempts at forcible assimilation of the ethnic Turkish minority, sometimes involving whole villages, this was not pursued by the authorities on a consistent countrywide basis before December 1984.

The name-changing campaign of December 1984 to March 1985

The situation radically changed in late 1984 when the Bulgarian authorities initiated a countrywide campaign to forcibly change the names of all ethnic Turks in Bulgaria. On the grounds that the roads were blocked due to adverse weather conditions, access to the regions where the ethnic Turks predominate was not allowed to foreign observers or visitors and these restrictions remained in force for certain areas, notably those around Kardzhali in the south and Yablanovo in the eastern Stara Planina until 1989.

After an initial period of complete silence in this matter which lasted until reports of the campaign began to appear in the news media outside Bulgaria in early 1985, the Bulgarian authorities stated that the ethnic Turks were in fact descendants of Slav Bulgarians who had been forcibly converted to Islam under Ottoman rule (ie. that they were Pomaks). The authorities further stated that these 'Slav Bulgarians' were all 'voluntarily' and 'spontaneously' requesting new Bulgarian names as a sign of their 'rebirth in the Bulgarian nation'. The authorities have called this name-changing campaign 'the reconstruction of Bulgarian names' and have repeatedly denied that there has been any element of force or coercion involved. There is no doubt that some ethnic Turks did voluntarily request new names, especially those in the party/state apparatus but such cases were rare compared to the majority where these 'voluntary' and 'spontaneous' requests were made under severe duress.

The methods used by the authorities were similar to those used in the past against the Pomaks. Villages with predominantly Turkish inhabitants were surrounded by police with dogs and troops with tanks, often in the early hours of the morning. Officials with new identity cards, or in other cases with a list of 'official' names to choose from, visited every household and the inhabitants were forced, in some cases at gun-point, to accept the new cards and to sign 'voluntary' forms requesting their new names. There are many reports of violence and rape by the security forces. In other instances the inhabitants of ethnic Turkish villages were assembled in the main square of the village where they were then obliged to accept the new identity cards. In villages with mixed populations, for example Preslavets near Harmanli in Haskovo district whose population is approximately 50% Turkish, similar methods were used by the authorities. However, in areas where the ethnic Turkish population constitutes only a small minority of the population, especially in cities, the operation was more low-key. For example, in Harmanli itself which has a population of 25,000 to 30,000 with at most 1000 ethnic Turkish inhabitants, the name-changing and the issuing of new identity cards were carried out at the work-place, and in some instances ethnic Turks were given a period of days to accept the new cards or else lose their jobs.

The campaign began in the southern regions of the country in December 1984 and then steadily worked northwards reaching around Varna and the Dobrudzha in the north-east by January/February 1985. By the end of March the operation had apparently been completed and Stanko Todorov, then Chairman of the National Assembly, in a speech of 28 March 1985 reported that the 'resumption' of Bulgarian names by citizens with 'Turkish-Arabic' names had been 'completed safely', stressing that Bulgaria was a 'one-nation state' and that in the 'Bulgarian nation there are no parts of any other people and nations'. This operation had, he said, taken place 'speedily, spontaneously and calmly'.[265]

Other aspects of the assimilation campaign: Religion and religious customs

Article 53, paragraph 1, of the Bulgarian Constitution guarantees freedom of conscience and creed to citizens who also 'may perform religious rites'. The same paragraph also allows 'anti-religious propaganda' and as noted above the authorities attacked Islamic traditions and Islam in general with growing frequency in official publications over a long period. Paragraph 2 of the same article states that 'the church shall be separated from the state'. In practice, however, all religious officials were paid by the state and the state was responsible for the preservation and maintenance of all churches and mosques.

Since the campaign of December 1984 there were a number of

reports of mosques forcibly closed or destroyed although the number which were actually destroyed was apparently small. These include the mosque in Gorski Izvor near the border with Greece which was forcibly closed by officials on 15 January 1985; the minaret destroyed and the building turned into a tobacco warehouse; and one of the two mosques in Haskovo, the minaret of which was destroyed at the end of 1986. More common was the practice of closing local mosques and ostensibly turning them into museums usually with the sign 'Museum of Bulgarian Mussulmen' on the locked doors. The half-crescent habitually found on the top of minarets was in most instances removed, apparently as being too associated with the Turkish national symbol.

According to a report by one of the very few foreign journalists allowed by the authorities to visit areas where ethnic Turks predominate while the campaign was fully underway, Islamic clerics who voluntarily changed their names were granted a salary increase in January 1985 of 50 leva ($50), making their total salary about 200 leva per month. The same source asserted that mosques in Bulgaria have been divided into two categories: 'official' and 'non-official'. 'Official' mosques were those which had an 'official' imam recognized as such by the authorities, that is those where the local imam cooperated with the authorities in the name-changing campaign. Mosques in the other category of 'non-official' mosques were closed.[266]

Another journalist who visited Bulgaria in this period was the Turkish journalist Kamil Taylan. He was given special permission by the Bulgarian authorities to make a film report within Bulgaria in September 1986 for West German television apparently because of his left wing stance and previous criticism of Turkey. His experiences demonstrated the constraints imposed even upon journalists whom the Bulgarian authorities might have viewed as sympathetic. He was permanently accompanied by 'guides' who refused to let him use the term Turks but rather 'reborn Bulgarian Muslims'. He was also strongly discouraged from conducting interviews in Turkish although in practice this was often unavoidable as some of the subjects for interview knew no other language. He was also refused permission to visit Kardzhali, one of the main ethnic Turkish areas, and the authorities admitted to him that there had been violent clashes between security forces and demonstrators against the name-changing campaign in Haskovo. Despite these and many other restrictions he was able, often in conversation when he had succeeded in temporarily losing his 'guide', to compile much information, especially regarding the religious aspect of the assimilation campaign.

He was allowed to visit Shumen, an ethnic Turkish area in the north-east of the country. There he was informed: that the authorities had replaced the previous *mufti* who had reportedly opposed the name-changing campaign, with one who would support the authorities' assimilation campaign; that young people were not allowed to go to mosque and that those who tried faced harassment and possible arrest; that all religious classes and teachings of the Koran in mosques was forbidden; that circumcision of male infants was strictly forbidden and that those who had this operation performed were imprisoned; and that all separate Muslim cemeteries had been abolished. The number of mosques in Shumen had been reduced to three, with seven others demolished in the preceding years and from January 1987 the main mosque in Shumen would be closed for restoration, apparently for some years.

Kamil Taylan also visited Plovdiv where again he was informed that young people faced arrest if they attempted to go to mosques which were open only for prayers on Fridays at noon. There an *imam* informed him that 'There are two mosques left in Filibe [Plovdiv] district. We are imams without mosques. We are paid a salary for show. They gather us to show to delegations like yours from other countries to prove that religion is free.' The imam also told Taylan not to believe what the mufti of Plovdiv told him stating that 'he is definitely their man'.

From this and many other such reports by refugees and others it appeared that Islamic religious practice was, while not completely banned, severely curtailed and that only old people were allowed to pray in the few mosques left open and then only once a week. It appeared that the Bulgarian authorities were not prepared to unduly antagonize Islamic world opinion by an outright ban as this would have jeopardized foreign relations with a number of then friendly Arab states, for example Syria whose Grand Mufti visited Sofia in July 1985 and declared that he was satisfied that there was religious freedom in Bulgaria for Muslims. Less convinced was the delegation from the Organization of Islamic Countries led by Abdullah Omar Nasif of Saudi Arabia which visited Bulgaria in 1987, and the UN Special Rapporteur on Religious Intolerance for the Human Rights Committee, Angelo Vidal D'Almeido who named Bulgaria as one of seven countries systematically preventing the peaceful practice of religion.[267]

On 6 March 1985 the Bulgarian authorities publicized a letter signed by leading Islamic officials with their new Bulgarian names. The signatories were the Chief Mufti, the regional mufti for Plovdiv (who also signed as 'interim in charge of the mufti of Kardzhali' which meant that at the time there was no mufti for Kardzhali – the district where most of the major demonstrations by ethnic Turks had taken place), and the regional muftis for Shumen, Tolbuhin, Razgrad, Smolyan and Aytos. This letter denied that the practice of Islamic religious rites had in any way been infringed.

Despite this and other public assurances of freedom to practice Islam and events like the appearance of the mufti of Plovdiv at a press conference held for foreign journalists in Sofia on 6 February 1985 to counter allegations of his death, it was obvious that there was some opposition from imams against the religious restrictions. As noted above the mufti of Shumen was replaced apparently due to his opposition to the assimilation policy and in July 1988 the mufti was again replaced apparently because the new man also was not sufficiently amenable to the authorities' policies – when asked outright by a western diplomat in the presence of Bulgarian officials whether the allegations concerning the assimilation campaign were true or not, he had answered by an eloquent silence.

On 11 November the Chief Mufti, Mirian Topchiev, was replaced but this is not seen as due to his opposition. The new Chief Mufti Nedyo Gendzhev, was regional mufti for Kardzhali from 1986 to 1988 and therefore undoubtedly loyal to the new policy. This was confirmed by demands in January 1991 by Muslim clerics and the DPS for his resignation, and revelations by security officials that he was a collaborator.[268]

Other local imams were arrested, like Yusein Kabov of Gorski Izvor, and in at least one other case allegedly killed. Enbiye Omerov Mahmudov, the Imam of Podayva village near Razgrad was, according to the Turkish newspaper Milliyet, killed by security forces. The Bulgarian journal Nova Svetlina on 11 June 1985 published an article purporting to refute this claim and showed a picture of a man named Biser Albenov, who said that he had been imam of Podayva for 15 to 20 years and denied any human rights violations had occurred during the name-changing campaign. The article strongly implied that Enbiye Omerov Mahmudov was now named Biser Albenov and was alive and well. However, a relative of Enbiye Mahmudov, who also lived in Podayva before emigrating to Turkey, states that the man in the photograph had not been imam prior to the name-changing campaign and that his name had been Basri Ahmedov Mollamedov and that he had been employed in the peasant cooperative in Podayva and was not imam prior to the campaign. The same source asserts that Enbiye Mahmudov was killed by the security forces. Further confusion is spread by the fact that Nova Svetlina in the same article states that the regional mufti from Razgrad is called Ilia Dimitrov when all other official publications, including the above-mentioned letter of 6 March 1985 by the muftis, name him as Ilia Georgiev.

Official pressure on religious figures continued. On 11 May 1989 there was a meeting of imams with the Chief Mufti where they were once again told to only use Bulgarian in all religious services and in general conversation, or face punishment. The imams were further informed about a forthcoming visit by a foreign delegation (believed to be a delegation from the Parliamentary Assembly of the Council of Europe which was due to visit Bulgaria on 13 July 1989) and that they were to say that they were happy with their lives, suffered no religious restrictions, and that there was no problem during the name-changing campaign. The imams were warned that government officials would be accompanying the delegation and any imam who did not follow these instructions would be punished.

Despite such public assurances of freedom to practice Islam as the muftis' letter, there were many official attacks on Islamic practices, especially the circumcision of male infants. The position regarding circumcision of the small but officially recognized Jewish community in Bulgaria whose religion also calls for circumcision of male infants was unclear; however, there was no ambiguity regarding the ethnic Turks. Georgi Tanev, First Secretary of the Kardzhali District Party Committee, stated in a speech on 15 May 1985 in Kardzhali, that 'Turkish reactionary forces in their subversive anti-Bulgarian propaganda in connection with the process of rebirth [ie. the name-changing campaign] rely first of all on the religion of Islam'. He went on to call for the total abolition of circumcision and for 'energetic measures' to be taken against 'all those involved, and (that) the parents who allow it, all those who carry out or assist circumcision should be held strongly responsible'.[269] This speech was typical of many by BCP activists in the period April to August 1985.

In practice this meant that the authorities made periodic checks on the population to make sure that male children were not being circumcised. In early 1985 in the south of the country some parents were obliged to sign forms stating that prosecution under Article 324(2) in connection with Article 20(2) of the Criminal Code would result if their sons were circumcised. Article 324(2) deals with practising a profession connected with public health without suitable qualifications or permission and Article 20(2) deals with instigating a crime. People convicted under this legislation face punishment of up to three years' imprisonment or a fine of up to 1000 leva (US$1000).

Although Bulgarian officials reportedly stated that circumcision was illegal only if performed by untrained people outside the medical profession and that circumcision was freely available in hospital under proper medical supervision, in practice this was not the case and the authorities heavily penalized those involved in circumcision. Initially fathers whose children were found to have been circumcised since the last monthly check were imprisoned as were the doctors who performed the operation. However, this was apparently not enough to deter the population and in 1986 the pressure was stepped up by imprisoning mothers and even grandmothers, reportedly for up to five years. The repressive measures seem to have been successful and circumcision of male infant Turks by all accounts ceased until the change of policy in late 1989.

The authorities also attacked the practice of fasting in Ramadan and attempted to stop the traditional celebrations of Bayram when the head of the household traditionally slaughters a sheep, even going as far as searching houses during Bayram in the Kardzhali district and searching refrigerators for sheep's carcasses. In August/September 1986 a 49-year-old man was imprisoned for one year after such a search found a sheep in his refrigerator.

The Islamic custom of washing the body of the deceased prior to burial was also forbidden and separate Muslim cemeteries abolished with many such cemeteries destroyed and the headstones smashed, eg. the Turkish cemetery in Ardino which was flattened by heavy plant machinery at the beginning of 1986.

Language and traditional clothes

As noted above all schooling in Turkish ceased by the mid-1970s. At the 23rd session of UNESCO's general conference on 14 October 1985, Academician Blagovest Sendov, replying to a statement made by a member of the Turkish delegation, stated that emigration to Turkey had 'objectively eliminated the need for instruction in a language [Turkish] which is alien to the Bulgarian nationals'. However, there were a number of official Turkish-language publications which ceased during the name-changing campaign. For example, the bilingual publication *Nova Svetlina* (Bulgarian) or *Yeni Isik* (Turkish) was available only in Bulgarian after January 1985.

In association with the name-changing campaign there was a blanket ban on the speaking of Turkish in all public places on pain of a summary fine. The amount of the fine initially varied from five to 10 leva but steadily increased from early 1985 to a fine of 50 to 100 leva for a first offence; one month's salary if repeated, followed by dismissal from work or even reported imprisonment of up to two years. All Turkish music was banned and similar punishments meted out to those caught listening to Turkish radio or listening to Turkish music cassettes with the additional punishment of confiscation of the radio or cassette player.

On 14 October 1986, during a visit by an Amnesty International delegation, Bulgarian embassy officials in Bonn, West Germany, claimed that the widely reported ban on the speaking of Turkish was 'nonsense' because 'there are old people who don't speak Bulgarian'. Referring to the official document signed by the Mayor of Gledka. banning the use of Turkish in public places on pain of 'sanctions', the officials admitted that 'some mayors' had initially made 'mistakes' but that this had been quickly rectified. However, further documents contradict this. For example, Order No.144 dated 9 July 1986, issued by the director of the Cherno More mine in Burgas, explicitly forbids the speaking of Turkish throughout the entire mine complex and on the buses to and from the mine on pain of a fine.

Women wearing shalvari (traditional Turkish trousers) or other ethnic clothing were harassed in the street and also faced fines. A document dated 20 September 1985 related to all villages in Kardzhali district and was a standard letter from the mayor to all heads of families in the villages. This document stated:

'In accordance with Article 2 of Order No.1 of the (village name) People's Communal Council, it is prohibited to wear shalvari, pyjamas, veils, yashmaks (traditional Islamic veils) and other non-traditional Bulgarian clothes or to speak a non-Bulgarian language in a public place. This tradition, inherited from five harsh centuries of slavery, has been forever rejected by the whole people, including the Muslims. Therefore we remind you that the time has come to end conservative modes of life and to adopt more appropriate and pleasant clothing and the pure Bulgarian tongue. We hereby warn that after 7 October those who do not abide by these requirements will be sanctioned.'

Employment and education

In the initial phases of the campaign, ethnic Turks who had not 'voluntarily' changed their names were not allowed to work in state enterprises, neither were they allowed to use their old names in any contact with the all-pervading state bureaucracy – for example they could not draw money out of the banks etc. without using their new names. As noted above such measures were often used as an alternative to brute force to induce ethnic Turks to change their names. A document dated

16 January 1985 relating to the Asenova Krepost works in Asenovgrad, south of Plovdiv, illustrates this. This document, Order No.21, states that all work forms, travel cards, sick records and other administrative documents had to be filled out with 'reconstructed Bulgarian names' and that 'all those with Arabic names who do not produce the necessary documents for name-changing will not be admitted for work'. The order also forbade the use of Turkish in work places.

It is not surprising that the Bulgarian authorities did not neglect the vital area of education in pursuing the assimilation campaign. Many ethnic Turkish teachers who were seen as unreliable by the authorities were replaced and often sent into manual labour instead like Ziya Osmanov, the school director in Kroyachevo, and his brother Selhattin Osmanov, a geography teacher, both of whom were sacked and sent to be miners in Maden. An official document dated 7 May 1985 from the District People's Council of Varbishta states that Sevda Rafailova Ognyanova, an ethnic Turk formerly named Saver Rifat Ahmetova, was relieved from her position, held since 1979, as director of a school in Lovets village, Shumen region, due to her attitude to the 'rebirth process' – this despite her acknowledged worth as a teacher and diligence in her job, and her membership of the BCP since 1975. The scale of replacement was particularly high in the south around Kardzhali in 1985. However, it appears from speeches made at the National Party Conference held on 28/29 January 1988 and reported in *Rabotnichesko Delo* on 31 January that the authorities found it hard to keep such specialists who had been sent into Muslim areas on double salaries in 1985 to bring the 'patriotic revolution' there, from leaving these areas.

Despite these apparent set-backs major emphasis was made within the secondary school system and *Nova Svetlina* on 15 November 1988 reported on sessions organized in the schools at which pupils met 'Bulgarians' who had returned from living in Turkey to describe their 'bitter experiences' in 'capitalist Turkey' and their feelings of gratitude to be back in Bulgaria and to have rediscovered their 'true' national identities.

In addition there were formed numerous genealogical, folklore and local historical societies which aimed to involve the Muslim population, especially school children, in programmes to indoctrinate them. For example, Nova Svetlina on 23 February 1988 described how the Koleduvane folklore society in Razgrad, one of the main ethnic Turkish areas, had 'revived' traditional celebrations of Christmas among local Muslims.

Thus it can be seen that the Bulgarian authorities used the education system in the scheme to attempt to eradicate a Turkish identity over a matter of a few generations. This time scale was confirmed by an article from a Razgrad newspaper, *Novo Ludogorie*, on 18 June 1987 which said that full assimilation of Bulgaria's Muslims would be achieved 'in several decades – a short historical period'.

Resistance to the name-changing campaign

Major demonstrations against the name-changing campaign took place in a number of places. In Benkovski, a town in Karzhali district near the border with Greece, according to eye-witness accounts, on 24 December 1984 demonstrators numbering some thousands of ethnic Turks from neighbouring villages and including women and children, marched to the town hall which was protected by 20 to 30 members of the elite special security forces known as the 'red berets' after their distinctive headgear. The security forces initially fired into the air above the crowd in an attempt to make them disperse. When this failed they fired into the ground in front of the advancing demonstrators who began to attack them and tried to disarm them. The security forces then opened fire into the crowd at point-blank range, killing at least six including a two-year-old child and wounding 40.

Eyewitnesses described a similar demonstration which took place outside Momchilgrad Town Hall on or about 27 December 1984. These reports state that initially army units supported by tanks attempted to stop a large crowd of ethnic Turks, again including women and children, from approaching the town hall. When this failed, 'Red Beret' security forces attacked the demonstrators with iron truncheons covered in rubber. The crowd retaliated and attempted to storm the town hall, breaking some windows and tearing up pictures of Todor Zhivkov (the Bulgarian leader). The security forces then used water canon on the crowd, the majority of whom dispersed. Those who did not disperse were arrested. The authorities apparently photographed the demonstrators and a number of people suspected of being organizers were subsequently arrested. A strict curfew was imposed.

On 1 April 1988, Stefan Solakov, a journalist who has written a number of pamphlets strongly denying any human rights abuses (eg. *Dangerous Play* and *The Investigation*) for the official news agency Sofia Press, reportedly told a *Reuters* correspondent that 40 people including 10 militia members had died in a series of clashes in and around Momchilgrad in December 1984 and January 1985, when ethnic Turks confronted the authorities in protest at the name-changing campaign. Solakov reportedly stated that the militia had used water canon and tear gas against the demonstrators and that most of the victims had been crushed to death, apparently in a stampede that ensued. However, this report was almost immediately denied by the Bulgarian Foreign Ministry and Solakov himself subsequently denied making the statements.[270]

Other violent demonstrations apparently involving loss of life are reported to have taken place in a number of places including: Gorno Prahovo; Mlechino, involving ethnic Turkish inhabitants from Gorno Prahovo and Dolno Prahovo as well as Mlechino; Dzhebel; and Ivaylovgrad near the border with Turkey where, according to an embassy official at the Bulgarian Embassy in Bonn, three 'Muslims' (ie. ethnic Turks) were killed by the security forces during a demonstration against the name-changing campaign when a crowd again attacked the town hall.[271]

Information on these and other reported violent incidents are hard to come by and the exact number of deaths is impossible to accurately assess. However, it appears that most of the violent demonstrations took place in the southern regions of the country where the campaign began and that mass organized demonstrations were not so prevalent in the north as reports of how the authorities had dealt with such demonstrations spread ahead of the actual campaign. Violent clashes were reported, however, in Razgrad district.

The campaign reached the Stara Planina – the central mountain range – in late January/early February 1985 and it was here that perhaps the most spectacular event of the whole campaign took place – the three day siege of Yablanovo in the eastern Stara Planina. According to a participant in the siege, Mustafa Suleymanov, the inhabitants of the ethnic Turkish town of Yablanovo comprising of about 1500 households or some 6000 people, had received reports of the events in December 1984 in Momchilgrad and other places. As a result the inhabitants along with some ethnic Turks from nearby villages including Vrani Kon, Obitel, Filaretevo and Velichka, erected barricades around the town when the authorities arrived on 18 January 1985 to implement the campaign.

Virtually all the inhabitants of the town were ethnic Turks including the mayor, two of the three local policemen, and other officials many of whom, such as the mayor, were involved in the resistance and used official vehicles to bring in wood for the barricades and for the five or six fires which were lit in the town square by the town hall to warm the inhabitants who congregated there for the three days and nights of the siege, despite the 20 cm. of snow and extreme cold.

The main entry to Yablanovo is from Kotel and the south-east and a barricade was erected in Malo Selo – a small village on the outskirts of the town. There was also a plan to use explosives from a quarry to destroy the bridge over the river Ticha at the entry to the town but in the event this did not happen. In order to prevent any informers in the village and also to prevent the police station from communicating with the authorities outside the town, the telephone wires were cut underground before the first house – one of the policemen's – on entering the town. The authorities had confiscated all hunting rifles a week previously and had removed all number plates of private cars to prevent the inhabitants from getting away. However, some inhabitants made molotov cocktails and armed themselves with sticks and stones.

For three days the authorities (at this time mostly police and civilians) attempted to reason with the demonstrators to peacefully disperse but to no avail and on the fourth morning troops with tanks and other armoured vehicles using tear gas and live ammunition forced their way in. One of the main tank training schools for the Bulgarian army is located in nearby Sliven but Suleymanov gained the impression that troops had been especially drafted in from other regions of Bulgaria and noticed that the number plates of some of the vehicles used were from Kyustendil district.

How many people were killed or injured in the ensuing violence is hard to assess. One report states that 34 were killed and 29 or 30 taken to Kotel hospital – the nearest – with gunshot wounds. Suleymanov stated that he personally saw one man shot in both legs and heard of other deaths, and estimated that perhaps six or seven had died but could not be sure as he escaped on the fourth morning for Sofia. All reports state that hundreds were arrested including one of the policemen, Ismail Alzhikov, and the mayor, Hyuseyin Nuhov, whose post was filled by a Bulgarian as were all other official posts in the town, even in the shops. Others arrested included Musa Musov, a teacher at the local primary school, and Fedal Fedalov, another senior official in the town. Many reports stated that the houses of some of the ringleaders were bulldozed, a charge which Suleymanov denies. According to Suleymanov the most serious material damage done was that a number of gardens including trees were destroyed by the advancing tanks. The mosque was locked up and entry forbidden but it was not destroyed.

Suleymanov himself, previously a photographer for the originally bilingual (Turkish and Bulgarian) official publication *Nova Svetlina* (*Yeni Isik* or *New Light*), had left Yablanovo on the fourth morning of the siege and gone to Sofia with 156 petitions from households in the town protesting at the compulsory name-changing. He left a copy of the petition at the Public Prosecutors office in Sofia and was then arrested and taken to Sofia Central Prison. The next morning he was transferred to Sliven Central Prison where he was detained for one and a half months. Sliven Central Prison was so overcrowded with ethnic Turkish prisoners, 90% of whom he estimated were from Yablanovo, that some had to be held in garages. He was interrogated and severely punched, kicked and beaten with rubber truncheons and officially charged with resisting the state and inciting the populace. However, he constantly pleaded forgiveness and was released without trial. Many of the others arrested were tried under Article 325 of the Criminal Code dealing with 'hooliganism' and sentenced to up to four years' imprisonment.

Suleymanov was allowed to return to Yablanovo where, in his own words, he kept a very low profile and managed on 3 April 1985 to take an official trip out of Bulgaria, first to Romania and then to the USSR where he applied for political asylum at the Turkish Embassy in Moscow. After 913 days at the embassy he was eventually allowed to go to Turkey. The Bulgarian authorities claim that he was a Turkish spy.

Assessing the number of ethnic Turks arrested during the name-changing campaign is extremely difficult and only vague estimates can be made. A Bulgarian who was detained in mid-1985 in Belene (a prison camp on an island in the Danube which was notorious in the 1950s for holding large numbers of political prisoners and where most ethnic Turks detained during the name-changing campaign were reportedly held) stated that there were at that time, in Camp Number 2 of Belene, 450 ethnic Turks detained in connection with the campaign. Other reports agree with the estimate that in early 1985 there were about 1000 ethnic Turks in the entire camp complex of Belene. Many of these were apparently released after a period of some months without trial, often followed by several years forced internal exile. Others were tried, often on charges of 'hooliganism' and sentenced to up to four years' imprisonment. Yet others were tried with more serious charges of espionage or 'anti-state agitation' and received longer prison terms.

In 1987 there was a mass hunger strike of ethnic Turkish detainees in Belene and some were subsequently removed to other places of detention, especially the penal mine in Bobovdol. By late 1988 it was reported that few detainees remained in Belene and that those who had been tried and sentenced had been removed to normal prisons like Stara Zagora prison where most political prisoners are held.

In addition to the large numbers of people imprisoned and even killed, many ethnic Turks, including whole families, were subjected to the administrative measure of internal banishment for protesting at the assimilation campaign. Under the terms of the 'People's Militia Law of 1976' Article 39(1), amended 12 August 1983, the authorities can, among other measures, apply without trial the 'preventive administrative measure' of 'compulsory residence in another place of habitation for a period of one to three years' on people who 'carry out anti-social activities affecting the security of the country'. These measures were often used as a supplementary punishment on ethnic Turkish prisoners after their release from Belene. Although such measures, which can be renewed indefinitely, cannot legally be applied to people under the age of 18, in some cases they were used against whole families including young children.

This internal banishment of dissenting ethnic Turks was tacitly admitted at the time by the Bulgarian authorities. In a speech of 28 March 1985, Stanko Todorov, then a member of the BCP Central Committee Politburo and Chairman of the National Assembly, after denying categorically that there would be any emigration to Turkey, stated that all those 'who dance to the tune of Ankara's propaganda and her nationalist agents in Bulgaria' and who 'do not wish to live in their native towns and villages can move out'. For cases of this kind, he added, instructions had been given to the appropriate Bulgarian organs to ensure speedy removal (reportedly within hours), 'not to Turkey but to other regions of Bulgaria, where these people will be able to live peacefully and happily'.[272] Such internal banishment had been similarly used in the past against the Macedonians and the Pomaks.

Protests against the campaign were also made by many leaders of the Turkish community in Bulgaria. Ethnic Turkish students at Sofia University held a protest meeting at the end of December 1984 but participants faced arrest and imprisonment. Other reports state that certain well-known ethnic Turks who the authorities saw as potential leaders of resistance were detained in advance. During the actual campaign leaders faced imprisonment or worse; for example, Nedzhattin Eminov, a mathematics teacher from Ardino who was also a high-ranking official of the local branch of the Communist Party. According to an eyewitness account he was shot in the head twice in Studen Kladenets quarter of Kardzhali and buried on 17 July 1985 in Ardino. His apparent assassination was allegedly due to his position as a leading member of the ethnic Turkish minority and his open espousal of nationalist views which had made him something of a leader for young ethnic Turks who opposed the name-changing campaign.

Other protest came from ethnic Turks holding high state posts, like Halil Ahmedov Ibishev, who at the time was a member of the Bulgarian National Assembly. Ibishev, now resident in Turkey, states:

'By the end of December 1984 rumours were spreading that the names of Turks living in the Kardzhali and Momchilgrad regions had been changed. Since it was said that these names were changed by force, the people in my constituency in Dalgopol asked me what was going on; so I conveyed their concerns to the Dalgopol Municipal Party Committee. The First Secretary of the party branch told me, "Don't worry – the changing of names does not apply to all Turks, only to Turkish women marrying Bulgarians". Later on I learned the horrifying facts. Bulgarian police and soldiers were raiding Turkish villages and assaulting the women. Some Turks had escaped to the mountains . . .

The main assault began in Kardzhali province in late December 1984. All the villages and cities where Turks lived were besieged by the military and police. It was forbidden for Turks to move in or out of the region. Anyone violating this would be taken to prison or killed. Then the campaign moved to other areas. Many houses were searched during the night, and many people tortured. The villages were besieged by tanks, military trucks, even fire trucks to ensure the completion of the name-changing campaign. Telephone conversations were interrupted, and it was made impossible for those in one Turkish village to phone other villages. You could not travel from one village to the next even by foot. In some areas the name-changing campaign was completed very quickly, in a couple of days, although it took longer in Kardzhali. Before the name-changing campaign got underway, young people and others who might fight the new policy were taken and put in special camps. There whereabouts were not known for 40 to 50 days. The schools were used as military headquarters. Anyone who asked questions or objected was taken away, and tortured.

The oppression came to our district in January 1985. The village filled with soldiers and police. Then I was called to the party committee and informed: "Turkish and Arab names will be changed to Bulgarian ones. You, as a Deputy and Representative of the people, will help us. You will explain that anybody who resists will be killed like a dog". I asked who had ordered this, and they replied that the Bulgarian Communist Party Central Committee had made the decision. So on 24 January they began to change the names. They . . . banned the speaking of Turkish and stopped Turkish language radio broadcasts, Turkish tombstones were taken down.

A month or two after the name-changing campaign had been complet-ed, circumcision was banned altogether. All children were examined, and it was recorded who had and who had not been circumcised. After that time, it was decreed that no further circumcisions could be carried out. Moreover, the examinations became periodic affairs, in order to ensure that circumcision was not carried out. And after the date when circumcision was banned, if a child was found to have been circum-cised, his parents and the doctor who performed the operation were fined or imprisoned. Also, anyone else who aided the ceremony was punished. From my own village there was the case of a young man who travelled to another village to bring the man who would do the circum-cision. This man was arrested and kept in prison 40 to 50 days, and he was still in prison when I escaped. It is just one example; there have been many similar cases.

At the end of 1984 at the time of the campaign in the south but before it reached my village, I requested to meet Todor Zhivkov [the Bulgarian leader] but this was refused. However I met Grisha Filipov [the then Prime Minister] and told him of the reports of force being used and asked him what would happen if we asked questions in the National Assembly and whether we could defend the rights of the ethnic Turks. Filipov replied that this was a question beyond the jurisdiction of our parliament and that the decision had been taken by the Politburo of the BCP and he warned me to avoid this problem and to keep silent, other-wise "you'll have problems with your family".'

Halil Ibishev also gave details of how he and other leading members of the ethnic Turkish minority had been forced to sign the open letter to Turgat Ozal, the Turkish Prime Minister, dated 27 November 1985[273] protesting at 'systematic attempts to interfere' into 'the internal affairs of our country' which was widely published by Sofia Press and dis-tributed by Bulgarian embassies in a number of countries:

'I was invited to Sofia to the National Council of the Fatherland Front building in Sofia. There I met before the meeting 40 to 50 other mem-bers of the Turkish intelligentsia who like myself had no inkling about what was going to happen. After we had entered, Kamen Kalinov, an ethnic Turk formerly named Fahrettin Halilov and who was the Direc-tor in Chief of Nova Svetlina, informed us that there was a political campaign against the Bulgarian state mostly led by Ozal and that we all knew that all Turks had willingly changed their names and so to prove this we all have to sign the letter. The letter was then read out by

Hristo Marinov, formerly Hamdi Mustafov, a secretary of the Father-
land Front, and we were all advised that anyone against the policy
would be put in prison, lose their jobs or be deported. Nobody said any-
thing and we all signed. The meeting was over in, at most, 45 minutes
and I immediately left Sofia.

I was also invited to go on television and make a speech in favour of
the new policy. I refused. After having refused I was told by a member
of the District Committee of the Varna BCP, Vasil Rusev, who was also
President of the District Committee of the Fatherland Front: "you are a
member of parliament, you refused to speak on television but don't for-
get that if you continue to refuse your title will be cancelled and you
maybe will not see your children and family again. Be careful from
now on and act according to government policy".'

Another ethnic Turk who signed this open letter to Ozal was Naim
Suleymanov – the world champion weightlifter who defected on 12
December 1986 during a sporting competition in Australia. On 13
December BTA claimed that it was suspected that he had been 'the vic-
tim of a terrorist act' and on 15 December *BTA* announced that he had
been kidnapped and that the 'Shalamanov Operation [his new 'Bulgarian' name was Naum Shalamanov] had been masterminded by the
Turkish secret services, not without help of their colleagues in other
countries'. Naim Suleymanov has since publicly stated that he left Bulgaria of his own free will because of the forced assimilation of the ethnic Turkish minority to which he belonged.
  On 24 January 1987, *BTA* announced that he had 'been treated with
psychotropic drugs to induce his anti-Bulgarian statements'. This
announcement by *BTA* followed publication of a number of press
reports, quoting Suleymanov stating 'they changed our names at the
end of 1984. In the District of Kardzhali 80-100 Turks were killed.
Many were thrown in jail... The mosques were closed. Speaking Turkish was banned.' The close relatives of Naim Suleymanov (now called
Naim Suleymanoglu) were allowed to emigrate and join him on 14
October 1988 after the Turkish government had paid a fee, reportedly
over one million US dollars, to the Bulgarian government – Suleymanoglu was by this time a Turkish national hero after winning a gold
medal for Turkey at the Seoul Olympics.
  Another ethnic Turkish athlete who was not so fortunate is Byun-
yamin Manchev, a wrestler from Plovdiv. On 8 May 1985, the Turkish
Broadcasting Authority broadcast a television interview with him
recorded secretly in Budapest, Hungary, during an international tour-

nament in which he was taking part. Manchev, apparently unaware that he was being filmed secretly, described how he and his family had been forced to change their names and alleged that ethnic Turks including children had been killed during the operation by the security forces. On 22 May 1985, however, BTA released a statement alleging that the interview with Manchev had been 'faked', and reported that in a written letter to BTA he stated that he had only spoken of rumours he had heard from Radio Free Europe.

However, on 24 January 1987, he and his wife, his brother and uncle and their wives visited the home of a Turkish consular official in Plovdiv requesting permission to emigrate to Turkey. On leaving the house they were arrested and beaten. Manchev was subsequently sentenced to one year's imprisonment and on release sent into exile to Nova Mahala near Pazardzhik where his wife and children had also been exiled. His brother and uncle and their wives were also exiled to different parts of the country.

Many ethnic Turks fled to the mountains in the first phases of the campaign but adverse weather conditions made such flight not a long-term possibility. Many others attempted to leave the country – some managed to cross the heavily guarded border with Greece, many more made the easier route to Yugoslavia, and yet others even managed to escape via Romania and then to Yugoslavia. Those unfortunate enough to be picked up by the Romanian authorities were returned to the Bulgarian authorities where they were imprisoned for attempting to leave the country without official permission under Article 279 of the Bulgarian Criminal Code. There have been unconfirmed reports that some were also returned by the Greek authorities before they could register as political refugees and have their cases examined, although in most cases such refugees were granted asylum by the Greek authorities. Those who fled to Yugoslavia were held for up to 14 days (as is Yugoslav practice) and then allowed to travel to Turkey without hindrance. Refugees reported that the Yugoslav authorities treated them well and were sympathetic to their plight.

Continued resistance

Although the largest incidents of active resistance to the assimilation policy occurred in the initial period of December 1984 to March 1985 and mostly in the south of the country, resistance continued. For example four people from Drandar near Varna were among the leaders of a group that produced thousands of leaflets which were distributed in early June 1986 to ethnic Turkish villages in the environs of Varna,

Tolbuhin and Silistra. These leaflets called on ethnic Turks to show their opposition to the assimilation campaign by boycotting the forth-coming elections to the National Assembly. They, along with the other leaders, including Ahmed Dogan were arrested and tried *in camera* and sentenced to between eight and twelve years' imprisonment. A number of other ethnic Turks involved in the actual distribution of the leaflets were also arrested and received milder sentences. The Bulgarian authorities stated that the four men were convicted for belonging to a group with terrorist aims although the available information contra-dicted this charge.

Ethnic Turks have, however, on occasion resorted to terrorism, apparently in protest at the assimilation campaign. On 8 July 1987 three men were killed in a shoot-out with anti-terrorist forces at a main tourist hotel in Varna during a siege after the men had taken schoolchildren as hostages. *BTA* on 9 July 1987 released only a mini-mum of information and gave the names of the dead men as N. Nikolov, O. Nikolov and N. Asenov. However, emigre sources state that this official unwillingness to disclose detailed information was because the three men were ethnic Turks from Dulovo in Silistra Dis-trict who were attempting to escape from Bulgaria. Other emigre sources in Turkey state that two of the men were named Apti and Orhan Nedzhibov (father and son presumably renamed Nikolov in the campaign) and again stated that all three were ethnic Turks protesting against the assimilation campaign.

Another case predates the name-changing campaign. On 25 April 1988 three men were sentenced to death and four others, including a woman, received sentences of between one and five years for being responsible for a series of bomb attacks in which eight people died, including two children, and 51 were injured. The attacks began on 30 August 1984 with an explosion in the waiting room of Plovdiv railway station and one at Varna airport. Other explosions occurred on a pas-senger train and at a hotel in Sliven. The last attack was on 9 March 1985. *BTA* in late April 1988 gave the names of the three men as Elin Madzharov, Altsek Chakurov and Sava Georgiev. Emigre sources in Turkey confirmed that these three men were ethnic Turks previously named Emin Aliev, Abdullah Chakirov and Safet Guney, respectively, and claim that their motives were to protest against the assimilation campaign. Again, lack of detailed information makes this hard to veri-fy but the inclusion of their names by the Bulgarian Deputy Foreign Minister Ivan Ganev (in a statement of 15 June 1989 to the Ambas-sadors of countries participating in the CSCE process at a conference in Paris) in a list of people alleged to have been operating under orders of the Turkish secret service would appear to confirm this. When the explosions began they were welcomed by some Slav Bulgarian emigre circles hostile to the then regime in Bulgaria like those in Paris centred around the journal *Badeshte* ('The Future') who implicitly claimed the actions as part of the Bulgarian Liberation Movement, which they supported. The appearance of leaflets stating '40 Years: 40 Bombs' after the August 1984 explosions perhaps shows that the outrages were more anti-communist than anti-assimilation – Bulgaria was just preparing to celebrate 40 years since the communist take-over of power in September 1944. *Badeshte* and the Bulgarian Liberation Movement were active in joining Turkish protests at the assimilation campaign. However, this has not been true of all such emigre groups. For example, a group in West Germany publicly applauded the assimilation campaign despite their antagonism to the then Bulgarian authorities – demonstrating again the depth of national feeling held by some Bulgarians against Turks.

Official information and disinformation

The Bulgarian authorities made no official statements about the name-changing campaign until reports began to appear in the foreign press in early 1985. Since then, until the fall of Zhivkov in November 1989, the authorities consistently denied both the existence of an ethnic Turkish minority in Bulgaria and that the name-changing was anything other than voluntary and spontaneous.

To support their claim to the non-existence of the minority, the Bulgarian authorities used carefully selected historical sources, especially an article by Midhat Pasha, the Grand Vizier of the Ottoman Empire, published in a French journal in 1878. This article states:

> 'Firstly, it must be borne in mind that among the Bulgarians who arouse so much interest there are more than one million Moslems. These Moslems did not come from Asia to establish themselves in Bulgaria, as is widely believed. They are themselves descendants of those Bulgarians converted to Islam at the time of the conquest and during the following years. They are children of one common country, from one common race, and share a common origin.'[274]

The Bulgarian authorities, however, ignored the many contradictory historical sources and since the start of the name-changing campaign, historians within Bulgaria were obliged to reflect the new policy. This was to the advantage of Professor Petar Petrov, a renowned anti-Turk whose work has played an important part in current official propaganda, while his opponents within Bulgaria were denied publication, for example, Strashimir Dimitrov whose book on the Turkish colonization was banned in 1985.[275]

Another facet of the policy was illustrated by the report in the official Bulgarian daily *Otechestven Front* in January 1986 which summarized the purported 'discoveries' of 30 years of studies by Bulgarian research anthropologists. Apparently, experts of the Bulgarian Academy of Science's Institute of Morphology carried out 'intensive research' in the districts of Blagoevgrad, Smolyan and Kardzhali on over 6000 men and women which showed, reported *Otechestven Front*, that all the inhabitants proved to be Bulgarians, Bulgarian-Moslems and descendants of a section of the Bulgarian population subjected to ethnic assimilation (by the Turks).[276]

Such 'research', apparently utilizing such methods as skull-measurements, was reminiscent of Nazi Germany and had little impact on outside opinion. More successful was the Bulgarian authorities' attempts to discredit accusations, many of which inevitably have originated from Turkey, by pointing to Turkey's own massive human rights violations and lamentable record regarding her own minorities, like the Kurds. The Bulgarian authorities also claimed that reports alleging a forced assimilation campaign were part of a concerted attempt to discredit socialist Bulgaria – an attempt which included allegations of Bulgarian complicity in the attempted assassination of Pope John Paul II and gun and drug trafficking.[277]

Additionally, beginning in April 1986 there were a number of statements in the official media rigorously denying all allegations of human rights abuses or that the name-changing was other than 'a benevolent, spontaneous and sincere process by persons who have taken cognizance of their Bulgarian origins'.[278] However, such statements at times contradicted each other. For example, in one statement, purported victims apparently did not exist and had never existed in Bulgaria after the authorities had apparently checked with the aid of the 'computers of the unified system of public records registration and administrative service (ESGRAON)' while in other publications the same people were reported to be alive and well in the villages where they were known to have originated.

In other instances letters signed under duress were published to counter human rights allegations as part of an official policy of disinformation. One example among many concerns the killing by security forces of Ayshe Myumyunova and her brother's child during the demonstration in December 1984 in Benkovski.[279]

The Bulgarian authorities resolutely denied such killings and produced death certificates and declarations to back up their claims that both Ayshe Myumyunova and Fatmen Yun's child died of natural causes – the Bulgarian authorities apparently knew which child was alleged to have died without even knowing the name as eyewitnesses only knew the first name of the mother. However, a variety of eyewitnesses testified to the contrary and one, who was expelled from Bulgaria on 19 May 1989, stated that Ayshe Myumyunova was shot in the heart while the child was shot in the head. He further stated that the grandfather was forced to sign a declaration that the child had died of natural causes and a doctor, Fikret Eyyubov, was pressured to sign a false death certificate but refused and as a result was sent to Belene camp for one year followed by internment in Bobovdol prison camp. It appears that other doctors had less qualms or were more susceptible to official pressure. Another refugee testified that he saw, on 7 March 1987 while he was employed at Kardzhali Hospital, officials in the morgue of the hospital burning documents relating to the deaths of ethnic Turks.

Despite these denials, statements made by leading Bulgarian officials implicitly acknowledge at the time of the campaign that the name-changing campaign met with resistance. For example, Stoyan Stoyanov, First Secretary of the Haskovo District Party Committee, stated in a speech in mid-1985 that some ethnic Turks 'had not yet matured sufficiently politically to accept new names' and that there had been 'sporadic instances of anti-social meetings' and of people 'favouring outdated traditions such as religious burials, circumcision and attendance at mosques'.[280] Other leading officials made statements referring to forced internal resettlement of objectors and penalties for circumcision, and a number of official documents have come to light which confirmed reported aspects of the assimilation campaign.

11

Bulgaria's ethnic Turks – mass exodus in 1989

The events of May 1989

The situation of small-scale sporadic protest arising out of a largely passive, albeit sullen, acceptance of the status quo by the ethnic Turkish population radically changed in early 1989 with the mass participation in various unofficial protest groups and large-scale protest action on a country-wide basis. The Bulgarian authorities responded with violent repression and mass expulsions of thousands of activists. This in turn was followed by a general exodus of ethnic Turks taking advantage of the previously unavailable opportunities of leaving Bulgaria for a new life in Turkey. In late June 1989 the number of refugees exceeded 60,000 with thousands more leaving each day and no sign of the flood abating. Official Bulgarian statements stated that 150,000 passports had been issued and another 100,000 applications received.[281] By late August over 300,000 ethnic Turks had left for Turkey.

The formation of opposition groups

On 16 January 1988 six Bulgarian dissidents set up an **Independent Association for the Defence of Human Rights in Bulgaria** (IADHR) and, despite severe harassment by the authorities with many founder members forced into internal exile or emigration, the association has continued to function and from the outset has taken up the issue of the repression against the ethnic Turks – this was in marked contrast to a group ostensibly with similar aims set up with official backing as a rival in June 1988 under the chairmanship of Konstantin Tellalov, a former ambassador to the UN and a significant figure in the Bulgarian power hierarchy, now retired.

The IADHR soon attracted Turkish members, such as 29-year-old Zeynep Ibrahimova from Kliment village in Shumen district who had refused to use her new Bulgarian name and who had served 17 months of a two-year prison sentence imposed on 23 August 1985 after attempting to flee to Turkey. Following her release from Sliven Prison for Women, she was interned in Botevo in Mihailvgrad district for two years along with her brother, Ibrahim Ibrahimova, who had been tried and sentenced with her for attempting to flee the country. They and two others were the first Turks to join IADHR in October 1988. She was elected the association's representative in the Varna region. On 31 January 1989 the association issued a list of 36 new active members willing to be publicly identified, 23 of whom were ethnic Turks using their illegal Turkish/Arabic names. When Zeynep Ibrahimova was expelled from Bulgaria on 3 February 1989 there were about 50 Turks in the IADHR out of a total of some 350, but by June the number of Turks exceeded that of Bulgarians due to their radicalization in May and June 1989.

Furthermore, a specifically Turkish civil rights group within Bulgaria was formed in late 1988, called the **Democratic League for the Defence of the Rights of Man** with the aim of, among other things, opposing the assimilation campaign and the repression of Islam. The chairman, Mustafa Yumerov, a philosopher, was internally exiled in Komarevo village near Vratsa, while the two secretaries, Sabri Iskenderov and Ali Ormanliev, were also subject to internal exile in Kameno Pole and Drashak, respectively – villages in Vratsa region – both men having served sentences in Belene prison camp in connection with the assimilation campaign. The Democratic League quickly attracted a very large membership and applied without success for legal recognition and sent an open letter containing its aims to Todor Zhivkov.

In addition on 30 January 1989 a third association – **The Association for the Support of Vienna 1989** – (ASV89) was set up in the village of Zornitsa in Haskovo region under the leadership of Avni Veliev – a former political prisoner sentenced in Kardzhali on 5 February 1985 to seven years 10 months' imprisonment for anti-state activities under Articles 108 and 109 of the criminal code and who had just been released from prison on 29 December 1988. This organization's name was due to the attempt to bring to the attention of the world public the plight of ethnic Turks in Bulgaria at the time of the CSCE Conference on Human Rights in Paris in early June 1989.

These three independent organizations (IADHR, The Democratic League, and ASV89) all had good connections with each other and quickly attracted thousands of professed members. The two primary Turkish organizations, the Democratic League and ASV89, in particular, were able to spread throughout the country mainly in the predominantly Turkish inhabited areas but also in other areas where there were large numbers of activist Turks in forced exile. An essential factor in their dramatic growth in support and the country-wide action they were able to undertake was the small amount of leeway afforded them due to the international climate of 'Glasnost' on the part of the USSR and the corresponding relaxation within Bulgaria – especially and vitally in the field of radio communications. Due to this changed international climate the Bulgarian authorities stopped jamming the *BBC*, *Deutsche Welle*, and *Radio Free Europe* (RFE) – although RFE occasionally was still jammed as was Turkish Radio. This, combined with the easing of telephone links with the west, allowed the new organizations to use foreign radio stations as essential means of communication which previously had been denied them.

The growth of support for ASV89 is an excellent example of this. After Avni Veliev set up ASV89 in January, with Ismet Emrullov Ismailov from Dzhebel as secretary, he managed to contact RFE on 2 May by telephone and informed them of the programme and aims of the organization. Between 5 and 11 May RFE repeatedly broadcasted his message and as a result many ethnic Turks from all over the country came to hear about it. Some made cassettes of the RFE report and these were distributed as far north as Shumen attracting support.

Mass protest – hunger strikes, demonstrations and violent repression

Hunger strikes had been used by many ethnic Turks in Belene and elsewhere as a means of protest against the assimilation campaign and the ensuing arrests, or in attempts to get permission to emigrate, but it was the publicizing of such actions within Bulgaria by foreign radio stations which was the crucial difference in 1989. The breaking of the authorities' monopoly on information within the country allowed the new organizations to coordinate mass protest which began again in May 1989 with hunger strikes by ethnic Turks in Silistra, Shumen and Razgrad and some other villages in the north-east.

The numbers on hunger strike rose from 30 to approximately 200 by mid-May[282] to over 1000 by mid-June and there were corresponding peaceful demonstrations in support by hundreds of ethnic Turks, mostly women and children, in Silistra and Shumen on 14/15 May. More hunger strikers publicized their actions via foreign radio stations and mass demonstrations occurred in late May throughout the north-east (Kaolinovo, Ezerche, Razgrad, Todor Ikonomovo, Tolbuhin) and

in the south (Dzhebel) of the country where ethnic Turks predominate. The authorities responded with force and many (reportedly the
number was as high as 60)[283] demonstrators were killed. Most deaths
were from gunshot wounds after troops opened fire on protesting
crowds or some from injuries received from beatings.

For example, on 24 May a demonstration of about 1000 people
including women and children took place in Ezerche near Razgrad in
the north-east at 10 pm. According to eyewitness accounts, the local
Communist Party secretary met the crowd and asked for their
demands, and the crowd replied that they wanted their old names
back etc. Three lorries arrived with troops and despite the fact that all
accounts state that the demonstration was peaceful, the troops opened
fire after orders from a Bulgarian official named Markov and two
demonstrators were shot dead: Ahmet Burukov, aged 38, shot in the
forehead and back of the head; and Sezgin Saliev Karaomerov, aged 18,
shot in the heart.

Another example is a demonstration in Kaolinovo on 20 May which
was the climax of a protest march which had begun in Pristoe and
continued through the neighbouring villages of Kliment, Naum and
Takach before arriving in Kaolinovo several thousand strong. Again
eyewitnesses state that the troops opened fire without provocation and
one eyewitness saw Nedzheb Osmanov Nedzhebov, a 47-year-old bus
driver from Kus, clubbed to the ground by blows from a rifle butt and
killed. The official cause of his death was reported to be heart failure.

Other deaths were reported following beatings which were
widespread and indiscriminate throughout all ethnic Turkish regions
in the north-east and south. Following the mass demonstrations
involving thousands of participants, most affected areas were quickly
put under martial law with troops and tanks and fire-engines (water-
canon was widely used as crowd control) installed. In the southern
regions, especially in Dzhebel, the authorities began widespread beatings, going from house to house and indiscriminately beating the
inhabitants. Similarly those caught in the streets faced arbitrary beatings and for three days, beginning on 22 May – 'Bloody Monday' –
nobody in the city of Dzhebel was allowed to leave their house.

On 23 May 1989, BTA issued a statement admitting that demonstrations had occurred but claimed that they were caused by misapprehen-
sion about the soon-to-be introduced new passport law, and incitement from foreign radio stations and extremists. BTA admitted that
three people had died but stated that one had died from heart failure
while the other two had died from ricocheting bullets fired as warning
shots.

On 15 June in a statement to the Ambassadors of countries participating in the CSCE process at the conference held in Paris, Deputy Foreign Minister Ivan Ganev gave a detailed list of demonstrations and 'disorders' which had taken place in Bulgaria between 20 and 27 May which had resulted in, he said, seven deaths and 28 people wounded. He said that demonstrations had taken place in Kaolinovo, Todor Ikonomovo, Razgrad, Dulovo, Vokil, Oven, Poroyno, Cherkovna, Vodno, Isperich, Dzhebel, Ezerche, Dulgopol, Beli Lom, Omurtag, Shumen, Medovets, Gradnitsa and Benkovski. However, he denied that the demonstrations were peaceful, alleging that in cases rioters had set fire to houses of 'Bulgarian Muslims' (ie. ethnic Turks) who did not want to emigrate and had vandalized cars and shop windows, and stated that the authorities had been obliged to resort to force to restore public order. He also denied that anybody had been expelled from Bulgaria and extensively blamed the activities of the Turkish secret services in fomenting trouble among ethnic Turks. On 1 June the Bulgarian authorities organized their own official demonstrations in Shumen, Pleven, Razgrad, Targovishte, Kubrat, Popovo, and Burgas against 'Turkish interference' in Bulgaria.[284]

Mass expulsions

In tandem with the policy of attempted intimidation through force, the authorities embarked on a policy of expelling activists from Bulgaria. All the initial Turkish leaders of the three organizations (IADHR, the Democratic League and ASV89) were expelled by the end of May and the expulsions soon grew into a flood. Some 500 had been expelled by 7 June but the number had risen to 14,000 by 14 June according to Turkish television and there were thousands arriving each day. By late June the figure had reached 60,000 and by late August it was over 300,000. The sheer size of the numbers involved indicated that while the first to be expelled were activists, many of whom did not want to leave but left due to the threat of imprisonment or other threats to them or their families, the authorities apparently seemed to be allowing large numbers to emigrate. Many ethnic Turks have decided that the policy of forced assimilation and the attendant official repression is such that there was no future for them in Bulgaria and despite having to give up, in many cases, a settled life of financial security have opted for a new life in Turkey.

Many, especially those expelled in or before May were given only a few hours notice and were not allowed to take more than a small bag and no money. All were obliged to leave houses and other valuables behind and some were informed by the authorities that if they returned within five years they could reclaim their property. Again, the later refugees had been able to leave with, in some cases, more possessions (cars, water heaters etc. and a limited amount of money) although the valuables left behind remained considerable. One state measure was to unlawfully redeem the state loan for a building insured through property mortgage forcing the occupants to sell at greatly reduced prices.[285]

The Bulgarian government officially recognized the economic problems incurred by the refugees as most of those leaving were highly skilled farmers who, with Bulgaria's labour shortage, would be difficult to replace. Ivan Angelov, a senior advisor to the Council of Ministers, told a press conference in Sofia that a decree had been passed introducing longer working hours and moving workers into the affected areas. This special decree on 'civil mobilization in times of peace' was only repealed on 15 December and its obligatory 12-hour working day caused great resentment against the departing Turks from ordinary Bulgarians. In addition Angelou stated that the refugees had removed huge amounts of savings from Bulgarian banks which could cause severe financial problems for Bulgaria.[286]

Refugees

Most of the large number of refugees came to Turkey where many had relatives due to the previous waves of emigration. In the beginning those expelled were often given passports with visas not for Turkey but for other non-Comecon countries like Austria, Yugoslavia or even Sweden, and were obliged to pay the authorities for their train tickets out of the country and then had to find their way to Turkey. Some, from the north-east, were even expelled to Romania and then had to make their way to Vienna. However, by early June the bulk of refugees were arriving directly in Turkey.

The arrival of such large numbers of refugees, often with only minimal financial means, has been problematic for the Turkish authorities. However, the Turkish government has proved to be extremely sympathetic to the plight of the Bulgarian Turks. On 7 June 1989 television announced that the government had passed a decree which would allow the refugees to be immediately accepted as Turkish citizens without the previous waiting period of two years and on 11 June it was announced that the Bulgarian currency, the leva, could be changed at Turkish banks. At a meeting of emigre associations on 7 June the mayor of Bakirkoy – one ofIstanbul's largest districts – promised substantial material help for the refugees in the shape of employment and housing, and the government helped to establish 'tent cities' (like that in Kirklarele near Edirne at the border with Bulgaria, which was announced on Turkish television on 10 June 1989) for those temporarily without accommodation. Similarly, the emigre associations worked around the clock to try and cope with the huge flood of refugees. Additionally, the Turkish government announced that it would raise the question of possessions and property which the refugees have been forced to leave behind in Bulgaria.[287]

Over 300,000 had arrived by late August and there were reports of Bulgarian troops entering villages, especially Pomak villages, to prevent the exodus. At the same time Turkey closed the border and reimposed visa restrictions on citizens from Bugaria. By mid-September over 13,000 had returned to Bulgaria.

By January 1990, over 130,000 had returned due no doubt to the unfavourable economic situation in Turkey but also due to the changes in Bulgaria. The returnees often faced great problems on their return. In the Hisarya district of Haskovo, local officials led by Dimitar Velev ordered the destruction of over 1000 homes after the majority of the residents, all ethnic Turks, had left. Those who remained were given only three days to leave, reportedly without compensation. Those who returned from Turkey- officially the authorities claimed that such people were not emigrants but tourists with three month visas and so had the right to come and go as they pleased – found their homes bulldozed and were forced to live in homes made from plastic sheets throughout the winter. Others told of similar tales.

Two ethnic Turks from Popovo in the north-east near Targovishte, had been informed by the authorities that if they wanted to join the exodus to Turkey, they had to sell their apartment first. They eventually sold it on 20 September for 19,000 leva having brought it six years previously for 24,000 leva and done considerable work on it. However, by this time, they were unable to leave a the borders were closed and were subsequently forced to live with their two children in an old barracks but were facing eviction even from that in February 1990, although their old flat was still empty. They had sold to a private buyer, but some 4000 were apparently sold to the government, otherwise the occupants could not get documents.[288]

Many who returned were forcibly sent to other parts of the country and those with qualifications, eg. teachers and doctors etc., were obliged to do manual work. Such measures were lifted after 10 November, although housing shortages and unemployment remained a problem and many still wanted to leave. In March 1990, over 6000 ethnic

Turks a month were receiving exit visas from the Turkish Embassy in Sofia and a ticket system was instituted to cope with the large queue which waited outside everyday hoping to get interviews for visas.

Support for ethnic Turks by Bulgarians

The alliance between ethnic Turks and Bulgarians shown in the membership of the IADHR has been mirrored by the presence of Bulgarians participating with ethnic Turks in some of the demonstrations, such as that of 27 May in Targovishte when about 100 Bulgarians joined the demonstration. In addition, there have been a number of declarations by Bulgarians deploring the use of violence by the authorities against ethnic Turkish demonstrators and calling for an end to the assimilation policy, eg. that of 22 May by the national leadership of the IADHR and again on 23/24 May by Anton Zapryanov of the IADHR and Father Hristofor Sabev of another newly formed independent group – **The Committee for Religious Rights**.[289] This latter group was set up by provincial Orthodox priests; Sabev is from Veliko Tarnovo, and calls for religious freedom for Muslims as well as greater freedom for Christians of all denominations. Amnesty International reported that Anton Zapryanov and Konstantin Trenchev, president of an underground trade union movement set up in February 1989, were arrested in late May apparently on charges of having fermented the wave of unrest amongst the ethnic Turks.[290]

Many ethnic Turk refugees state that they encountered little animosity from ordinary Bulgarians but reported that many Bulgarians living in regions predominantly inhabited by Turks, especially in the south around Kardzhali, viewed the mass demonstrations with considerable unease due to government propaganda which implied that the Turks would attack them. Despite this, all the protests have been directed at government policy and there have been no reports of such inter-ethnic violence. However, the change in government policy after the fall of Zhivkov and the attendant recognition of the ethnic Turkish minority resulted in a nationalist backlash.

The international response

Bulgaria is a small country widely viewed as one of the USSR's most loyal allies. As such it enjoys less world press coverage than, for example, Poland. The assimilation campaign has been widely reported but the difficulties in obtaining information prior to the events of May 1989 – due to extreme official censorship – made such reporting problematic. Inevitably, perhaps, the Turkish government has been the main foreign power to raise the issue at international forums but Turkey's treatment of its own minorities, such as the Kurds, and its record on human rights abuses, have allowed the Bulgarian government to deflect criticism; statements made by Turgut Ozal, the Turkish Prime Minister at an election rally in Bursa, threatening action against Bulgaria similar to that taken by Turkey in Cyprus have not helped.

However, various human rights groups have repeatedly raised the issue both with the Bulgarian government and in the UN. Amnesty International twice, in June 1986 and May 1987, submitted its concerns in Bulgaria to the UN under the procedure for confidentially reviewing communications about human rights abuses (the so-called '1503 procedure') and the organization visited Bulgaria and met with officials to discuss these concerns. The Bulgarian government made available a large amount of information on individual cases but Amnesty International remained concerned and has pointed out the unreliability of some of the information received from official Bulgarian sources.[291] It can hardly be coincidence that Bulgaria is some seven years overdue, despite repeated reminders by the UN, in her second periodic report to the Human Rights Committee of the UN on Bulgaria's compliance with the terms of the International Covenant on Civil and Political Rights which she ratified on 21 September 1970.

Western governments have also raised the issue on many occasions, but not with the vehemence that others – like Turkey – would have preferred, although the events of May and the expulsions have prompted greater censure. On 13 June the US State Department refused to meet Konstantin Glavanakov, Deputy Minister for Foreign Trade, due to 'Bulgaria's violent actions against its ethnic Turkish minority', and Western diplomats at the Paris CSCE conference were reported as trying to persuade Bulgaria to accept neutral mediation, either by Austria or Switzerland, on the ethnic Turkish issue, but the Bulgarian delegation adamantly refused.[292] Various Islamic countries have condemned Bulgaria and the OIC sent a delegation to Bulgaria which reported on religious restrictions for Muslims. However, some Arab countries like Syria, which were more closely allied to Bulgaria, have supported Bulgaria in the international propaganda arena. It has also been noticeable that there was little support for Bulgaria from her erstwhile allies in Comecon on this issue.

12

ETHNIC TURKS IN POST-TOTALITARIAN BULGARIA

The fall of Todor Zhivkov

On 10 November 1989 Todor Zhivkov was ousted as Bulgarian leader and replaced by his erstwhile foreign Minister, Petar Mladenov. Zhivkov had been looking increasingly out of step with Gorbachev's policies in the USSR and the events in Eastern Europe, and perhaps it was not coincidental that the coup from within the BCP came from the foreign ministry which had somehow to justify the assimilation campaign and the mass exodus to the outside world.

Immediately there was relaxation in the policy and returnee Turks, who in cases had been sent to other parts of the country under the People's Militia Law were allowed freedom of movement and could return to their home territories. Article 273 of the criminal code, which was used to penalize those who criticized government policy, was abolished and those sentenced under it, including some ethnic Turks, were released. A further 50 or so ethnic Turks were released in December when another amnesty was announced for those sentenced under Articles 108 and 109 dealing with anti-state agitation and propaganda and forming anti-state groups, respectively. Among those released was Ahmed Dogan – also known as Medi Doganov, Ahmed Hasanov Aptullov or Ahmet Ismailov Ahmedov – a former research fellow at the Institute of Philosophy in Sofia, sentenced to 12 years' imprisonment for leading a group opposed to the assimilation campaign.

On 14 November Mladenov had met leading intellectuals and told them that the assimilation policy was to be stopped but that the government wanted to move slowly on this issue due to the potential of a Bulgarian nationalist backlash.[293] However, mass protests by ethnic Turks and Pomaks took place in Sofia on 11 December and continued in other places as well as Sofia throughout the month and on 29

December the government announced that those who had had their names forcibly changed could use their original names again, practice Islam and Islamic customs and speak Turkish in their everyday lives. On 10 January 60 historians of The Bulgarian Academy of Sciences, Sofia university, and the National Library hailed the restoration of Muslim names and stated that they had been forced by the BCP to back the 'absurd' name-changing campaign.[294]

The Bulgarian nationalist backlash

However, not all sections of the population welcomed the new policy and there was an instantaneous backlash from nationalist sections of the Bulgarian population. In areas where ethnic Turks predominate the assimilation campaign and the mass-exodus had stirred up nationalist passions. Many Slav Bulgarians viewed the mass exodus as unpatriotic and the special decree on 'civil mobilization in times of peace' which the authorities had introduced to cope with the labour shortage at harvest time brought about by the exodus, was blamed on the Turks. Additionally, many people, often the local *nomenklatura*, had profited from the exodus in the form of buying cheap housing etc. and now feared that the new policy would change this as well as the general fear of the local party 'barons' to the prospect of democracy and accountability, especially in areas where ethnic Turks predominated. In Kardzhali, many of the Slav Bulgarian inhabitants are descendants of refugees from Turkish or Greek Thrace who fled in the Balkan Wars and thus tend to be very nationalistic. Mass demonstrations took place against the government decision which had been taken by a closed party session and then rubber stamped by a joint session of the Ministerial and State Councils. Such 'old' methods gave the protestors, as well as protesting about the restoration of Muslims' rights, the opportunity to object to the lack of democratic procedures.

The demonstrations began in Kardzhali on 31 December 1989 and on 1 January 1990 over 10,000 had joined the demonstration. About 2000 ethnic Turks staged a counter-demonstration with the security forces barely keeping order in the town.[295] On 2 January the demonstrations had spread to Plovdiv and Sofia, and subsequently spread to Smolyan, Shumen, Ruse, Targovishte, Haskovo, Devnya, Provadiya, Sliven, Preslav, Dulovo, Silistra, Novi Pazar and Pleven. There were reports that local party officials were helping to incite the nationalist backlash and were supplying the demonstrators with buses, cars and food etc. Strikes began in Kardzhali on 4 January.[296]

The democratic opposition, the Union of Democratic Forces (SDS) which included the IADHR, was also a target for the demonstrators. Already at an anti-government rally in Sofia on 18 November 1989 IADHR members had been booed when the defence of ethnic Turks was raised[297] and the SDS support on 4 January for the authorities' restitution of Muslim rights further angered the demonstrators. The force of the public reaction on this issue caused the SDS to distance itself somewhat on the ethnic Turk and Muslim issues.

The nationalists soon set up their own organization, the Committee for the Defence of National Interests (KZNI), with district committees (OKZNI) throughout the country, especially where there were mixed populations of Bulgarians and ethnic Turks. Mincho Minchev, a taxi-driver and a former State Security officer from Kardzhali, was the spokesman. There is no doubt that Bulgarian nationalism is a potent force and not merely a front for old party bureaucrats to protect their position.

The situation calmed somewhat after talks between all sides were held on 8-12 January at a forum named 'The Public Council on the Various Aspects of the Ethnic Issue' held at the National Assembly and presided over by its chairman Stanko Todorov who admitted that he was to be blamed for not having protested against the name-changing campaign although he was among those who approved it.[298] The council confirmed the 29 December decision but to appease the nationalists it recommended that separatist or autonomist organizations be banned as should public displays of the Turkish flag. Bulgarian was confirmed as the official state language. The council proposed that the National Assembly adopt a special statute on minority rights by the end of February 1990.[299]

A further amnesty was announced in January for those imprisoned in connection with the name-changing campaign since 1984 which covered all those ethnic Turks imprisoned, except those 50-60 sentenced for 'sabotage' or 'espionage'.[300] Most, if not all, of the latter were also released early during 1990 in the continual re-evaluation of 'crimes' committed by ethnic Turks in the assimilation campaign.

Responsibility for the assimilation campaign

On 18 January 1990, Todor Zhivkov was arrested and charged with, among other things, 'incitement of ethnic hostility and hatred' for his part in the assimilation campaigns.[301] However, investigations have been slow and on 14 May the Parliamentary Commission Investigating the Abuses and the Violations of Law in the Period of Totalitarianism announced that for the time being the so-called 'entourage' of Zhivkov who played a prominent part in the 'crimes' in this period was reduced to one – former Politburo member and close Zhivkov associate Milko Balev. Prosecutor General Evtim Stoymenov said that several months before the 1984-5 name-changing campaign, the Politburo approved a report presented by a special commission which suggested gradual reintegration by peaceful means of the Muslim populations and which rejected the other two options of forced name-changing, or deportation to Turkey. Evtim stated that Zhivkov then went ahead anyway and personally gave the order for the name-changing campaign. The parliamentary commission also agreed with the Minister of Interior, Gen Atanas Semerdzhiev's suggestion to rehabilitate 517 ethnic Turks arrested and imprisoned on Belene or exiled without trial or charge in the name-changing campaign of 1984/5.[302]

Balev responded to this attempt by the authorities to put all the blame on Zhivkov and himself by stating that the idea of the campaign was given by Zhivkov, Georgi Atanasov, Dimitar Stoyanov, Pencho Kubadinski, Petar Mladenov, Stoyan Mihailov, Chudomir Aleksandrov, Yordan Yotov and other senior BCP officials who participated in the campaign. He claimed that major decisions were written in secret documents of the then Politburo and Central Committee of the BCP.[303] Zhivkov himself also denied sole responsibility but said that he felt no guilt for the campaign as, he claimed, Bulgaria was threatened by Turkish terrorist groups and demands for autonomy. He also said that 'in 10 or 20 years Bulgaria could repeat the fate of Cyprus'.[304] Dimitar Stoyanov, who was Minister of Internal Affairs at the time of the campaign, disclaimed responsibility but noted that 'the USSR kept silent and we took it as consent'.[305]

At the beginning of 1991, nobody had been prosecuted for the assimilation campaign despite the often-repeated official description of it as 'criminal'. With the Bulgarian Socialist Party (BSP) [formerly BCP] winning the elections in June and with the undoubted complicity of many of its leading figures in the campaign this delay is perhaps not so surprising. With the SDS in early 1991 apparently dominant over the BSP the situation should change.

The Movement for Rights and Freedom (DPS)

The DPS was formed by Ahmed Dogan on his release from prison on 22 December 1989. It was officially registered on 4 January and was specifically concerned with ethnic and religious freedom for ethnic Turks and Muslims. It claimed initially not to be a political party – the January agreements had forbidden parties based on ethnicity or religion specifically to counter such organizations as the DPS – but an organization for rights. The DPS in February had a five-person central leadership and three coordinators – one for the south, one for the north-east, and one for the centre of the country. Pomaks in the south-west also belonged to his organization although some belonged to other parties.

The organization claimed 100,000 members in February 1990 – a huge figure for an organization which had only just begun but Dogan claimed that he had been organizing underground structures since 1985. It appears that Dogan and the DPS inherited the previous mass ethnic Turkish organizations which led to the demonstrations in 1989 and the resulting mass exodus. As all the leaders of these organizations, along with most activists, were expelled in the first stage of the exodus, Dogan was in a good position to take control on his release. This is somewhat confirmed by the return of Mustafa Yumer in November 1990 and the restoration of his organization set up in November 1988 – The Democratic League for the Defence of the Rights of Man. Yumer (formerly Yumerov) accused Dogan of claiming undue credit for previous protest actions by Turks, especially the actions of May and June 1989 (when Dogan was actually in prison).[306]

Initially the DPS had formal ties with IADHR and supported the SDS. However, strains quickly showed especially with the nationalist backlash which showed how vulnerable the SDS was on the nationalist issue. The IADHR virtually split over the ethnic issue with Iliya Minev arguing against further taking up the Turkish issue. His main rival for leadership at the time, Rumen Vodenicharov, also attacked the DPS in the run up to the elections in June as SDS leaders feared that the Muslim vote would go almost entirely to Dogan's party.[307] On 6 June Dogan claimed that Petar Berun, one of the SDS leaders, had presented a proposal for banning the DPS to the Bulgarian Presidency on the grounds that it was an ethnic party – a claim Dogan denied, stating that the DPS had Bulgarians, Jews and Roma among its members.[308] Despite the rift between SDS and DPS, Dogan advised his supporters to vote for the SDS in regions were there were no DPS candidates.[309]

On 28 June the government, in connection with numerous protests it had received against the DPS, stated that it had been registered for the elections on the basis of the new electoral law which allowed organizations and movements that were not parties to take part. This registration did not, however, give the DPS the status of a political party once the elections were over.[310] However, despite this ruling, and despite its claims which it has consistently repeated, the DPS was the ethnic Turks political party to all intent and purposes and in the elections to the 400 seat Grand National Assembly (GNA) won 23 seats. Dogan stated that the DPS only won about 370,000 votes due to what he claimed to be attacks on his organization, especially by the SDS, which resulted in many Muslims voting for the BSP.[311] Bulgarian nationalist groups tried to prevent Dogan and his fellow DPS members from taking part at the ceremonial convening of the GNA in the old historic capital Veliko Tarnovo on 10 July.

Dogan has shown himself to be a skilful leader and the DPS has avoided taking up provocative positions. At the same time it has successfully pushed for the adoption of a simplified administrative procedure for Muslims to restore their names, and has succeeded in introducing Turkish media and education measures. The careful approach has been criticized by some in the DPS and one of its members, Aden Kenan (formerly Alyosha Keranov), accused Dogan of being too slow. He was instantly disowned by the DPS leadership which stated that they opposed nationalism, chauvinism, extremism and fundamentalism, and that Kenan had been dismissed the DPS leadership two months previously.[312]

The restoration of Muslim names and media/educational progress

In early March 1990 the National Assembly met to discuss laws on the restoration of Muslim names. A variety of options were discussed some of which were clearly aimed at splitting the Pomaks from the ethnic Turks by allowing only those whose names had been changed after 1984 to go through a simplified administrative procedure. The others (mostly Pomaks) would have to go to court. Intense negotiations went on throughout the night of 4/5 March with a crowd of about 3000 ethnic Turks and Pomaks, some with handwritten signs saying eg. 'Our names were taken from us with blood – we don't want to buy them back in a court', camped in the cold outside the assembly building.

On 5 March the Bulgarian Citizens Names Law was unanimously passed by the National Assembly. It was something of a compromise and there were vocal protests from the Muslims outside the building when Prime Minister Andrey Lukanov addressed them through a microphone. The law included the Pomaks as well as the ethnic Turks but stipulated a simplified court procedure up to 31 December whereafter a more complicated procedure with a fee would be obligatory. A sticking point had been the mandatory -ov, -ev, -ova, -eva endings of last names which is characteristic of Bulgaria (Dogan had refused to use this ending). Article 6 of the law stated that these suffixes must be used 'unless the father's first name makes it impossible to add such a suffix, or else the suffix conflicts with name-assigning traditions.'[313] This was sufficiently vague to give rise to some controversy.

Despite its shortcomings the new law did allow many to restore their names legally. Pencho Penev, the then Minister of Justice, announced that by 21 May 1990 over 220,000 applications had been filed of which over 180,000 had been considered. The government also decided that the old name-changing applications which ethnic Turks had been forced to sign be destroyed and citizens who restored their names be given backdated birth certificates. Compensation would be paid to 'the heirs of people who had died in the riots which broke out over the name-changing campaign and in the exodus of Bulgarian citizens to Turkey'.[314]

The name-changing was brought up again in the parliament by the DPS in November and after much heated debate – Dogan told the GNA that he would not assume responsibility for events if a rider making it possible to restore names without the Bulgarian suffixes was not adopted[315]; in late November the GNA allowed Muslims to restore their names administratively rather than through a court procedure. The absurd name-changing campaign had finally been buried.

Along with the restoration of names went the opening of all mosques and freedom of religious practices. However, there were some problems with the Islamic custom of circumcision. Although it was now allowed, hospital authorities did not allow *hodzhas* into hospitals to perform the rite during the operation so that as a consequence many still relied on performing it outside of hospitals with the added risk of infection.[316]

The next step was the media and education. At the end of April 1990, the first edition of the twice-monthly paper *Muslim*, published in Bulgarian and Turkish, appeared with the Chief Mufti, Dr. Hadzhi Nedim Hafiz Ibrahim Gendzhev, on the editorial board.[317] The use of Turkish for publication prompted protests and condemnation from the army paper *Narodna Armiya* as well as from the National Radical Party which appealed to the Prosecutor General's office at this 'unlawful act'.[318] On 1 October an Islamic institute – the first establishment of its kind in Bulgaria since 1948 – was inaugurated in Sofia with 45 students chosen from 700 applicants[319] and on 4 October a Muslim secondary school was opened in Shumen.[320] On 11 October, *Alev*, a Muslim cultural and educational organization in Varna, was founded.[321]

The DPS announced that in December 1990 it would publish its own newspaper, 'Rights and Freedom', in 150,000 copies of which 50,000 would be in Bulgarian and the rest Turkish. Agreement had also been reached for a new law on education for four classes a week study of Turkish in the school curriculum for areas where there were ethnic Turks living in compact masses. A minimum of 10 children in a class was seen as the lower limit. Textbooks up to the fourth grade were to be produced by January and radio and TV of three hours a day (this was the airtime for Turkish language programmes in the 1970s) was planned.

These great strides towards emancipation of the ethnic Turkish minority have continued to elicit protests from Bulgarian nationalists, often in the form of short-lived strikes. On 25 October the DPS club in Shumen was bombed by unknown assailants.[322] Nationalists have alleged that Muslims are driving out Bulgarians from some areas (this is a strikingly similar claim to the Serb claims against Muslim Albanians in Kosovo) and while the GNA discussed the November 1990 legislation on restoration of Muslim names some 200 protested outside the building and stated that the new law could trigger 'an irreversible process of Islamization of Bulgarian citizens'.[323] A more serious outbreak of nationalist protest at the new law occurred in Razgrad – a city composed of about 75% Slav Bulgarians in an ethnic Turkish area of the country – with the declaration of a 'Bulgarian Republic of Razgrad' in protest at 'the treacherous pro-Turkish policy of the Bulgarian Parliament'. A crowd of supporters of the Razgrad Committee for the Defence of National Interests, which reportedly included many schoolchildren, besieged the Regional People's Council for over an hour on 22 November. Allegedly former BCP nomenklatura members responsible for abuses in the 1984-5 period were behind the protest.[324]

Similar civil disobedience surfaced in Shumen where the municipal leadership, bowing to demonstrators' pressure, rejected the teaching of Turkish in schools, and in Kardzhali the OKZNI called for the establishment of civil self-government.[325] Nationalists also threatened to remove their children from schools if Turkish language education was reintroduced. Faced with these threats of local refusal to accept the authority of the GNA on the ethnic issue, the central authorities wavered and delayed implementing the agreement on Turkish education measures and publishing. In protest, ethnic Turkish schoolchildren in the south-east boycotted schools.

The BSP entered the debate by warning of possible 'unconstitutional' extension of Turkish language education to Pomaks.[326] Dimitar Popov, who replaced Andrey Lubanov as Prime Minister in December 1990, has publicly warned of 'Moslem aggression' in Bulgaria in an interview published in December 1991 by *Ruse Dnes*, a Bulgarian newspaper. However, after his becoming Prime Minister, he somewhat retracted his views.[327] On 13 February, the DPS newspaper finally appeared and on 14 February, Education Minister Matey Mateev announced that Turkish would be offered in certain elementary schools from March and in all elementary schools by the beginning of the next school year.

The situation of the ethnic Turks and other minorities (except perhaps the Macedonians) in Bulgaria has improved dramatically in the little over a year since Todor Zhivkov's downfall. However, widespread are the fears of Turks and Islam in general by large section of the Bulgarian population; fears which have been amplified by Zhivkov's disgraceful policies of forced assimilation remain and will continue to play an important part in the future. The current desperate economic situation (which can be seen as being in part caused by the campaign and the resulting exodus which so devastated the Bulgarian economy) is a dangerous background for nationalist passions. However, despite the occasional wavering in the face of outraged Bulgarian nationalism, the authorities have shown commendable resolve in reversing the previous ruinous policies as quickly as possible.

The future may well be problematic. Educational and cultural provisions may be superceded by demands for political and even territorial autonomy which may produce a backlash which will be uncontrollable. The role of Turkey, especially following the disintegration of the Warsaw Pact, in such a future scenario will be of course crucial, but perhaps even more so will be the role of other European states.

13

GREECE AND ITS MINORITIES

Greece in Outline

The Republic of Greece, *Eliniki Dimokratia* has an area of 131,957 sq. kms and shares borders with Albania, the Republic of Macedonia in Yugoslavia, Bulgaria and Turkey. It has 166 inhabited islands and a coastline as long as much larger France, along with a largely mountainous mainland area. In 1985 Greece had a population of 9,950,000 with over one third living in Greater Athens. Formerly a largely rural society, in the post-war period it has experienced rapid urbanization and also emigration, to Western Europe, North America and Australia.

The beginnings of the modern Greek state were in 1830 when the southern areas and some islands became a republic (and soon after a monarchy) after winning independence from the Ottoman Turks. The boundaries were extended, most notably after the Balkan Wars of 1912/13 but the massive exchange of populations between Greece and Turkey after the 1923 Treaty of Lausanne, lead to a dramatic change in the human geography of Greece. In the period between the wars Greece had periods of monarchial, republican and military rule. During World War II, Greece was invaded by Italy and, later Germany and Bulgaria, who were fiercely resisted by the population lead by the National Liberation Front (EAM). Perhaps half a million Greeks died, most of starvation. Civil war broke out, even before the end of the war, and continued until 1949.

Greece remained a monarchy from 1950 to 1967, when the military, concerned by the imminent re-election of a radical government, launched a coup in April 1967. The resulting seven years of military rule saw a banning of political activity and thousands of left-wingers imprisoned. The junta collapsed in 1974 after an abortive adventure in Cyprus and an army mutiny; civilian government was restored and the monarchy was abolished after a referendum. Greece was ruled by the conservative government of Constantine Karamanlis and from 1981 to 1989 by the Pasok Socialist party of Andreas Papandreou. Since 1989

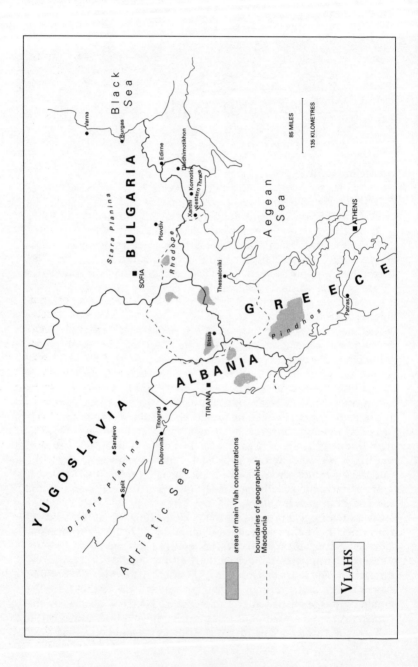

and after three, largely indecisive, elections, Greece is once again governed by Karamanlis's Conservative Nea Demokratia party. In 1980 Greece joined the European Economic Community.

Modern Greece is the sum of a diversity of influences from different civilizations and peoples; the Roman, Byzantine and Ottoman Empires, merchants from the Near East, France, Venice and Italy, settlers and invaders from the Slavs, Albanians, Turks, Italians and British. While the majority of the population – perhaps 95% – is ethnically Greek, there remain substantial, often unacknowledged and considerably Helleniczied, minorities – Vlahs, Turks, Pomaks, Roma, Albanians, 'Macedonians' and others. However the only minorities recognized by the government are those with a religious, rather than ethnic or cultural, identity, and even here treatment accorded to them is not, in practice, always equal to that given to Greek citizens of the Orthodox Church.

The Slav Macedonians

The Greek authorities have, from the outset of the modern Greek state, consistently denied the existence of the Slav Macedonians as a separate people from the Greeks and instead officially referred to them as Slavophone Greeks while the Bulgarians claimed them to be Bulgarians – in common speech the Greek population referred to them as Bulgarians and the notion of them as a separate people, the Macedonians, only really came later.

Assessing population figures is problematic due to the tendency to exaggerate the number of the Greek or Slav populations, depending on which side is making the assessment – the Greeks, the Bulgarians or the Yugoslavs. One of the most detailed assessments is a Yugoslav one[328], using Bulgarian and Greek sources, just before the Balkan Wars of 1912, which saw the liberation of the areas from Ottoman rule, that there were in Aegean Macedonia: 326,426 Macedonians; 40,921 Muslim Macedonians (Pomaks); 289,973 Turks; 4240 Christian Turks; 2112 Cherkez (Mongols); 240,019 Greeks; 13,753 Muslim Greeks; 5584 Muslim Albanians; 3291 Christian Albanians; 45,457 Vlahs; 3500 Muslim Vlahs; 59,560 Jews; 29,803 Gypsies; and 8100 others, making a total of 1,073,549 inhabitants. However, it must be stressed that this is merely one among many rival assessments of the population at that time.

However, from 1913 to 1926 there were large scale changes in the population structure due to ethnic migrations. During and immediately after the Balkan Wars about 15,000 Slavs left the new Greek territories for Bulgaria while many Greeks from Thrace, Bulgarian and

Yugoslav Macedonia moved to be under Greek rule. More significant was the Greek-Bulgarian convention of 27 November 1919 which allowed voluntary population exchange in which some 25,000 Greeks left Bulgaria for Greece and between 52,000 and 72,000, depending on which estimate is used[329], Slavs left Greece for Bulgaria, mostly from Eastern Aegean Macedonia which from then onwards remained virtually Slav-free. Most Slavs living west of the Vardar river especially bordering on Yugoslavia chose to remain. Greece was obliged to protect its Slav minorities and these obligations were further stipulated in the Agreement at Sevres in 1920 with educational rights and guarantees for the use of their mother tongue for official purposes.

In September 1924 Greece and Bulgaria signed a protocol known as the Kalfov-Politis Agreement which placed the 'Bulgarian' minority in Greece under the protection of the League of Nations which prompted the Yugoslavs to renounce the Greek-Serbian treaty of 1913 in protest. On 15 January 1925 Greece announced that they would not follow the protocol and henceforth treated the Slavs as Greeks. In 1926 the Greek government ordered in decree No. 332 of November 1926 that all Slavonic names of towns, villages, rivers and mountains should be replaced by Greek ones.[330]

Up until the Balkan Wars there were in Greek Macedonia under the control of the Exarchate Church 19 primary schools in towns and 186 in villages with 320 teachers catering for 12,895 pupils in the Bulgarian language. In addition, there were 4 Serbian schools and some 200 or so other Slav primary schools supported by village communities. All these Slavonic schools were closed and the inventories destroyed while in the Slavonic churches the icons were repainted with Greek names.[331]

Larger population exchanges took place between Greece and Turkey following the Greco-Turkish war of 1920-22. The peace treaty of July 1924 stipulated that the Greek and Turkish populations of Turkey and Greece, respectively, were to be exchanged, except for the Greeks of Istanbul and the Turks of Western Thrace. Again, as so often in the Balkans, religion was the criteria used to define 'Greek' or 'Turk' which resulted in many non-Turkish Muslims (Slavs and Greeks) emigrating to Turkey and, conversely, Turkish-speaking Christians to Greece. In this exchange some 390,000 Muslims (mostly Turks) emigrated to Turkey and over 1,200,000 Greeks left Turkey of whom some 540,000 settled in Greek Macedonia along with approximately 100,000 more Greek refugees who settled there before 1920.

Thus, there was an influx of over 600,000 Greek refugees into Greek Macedonia while the Turkish and Pomak population outside of Western Thrace mostly emigrated. The official Greek census of 1928 recorded 1,237,000 Greeks; 82,000 Slavophones; and 93,000 others, although this census almost certainly exaggerated the number of Greeks.

The position of the Slav minority worsened in the period 1936-41 under the Metaxas regime which viewed the minority as a danger to Greece's security and large numbers (Yugoslav sources allege over 5000) of Macedonians were interned from the border regions with Yugoslavia; night schools were opened to teach adult Slavs the Greek language.[332] The repression was further stepped up after the beginning of the Greco-Italian war in October 1940, despite the numbers of Macedonians fighting loyally in Greece's armies, with, according to Yugoslav sources, some 1600 Macedonians interned on the islands of Thasos and Kefallinia (Cephalonia).[333]

After the defeat of Greece by the Axis powers in 1941, Bulgaria occupied the eastern portion of Greek Macedonia, excepting Salonika which was occupied by the Germans, and a small part of the western portion. The remainder was under the Italians. In the portions under Bulgarian rule the Bulgarians imported settlers from Bulgaria and acted such that even a German report of the time described the Bulgarian occupation as 'a regime of terror which can only be described as "Balkan".' In Kavalla alone over 700 shops and enterprises were expropriated and large numbers of Greeks expelled or deprived of their right to work by a license system that banned the practice of a trade or profession without permission from the occupying authorities.[334] The Bulgarians acted with such ruthlessness that the Greek population, many of whom were previously emigres from Turkey and who were understandably hostile to being once more ruled by a foreign power, became bitterly anti-Bulgarian. Thus Bulgaria, in the brief period when she finally controlled some of the areas in Greek Macedonia she always claimed, succeeded in alienating the populations under its control while loosing influence to the Yugoslavs in Western Greek Macedonia.

Another product of the brutal Bulgarian rule was that the Greek population became more violently opposed than ever to the idea of a 'United Macedonia' which, up until the change of line of the Comintern in the mid-1930s to that of the Popular Fronts following Hitler's rise to power, had been the Greek Communist Party's (KKE) line. This line, which was always unpopular with rank and file Greeks, was resumed by the Communist controlled resistance movement, the National Liberation Front, EAM, and its military wing, ELAS, and in 1943 EAM-ELAS tried to organize resistance in Aegean Macedonia. Tito's aide Vukmanovic-Tempo, who was very successful in Yugoslav Macedonia, set up SNOF, the Slav National Liberation Front, which comprised of Macedonian Slav Partisan units allied to ELAS but this provoked prolonged resistance from non-Communist Greeks, especially from a movement called 'the Protectors of Northern Greece'(YVE), and relations between ELAS and SNOF were strained.

The Greek civil war which began in earnest, after a brief 'First Round' in the winter of 1943/4, in December 1944 between the Communist-controlled ELAS and non-Communists supported by Britain and, later, USA, saw the exodus of many Slavs and Greek Communist Party members fleeing to Yugoslavia. The last round of the civil war which lasted until 1949 saw SNOF reformed as NOF (National Liberation Front) and up to 40% of the Communist forces comprising of Slav Macedonians.[335] However, the struggle at the top of the KKE between Nikos Zachariades and Markos Vafiadis, who had close links with Tito which even survived the initial Stalin-Tito break of 1948, which ended in Markos's retirement due to 'ill-health' on 31 January 1949, was followed by an attempt by the KKE to set up an anti-Tito NOF – but by now the war was virtually lost for the Communists and only gestures remained. On 1 March 1949 'Free Greece', the communist radio station, broadcasted a declaration of an Independent United Macedonia which was not recognized by the USSR or its allies and only caused alarm in the rank and file of the KKE. On July 1949, Tito closed the Yugoslav-Greek frontier.

During World War II and the ensuing civil war the Slavs of Greek Macedonia enjoyed language rights such as education in Slavonic which had been denied them before, except for the brief appearance of a Slavonic primer using the Latin script, Abecedar, in September 1925.[336] By this time the Slavs were called Macedonians by the Yugoslav side, a name which has caused great offence to Greeks ever since, as Macedonia and the term 'Macedonian' has great historical connotations for Greeks which predate the arrival of Slavs (whoever they may have been) into the area. The apparent appropriation of this name by a Slavic people outside the country was bound to offend Greek sensibilities.[337] Similarly, the use by Yugoslavia of the adjectives 'Vardar' and 'Aegean' to describe Yugoslav and Greek portions, respectively, offends Greeks although the reasoning behind this is not so apparent.

In the period after the civil war the Macedonians were, unsurprisingly, seen as potentially disloyal to the Greek state and steps were taken to try and remove such 'undesirable aliens' from the sensitive border regions with Yugoslavia. In 1953 Decree No. 2536 was enacted to colonize the northern territories 'with new colonists with healthy national consciousness'[338] – the anti-Macedonian element in this law was evident by the exclusion of the Turks in Western Thrace from such measures.[339] In this period it was forbidden for Macedonians to use the Slavonic forms for their names and henceforth only Greek forms could be used for official purposes – a measure with obvious parallels to recent Bulgarian measures against its minorities.

In the beginning of 1954 the Papagos government resolved to remove all Macedonians from official posts in Greek Macedonia. In the border regions with Yugoslavia peasants were not allowed to move from their villages and in 1959 in the villages around Lerin, Kostur and Kajlari the inhabitants were asked to confirm publicly in front of officials that they did not speak Macedonian. Such measures led to many emigrating to Australia or Canada.[340]

Since the civil war, the official denial of a Macedonian minority in Greece has remained constant regardless of the government in power, whether democratic or the military dictatorship of 1967-74. The return to democracy in Greece saw an improvement with the abandonment of official terror which had held sway over the whole population. However, the education system and the lack of job opportunities for those who declared themselves to be Macedonian in any branch of the state bureaucracy have greatly aided assimilation into the Greek majority and the Greek authorities have apparently been successful in going a long way in achieving this aim. It is noticeable that Macedonian nationalism appears much stronger in emigres from Greek Macedonia, not merely in Yugoslavia but also Australia or Canada, than in the area itself.

There have been some recent internal manifestations of Macedonian nationalism, though. In 1989 an organization calling itself the Central Committee for Macedonian Human Rights which claimed to be based in Thessalonika appeared. Five of its members from Greece, joined a delegation of Macedonians which visited the UN Centre for Human Rights in Geneva, the Council of Europe, and the European Parliament in May 1989, claiming that by doing so they risked 'severe reprisals for both themselves and their families' from the Greek authorities.[341] However, it is possible that emigres, rather than internal dynamism, are the driving force behind this organization. On 20 July 1990, the local authorities reportedly forcibly disrupted a Macedonian 'national day' in the village of Meliti in Florina district, and emigres allege that similar incidents took place in other Macedonian areas during that week, and, similarly to Turkish claims in Western Thrace, some Macedonians in government employment have been forced to transfer to distant regions of the country on pain of dismissal.

However, the massive dilution of the Macedonian population by emigration on the one hand and influx of Greeks on the other combined with natural assimilation into the majority aided by a shared religion, and the experience of the civil war, has made the aim of some kind of Macedonian state incorporating Greek Macedonia a notion predominantly held by those outside of Greece.

Refugees and relations between Greece, Yugoslavia and Bulgaria

A continuing legacy of the civil war has been the numbers of people who fled from Greece, including some 25-30,000, according to the Association of Refugee Children from Greek Macedonia and Red Cross estimates, of children aged between two and 14 – the Greek government alleged that many of these children were virtually kidnapped by Communists but the number of parents requesting Red Cross help for their return was relatively small.[342] Many of these refugees were Macedonians who went to Yugoslavia or other East European Communist countries. From 1955 onwards Yugoslavia made efforts to attract the refugees from other countries to Greek Macedonia. Borba, published in Belgrade on 6 June 1988, stated that there were 150,000 such people who were full citizens of Yugoslavia; however, other Yugoslav sources put the numbers of Macedonians who emigrated in the period 1945-9 from Greek Macedonia as only some 40,000 to 50,000 out of a total of 60,000 to 70,000. Again there appears to be confusion about actual numbers as there is about the numbers of Macedonians in Greek Macedonia at present: some Yugoslav sources allege a figure of 350,000 but more sober estimates are about 200,000.

The property of these refugees was confiscated by the Greek government by Decree 2536/53 which also deprived them of their Greek citizenship.[343] The Greek government later enacted a law so that the property would be returned to refugees who are 'Greek by birth' ie. to those who renounce their Macedonian nationality and adopt Greek names.[344] Greece also has consistently denied entry visas to these refugees except in a few cases to attend funerals but even then with difficulty. In July 1988, following a reunion in Skopje, over 100 of these former refugees attempted to visit northern Greece but were turned back at the border after Greek officials refused entry to some of them, and one participant at the reunion, Lefter Lajovski, who was by then a Canadian citizen, claimed that the authorities had asked him to change his name to a Greek one if he wanted to enter Greece even though no visa is required for Canadian citizens.[345]

Such actions by the Greek government against Macedonians and the Yugoslav Socialist Republic (SR) of Macedonia escalated after Andreas Papandreou and his Greek Socialist party PASOK, came to power in Greece in 1981. Skopje's Kiril i Metodija university was taken off the list of foreign academic institutions whose degrees are recognized by Greece as the instruction at the university was in a language, Macedonian, not 'internationally recognized'.[346] Greece has repeatedly refused Yugoslavia's initiatives to bilaterally abolish visas and while Serbs, Croats or other Yugoslav nationals have few problems, Tanjug on 12 July 1984 reported that the Greek Consulate in Skopje was asking for special proof from Macedonian entry visa applicants that they were not born in Greek Macedonia.

Papandreou himself has explicitly denied the existence of a Macedonian minority in Greece and stated that he would not accept any dialogue on this matter.[347] An example of the lengths to which this is drawn is the last minute cancellation in September 1987, when the players were already on court and 5000 spectators present, of a friendly basketball match between Aris of Thessalonika and Metalno Zavod Tito of Skopje due, according to the Skopje paper *Vecer* of 1 October 1987, to the letter 'M' in the name of the Skopje team being seen by the Minister for Northern Greece as standing for Macedonia.

The Greek conservative party, *Nea Demokratia*, also continued its hostility to SR Macedonia and set up in early 1986 a monitoring centre in Florina to monitor broadcasts from Skopje for anti-Yugoslav commentaries. Papandreou himself was attacked by some Greek newspapers for travelling to Yugoslavia in January 1986 'at a time of an allegedly stepped up Yugoslav propaganda drive concerning the so-called Macedonian question' and the Greek newspaper Stohos (an extremist small circulation newspaper) which is very nationalistic on minority matters and has alleged that Greek students in Skopje have been pressured to declare themselves as Macedonians, urged Greeks to fight with all available means against those who speak Slavo-Macedonian.[348]

Relations between the Papandreou government and Bulgaria, on the other hand, were very good. It appears that the Bulgarians have acquiesced to the loss of Aegean Macedonia to Greece and united with Greece in denying the existence of a Macedonian nation as espoused by the Yugoslavs – the Bulgarians even going as far as to exclude from Bulgarian television the Yugoslav entry, a Macedonian song, to the 1988 Eurovision song contest along with the Turkish and Israeli entries.[349] The shared problem of enmity to Turkey and Turkish minorities is another factor in the present Greek-Bulgarian friendship well illustrated by the visit of the Greek foreign minister to Sofia and subsequent public thanks to the Bulgarians, a Warsaw Pact member, for their support in 1988 during a confrontation with Turkey, ostensibly Greece's NATO ally, over territorial problems in the Aegean.

The Greeks apparently do not react with the same outrage as the Yugoslavs to the perennial Bulgarian statements about the 'unjust' annulment of the 'Greater Bulgaria' of the San Stefano Treaty of 1878 which included present-day Greek as well as Yugoslav Macedonia, and the Greeks do not claim historical events like the Ilinden rising of 1903 as both the Bulgarians and Macedonians do. Neither do Bulgarians antagonize the Greeks by making films like 'The Rescue' which won the highest Bulgarian honour, the Dimitrov prize, in 1986 and which claimed that the population of Ohrid in 1944 was Bulgarian.

Relations between Greece and Yugoslavia over the Macedonian question have continued to deteriorate following Papandreou's fall from power in 1989. One factor in this has been the rise of a more assertive Macedonian nationalism in Yugoslavia as the state appeared to disintegrate. A mass demonstration in Skopje protesting at the lack of minority rights for Macedonians in Greece and Bulgaria was organized on 20 February 1990 to coincide with Greek Premier Konstantin Mitzotakis's visit to Belgrade. In protest at Greece's continuing obstruction in granting visas to some of their citizens, Yugoslav Macedonians organized a series of rallies on the Yugoslav-border which were supported by the Presidency of the Macedonian Republic of Yugoslavia. These began in May and after a 10-hour blockade of the Yugoslav-Greek border by Yugoslav protestors on 16 June, Greece responded by obliging all Yugoslav travellers to Greece to show proof of possession of US$1000.[350] Additionally, on 3 June a new organization, 'Dignity', was founded in Skopje dedicated to the protection of the rights and freedoms of Macedonians living in the Republic of Greece.[351] Polemics between the two countries look certain to escalate in the forseeable future, compounded by rival claims over Orthodox citizens in southern Albania.

The Turks and Pomaks

Assessing the number of Turks and other minorities in Greece is problematic. The census of 1928 recorded 191,254 Turks while the 1951 census recorded 179,895 Turks of whom virtually all were either Muslim by religion, 92,219, or Orthodox, 86,838. While some live on the Greek islands neighbouring Turkey, most live in Western Thrace. The Pomaks, Muslim Slavs, or a small number of Muslim Greeks, tend to live also in Western Thrace in villages in the southern Rhodope and due to the official reticence to give figures for ethnic minorities, only for religious ones, it is hard to separate them from the Turks; however, the villages near the Bulgarian border in all three provinces of Western Thrace are predominantly Pomak with the exception of some like Mikron Dereion which have a mixed population of ethnic Turks, Pomaks and Greek Orthodox, or others which have a sedentary Muslim Gypsy population. Many Pomaks also live in Komotini and Xanthi and some also live in Dhidhimotikhon.

Official Greek sources tend to claim that the Turks are Pomaks or Muslim Greeks while, conversely the Turks claim the Pomaks as Turks. Estimates from the Information Office at the Greek Embassy in London based on the 1981 census figures give a total of 110,00 people belonging to religious minorities of whom some 60,000 are Turkish-speaking Muslims; 30,000 Pomaks; and 20,000 Athingani (descendants of Christian heretics expelled from Asia Minor during Byzantine rule) or Roma Gypsies. However, Turkish Muslim sources from Western Thrace claim a total of 100,000 to 120,000 Turkish-speaking Muslims in Western Thrace and most observers estimate between 100,000 and 120,000 Muslims out of a total population for Western Thrace of some 360,000 recorded in the census of 1971. Of the other minorities there are small populations of **Gagauz**, Christian Turkish-speaking people, for example around the city of Alexandroupolis, and **Sarakatsani**, Greek speaking transhumants, especially in the village of Palladion. Fieldwork by F. De Jong in 1979[352], to whom much of the above is indebted, notes that there are no longer any Circassians in Western Thrace.

Turkey is Greece's traditional enemy, despite being a NATO pact partner, and, similarly to Bulgaria, Greece fears Turkish expansion, especially after the example of Cyprus and huge billboards featuring a bleeding partitioned Cyprus with appropriate captions, were openly displayed in Thrace in 1987. Much of Western Thrace is a restricted area due to reasons of national security. These areas are the border areas with Bulgaria where many Turks and Pomaks live and in these militarized areas large portions of land has been expropriated from Pomaks and Turks. The inhabitants of these areas are severely restricted in their freedom of movement to 30 kms. radius of their residence. Decree 1366/1938 which forbids foreign nationals to buy land near border areas is still operational and it is claimed that this decree is used against ethnic Turks and Pomaks even though they are Greek citizens.

In the exchange of populations following the Greco-Turkish war of 1920-22 some 60,000 Greek refugees from Asia Minor were allowed, in contravention to the Treaty of Lausanne, to settle in Western Thrace, and under steady administrative and economic pressure from the Greek authorities a gradual migration of Muslims to Turkey ensued.

This is particularly noticeable in the previously Muslim province of Ebros where the population now is Greek Orthodox. World War II and the civil war saw a rise in the number of such emigres and some 20,000 left for Turkey in the period 1939-51 with emigration continuing to the present day.

The deterioration of relations with Turkey over the developing situation in Cyprus saw a corresponding deterioration of the situation of the Turkish minority in Western Thrace with increased pressure to induce emigration. At the same time the Turkish government began to raise the issue of the minority as a counterpoise to Greek claims for uniting Cyprus with Greece. (Successive Greek governments have tended to see any complaints from Turks in Western Thrace as being orchestrated by Turkey and have also pointed to the unhappy situation of the 100,000 or so Greeks allowed, under the Treaty of Lausanne, to remain in Istanbul. These Greeks have suffered severe harassment and their numbers have declined drastically, as a result, to under 10,000 by 1974, and their position seems serious in the extreme.)[353]

Under the military dictatorship of 1967-74 the situation worsened. Members of the Turkish minority community boards, elected under provision of Decree 2345/1920, were dismissed and replaced by non-elected people, appointed by government agencies, prepared to act contrary to the interests of the Muslim community. Examples are the appointment, without any qualifications, of a Gypsy Muslim, Ahmet Damatoglu, previously an imam, as Mufti of Dhidhimotikon (Dimotoka) in 1973, and a non-Muslim as chairman of the council for the administration of religious organizations in Xanthi in 1967. In this period Greeks, including many Sarakatsani – a Greek-speaking transhumant people akin to the Vlahs – were given financial inducement to move into Western Thrace to dilute the Muslim Turkish speaking population.

Despite the return to democracy in 1974 the trend continued aided by Greek reaction to the Turkish invasion of Cyprus. There has been no return to the former democratic practices as stipulated in Decree 2345/1920 and when the Mufti of Komotini died on 2 July 1985 he was replaced by a government appointee. When the new Mufti resigned almost immediately due to community protests he was replaced six months later by another appointee without consultation. From 1977 all the place names in Komotini were changed from Turkish forms to Greek forms and henceforth it was forbidden to use the old names for official purposes, apparently on pain of fine or even imprisonment. Mention of the Turkish name in parenthesis after the Greek names is also forbidden.[354]

Over a long period there have been growing complaints by Muslims, Turks and Pomaks, that: they, unlike Greek Orthodox Christians, cannot buy real estate, except for a few select people who cooperate with the authorities, neither can they negotiate loans or credits; that building construction for Turkish houses has been withheld for many years resulting in the Turks being forced to live in backward conditions (easily observable by a casual visitor), neither is permission to build or restore mosques forthcoming; Muslims have been particularly affected by expropriation of land for public use without adequate compensation, and the re-allocation of land in Western Thrace which began in 1967 has resulted in their receiving inferior land in exchange; Muslims are virtually excluded from the state bureaucracy and hindered in business matters by difficulties in obtaining business and driving licences and even subject to punitive levies; despite constitutional guarantees, Turks who leave Greece, even for a temporary period, have been denied re-entry under Article 19 of the Greek Nationality Law which states:

'A person who is of foreign origin leaving Greek territories without the intention of returning may be deprived of Greek citizenship', and obtaining normal five-year passports is difficult for many Turks. This last point is illustrated by a number of cases like one reported in the Athens newspaper Rizospastis on 19 May 1986 that 'two Muslim origin Greek citizens' from a village near Komotini were refused re-entry and deported after having visited their son who was studying in Istanbul. Additionally it is alleged that the authorities are attempting to disperse the minority by moving unemployed Turks and Pomaks to other areas, where once registered they are unable to return to Western Thrace, and are pressured under pain of dismissal to change their names to Greek ones.

Education

In the vital field of education the Greek authorities have steadily increased teaching in Greek at the expense of Turkish. From the 1960s onwards religious teachers from the Arab world have progressively been reduced while the employment of teachers from Turkey to Turkish schools in Western Thrace has been stopped. Since 1968 only graduates from a special academy in Thessaloniki can be qualified to teach in Turkish schools. This academy takes much of its intake from Greek secondary schools and, its critics claim, relies on an outdated religious curriculum deliberately to create an incompetent Hellenized education system in Western Thrace isolated from the mainstream of modern

Turkish culture. The situation has deteriorated with the authorities introducing an entrance exam for the two Turkish secondary minority schools in Komotini and Xanthi – there are some 300 Turkish primary schools – and a directorate from the government in March 1984 stipulating that graduate examinations from Turkish secondary and high schools have to be in Greek. The implementation of this law in 1985 with, in some cases, merely a few months' notice was extremely hard on the unfortunate students. The result of these measures has been a dramatic decline in secondary school students in Turkish schools from 227 in Xanthi and 305 in Komotini in 1983-4, to 85 and 42, respectively, in 1986-7. Greek history books portray Turks in crude stereotypes and while Turkish pupils are allowed some books from Turkey, there have been inexplicable delays resulting in long outdated textbooks having to be used.

The authorities have also prohibited the use of the adjective 'Turkish' in titles denoting associations etc. and the Turkish Teachers Association in Western Thrace was closed by order of Komotini court on 20 March 1986, a decision upheld by the Athens High Court on 28 July 1987.

Protest

As noted above, over a long period there have been many individual complaints by ethnic Turks at the deteriorating position of the minority in Western Thrace. Such protests are apparently gathering force. In the summer of 1988 there was a large scale demonstration by Turks in Komotini which was followed by two bomb explosions – one in the central mosque and one in a cemetery of a neighbourhood mosque. Nobody was injured in these attacks which Turks see as an act of provocation by the Greeks against the Turkish minority. Additionally, there have been a number of appeals by Turks in Western Thrace to outside bodies like the UN and Council of Europe.

In August 1986, Dr. Sadik Ahmet, a doctor of philosophy from Western Thrace, was arrested along with a collaborator and held for a few days. They were later tried in Thessaloniki and Sadik Ahmet was sentenced to two and a half years' while his co-defendant, Ibrahim Serif, a teacher of theology, received 15 months' imprisonment on charges of spreading false information and falsifying some five or six signatures after they had sent a petition containing around 13,000 signatures to the UN and the Council of Europe alleging a policy of assimilation and forced emigration by the Greek authorities and detailing many of the complaints already listed. Both were released pending appeal which was due to be held in December 1988 but was post-poned, apparently due to pressure by human rights groups like Amnesty International.

On 18 June 1989 Sadik Ahmet stood for Parliament as an independent Turkish candidate and was elected with some 32% of the vote, illustrating the support for him among the Turkish population. Sadik Ahmet and Ibrahim Serif were tried again on 25 January 1990 by Rodope Court of Petty Sessions and sentenced to 18 months' imprisonment and three years deprivation of civil rights. The charges related to an election communication they, along with Ismail Molla Rodoplu, distributed prior to the general elections in November 1989. Ahmet's candidacy in this election was disqualified on a technicality, but Rodoplu was elected and so immune from prosecution. In this manifesto they called on Turks to vote for them as independent Muslim candidates standing on a list called 'Trust'. They stated that the main Greek political parties 'spread an atmosphere of terror in the towns and villages' in order to intimidate the minority and gain their votes. Ahmet and Serif were charged with Article 163 of the penal code ('spreading false information') due to this claim of 'Terror', and Article 192 (which penalizes those 'provoking or inciting citizens to acts of violence amongst themselves or to mutual discord and disrupting the public peace') for claiming the existence of a 'Turkish' minority in Greece. This latter charge was made because of the violent clashes which had occurred. They were acquitted of the first charge but found guilty of the second.

On 29 January, further violent incidents occurred between ethnic Turks and Orthodox Greeks in Komotini in which 19 people were reportedly injured and Muslim property damaged. A Greek reportedly died following a fight with a Muslim in Komotini hospital.[355] The verdict against Ahmet and Serif was upheld on appeal on 30 March but their sentences were reduced to 15 months' and 10 months' imprisonment, respectively. They were both given the option of paying a fine instead of serving their sentences – Ahmet, 1000 drachmae per day of sentence, and Serif, 400 drachmae. This amounted to a total of 540,000 drachmae (about US$4,000). They both paid and were released.

On 8 April Dr. Ahmet was elected to parliament on the 'Trust' list and although he had been deprived of his civil rights for three years, a court in Komotini ruled he could stand in the elections. He still faces charges under Article 192 similar to those above relating to a declaration he made to the Turkish language newspaper *Guven* on 17 November 1989, and a leaflet of 22 November 1989 and in January there were reports that the Greek authorities were planning moves to remove his parliamentary immunity from prosecution.

Dr. Sadik Ahmet is now well established as the leader of the ethnic Turks in Western Thrace and the Greek authorities who persecute him have only served to reinforce his position. There have been reports that the Turkish government of Turgut Ozal viewed the pre-eminence of Ahmet and the worsening relations between ethnic Turks and Greeks in Western Thrace with some alarm and even contemplated a deal with Mitsotakis to remove Ahmet from the political scene.[356]

The situation appears to be becoming more serious with increased polarization of the communities in Western Thrace and while some of the complaints, like the alleged policy of resettling unemployed Turks in other areas being a deliberate policy of assimilation, may be exaggerated, the facts add up to an apparent deliberate policy of discrimination with a long-term aim of assimilation akin to that carried out against the Macedonians by successive Greek governments. Against this escalating policy there appears to be growing discontent among the Turks in Western Thrace which might explode in the future.

The Roma (Gypsies) and Albanians

The lack of statistics available for ethnic minorities and the official Greek position of classifying as Greeks all those who use Greek in everyday language, even if it is not their mother-tongue, especially if they are of Orthodox faith, again makes assessing the numbers of Roma, Albanians and Vlahs very hard. Estimates from official Greek sources give the figure for the Roma as far lower than outside observers who estimate the number at 140,000 of whom 45,000 are nomadic Muslims. Many Muslim **Roma** live in Macedonia and Western Thrace where there is a community of them, numbering 1500 to 2000, in Komotini alone.

A MRG report[357] commented on their plight especially that of the situation of Muslim Roma who lack citizenship and thus basic civil rights. A law passed in 1979 designed to enable them to obtain identity cards has had little apparent effect due to most lacking birth-certificates. The Panhellenic Romani Association has held council elections in Thessaloniki and Athens since at least 1980 and about 50 houses have been built for Roma in Serrai. Muslim Roma have in practice only been accepted as Greek citizens after baptism and admission to the Orthodox Church, and the Bishop of Florina in Greek Macedonia has continued to lead a church mission to convert Muslim Roma to Orthodoxy. The Ministry of Education is looking at the educational needs of

the Muslim Gypsy population but travelling Roma are still faced with
the 1976 law making camping illegal outside of organized sites – virtually all of which are for tourists and banned to Roma. The Roma, as is
so common elsewhere, are at the bottom of the social order.

While there is much comment focused on the position of the Greek
minority in **Albania**, there is very little information about the Albanian minority which remained in Greece after the founding of the Albanian state in 1913. Most of these Albanians were Orthodox by religion
although there were Muslim Albanian Cams in northern Greece up till
immediately after World War II. During the war attempts were made
by the Italian occupiers to harness them against the Greeks and as a
result there was a backlash against them after the war with many being
driven into Albania and mosques burnt.

The Orthodox Albanians, similarly with other Orthodox minorities,
tended to become Hellenicized due to the Greek control of the education system. Three generations ago there were many Albanian-speaking people in Attica, Boeotica, southern Euboea (Evvoia), and Hydra
while the Plaka district in Athens by the Acropolis was the Albanian
quarter of the city with its own law courts using the Albanian language.[358] The Federal Union of European Nationalites, based in Austria,
claims that there are 95,000 Albanians in Greece[359] while the Democratic League of Camuria, based in USA, claims the huge figure of over
one million of whom over 100,000 are claimed to be from the border
region with Albania (Camuria).[360] Such huge figures appear fanciful in
the extreme, and there is little sign of this minority today. It appears
that the shared religion under Greek control and the education system
has greatly facilitated their total and peaceful assimilation into the
Greek nation.

The Vlahs (Koutsovlahs or Aromani)

The **Vlahs** are a Latin-speaking people – they speak a form of Romanian – living south of the Danube in Albania, Bulgaria, Yugoslavia (predominantly in Serbia and Vardar Macedonia) and, primarily, in
Greece. They are an historically old people who antedate the more
modern arrivals to the Balkan Peninsula like the Slavs, Bulgars and
Turks. Perhaps because of this they, unlike other minorities, do not
appear to live in particularly concentrated areas, with the exception of
the 'Vlah capital' Aminciu (Metsovon) in the Pindus mountains at the
headlands of the five rivers of the Pindus range.

The censuses of 1935 and 1951 recorded 19,703 and 39,855 Vlahs,
respectively, although as noted above the classification as Greek, those

who use Greek as 'language of daily use' has tended to greatly underestimate the number of minorities like the Vlahs, who tend to be Hellenophile and are almost entirely Orthodox Christian by religion (hence, Greek Orthodox). Emigre Vlah sources claim a figure of 600,000 in Greece, although this would appear to be exaggerated. The Federal Union of European Nationalities puts the figure at 300,000[361] but this too seems to be exaggerated.

The Vlahs are similar to the Sarakatsani, Greek-speaking transhumant shepherds, but less mobile, and are seasonally nomadic as shepherds in the mountains while pursuing other fields of employment like medicine, law, taxi-driving etc. Traditionally the Vlahs have held an important position in inland Greece and under the Ottoman domination they, due to their traditional occupations of shepherding and transport of goods by caravan, tended to control overland trade in the Greek provinces of the Ottoman Empire while the Greeks controlled the sea trade. Many Vlahs identified themselves with Greeks, due to having received Greek education in Greek schools, and took a leading role in the struggle for Greek independence.

However some, influenced by the Romanian national movement and the close similarities between their languages, attempted to have church services and schooling in their vernacular – a move which, similarly to the Bulgarians, was strongly resisted by the Greek Orthodox hierarchy. This latter strand of Vlah distinctness from Greeks was soon patronized by the new Romanian state leading to the creation of Romanian churches and schools in Macedonia, which was then still part of the Ottoman Empire, funded by the Romanian state. In these schools children were taught the Vlah language, Aromanian, in the lower grades, and then later Romanian, as it was a recognized literary language.[362] By 1912 the Romanian state was subsidising over 30 such schools in Macedonia.

The savage internecine warfare in Macedonia from the 1890s to 1914 by rival armed bands of Serbs, Bulgarians and Greeks as the new national states competed for the decaying Ottoman Empire, was especially hard on the Vlahs who for the most part could not defend themselves well, and there were massacres of Vlahs with churches and villages burnt by Greek nationalists. This sorry period finished after the settlement of the Balkan Wars and in 1913 the Greek Prime Minister Venizelos signed an agreement with the Romanians to officially allow Romanian schools for Vlahs in the Greek state. The Vlah nationalist movement continued under Romanian tutelage but never recovered from the violence late in the 19th Century.

The rise of fascism in Italy and Romania led to attempts, especially during the Italian occupation of parts of Greece during World War II, to harness the Vlahs to the fascist cause and an autonomous 'Principality of the Pindus' was even declared by an extremist named Alcibiades Diamandi of Samarina consisting of Epirus, Macedonia and all of Thessaly, with Diamandi as Prince and a compatriot as head of the 'Roman Legion'- an army of Vlah fascists.[363] After World War II the new Romanian state chose not to carry on financing the schools and churches in Greece.

The majority of Vlahs who saw themselves as distinct from Greeks tended to emigrate with the result that separatist feeling is much stronger in the diaspora than in the homeland – similarly with the Macedonians of Northern Greece. There is no apparent nationalist or separatist feeling among the Vlahs of Greece despite the occasional hostility towards them from the more nationalistic sections of Greek society, usually manifested in objecting to the use of the Vlah language – it is frequently used in public places in Metsovon and elsewhere. An example of this hostility is an article in the Athens newspaper *Stohos* – notorious for such outbursts against Greece's minorities – of 18 October 1984 which under the heading 'The end justifies the means' pointed to such public use of Vlah (and Macedonian) 'in the street, in the cafes and at work' and called for its prohibition by 'employing all means' against 'the plans of the enemies of the nation'. Such pressure has in the past tended to intimidate Vlahs living in the cities in mixed communities from speaking their own language and under the dictatorship of the Colonels from 1967 to 1974 Vlahs were even threatened with imprisonment for speaking Aromanian.

However, since the 1980s the situation has improved as the Greek government apparently recognizes that the Vlahs, unlike the Turks or Macedonians, constitute no threat, real or potential, to the Greek state, and many 'Vlah Cultural Societies' have come into existence; since 1984 there has been a huge annual festival for all Vlah villages of Greece. Despite this improvement the Greeks are still very wary of acknowledging any minorities and hold to the position that the Vlahs are Greeks who speak an unusual dialect.

When Vlah activists in Germany contacted the European Community's Bureau of Lesser Known Languages which resulted in the European Community questioning Greece about the position of the Vlahs, there was a strong reaction within Greece involving leading Vlahs like Evangelos Averoff against this intervention from outside and a corresponding criticism of the burgeoning local cultural efforts. This has led to a severe limiting of previous efforts by Vlahs in Greece with only a few brave individuals speaking out against Averoff's view – eg. Zoitsa

Papazisi-Papatheodorou, a chemistry teacher from Trikala and a director of the Pan-Hellenic Vlah Cultural Society, who testified on behalf of the Vlah language to the European Community and as a result was vilified in the Greek press.

As noted above, large numbers of Vlahs emigrated during the course of the century and among these emigres there is some pro-Romanian feeling (due to linguistic and cultural similarities) and, conversely, some anti-Greek or anti-Yugoslav feeling. These emigres have formed Vlah associations in a number of places: France, USA, West Germany etc. and have held two international Vlah congresses in Germany – in September 1985 in Mannheim, and in August 1988 in Freiburg. A central question at these conferences has been the lack of a defined Vlah language (there is, however, a Vlah-Romanian dictionary) and Vlahs from Greece pressed for the use the Greek alphabet so as not to antagonize the Greek authorities; however, the other participants preferred the more obvious choice of the Latin alphabet – the antagonism between 'Panhellenes' and 'Superromani', often becoming a struggle between Vlahs in Greece and those in the diaspora, is a constant factor in Vlah matters.

14

ALBANIA AND ITS MINORITIES

Albania in outline

The People's Socialist Republic of Albania has an area of 28,748 sq. kms. and shares borders with Yugoslavia and Greece. It is bound to the west by the Adriatic and Ionian Seas and separated from southern Italy by the Strait of Otranto – less than 60 km. in distance.

Formerly a territory of the Ottoman Empire, the Albanian national awakening came in the second half of the 19th Century with the founding of the League of Prizren (in present- day Yugoslavia) in 1878 to combat the threat of partition of the Albanian inhabited territories by neighbouring Serbia to the north and Greece to the south. With assistance from the Great Powers, Albania declared its independence in November 1912. However, the new state was prone to internal difficulties and outside manipulation especially from Italy. During World War II it was annexed by Italy and occupied by Italian, and, later, by German forces. The most effective resistance movement was the communist-led National Liberation Front, which took power in November 1944 under the leadership of Enver Hoxha. In January 1946, Albania was proclaimed a People's Republic and the first post-war constitution was promulagated in March 1946.

At the end of World War II, over 70% of the population was Muslim; approximately 17% – including ethnic Greeks – belonged to the Orthodox Church mainly in the south and central areas; and about 10% to the Roman Catholic Church in the mountainous north. In 1967 Albania was officially proclaimed 'the first atheist state in the world', all religious institutions were closed, and religious officials were forbidden to exercise their functions. No current statistics on religious affiliation are available.

As of December 1981, Albania had a population of 2,752,300. The capital Tirane has some 250,000 inhabitants. Albania has the highest population growth rate in Europe. Assessing the numbers of ethnic minorities is problematic. No recent statistics for ethnic minorites

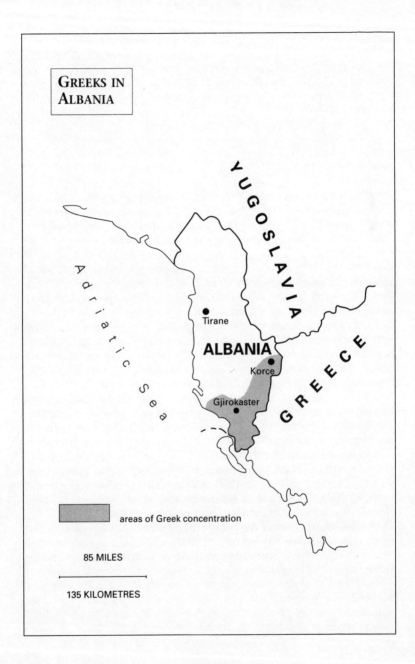

GREEKS IN
ALBANIA

YUGOSLAVIA

Adriatic Sea

● Tirane

ALBANIA

● Korce

GREECE

Gjirokaster ●

areas of Greek concentration

85 MILES

135 KILOMETRES

have been published but the largest is probably the Greek minority, concentrated mainly in the southern districts of Korce and Gjirokaster. According to the 1955 census, it then represented 2.54% of the population. In the 1961 census, 95% of the population was given as ethnically Albanian.[364] The remainder was estimated to comprise of 40,000 Greeks (2.4%), 15,000 Macedonians and Montengrins (0.9%), 10,000 Vlahs (0.6%), and about 10,000 Roma (Gypsies).[365] All these figures are contested. Small Jewish and Armenian groups also live in Albania.

Albania is a highly centralized state. The Albanian Party of Labour (the Communist Party) was the sole authorized political party until December 1990 when, following large- scale disturbances and, if somewhat belatedly, following the events in other East European erstwhile communist countries, an opposition party, the Democratic Party of Albania, was allowed to function.

At the end of World War II, Albania had close links with Yugoslavia, but these were broken after the latter's rift with the USSR in 1948. In 1961 Albania broke off relations with the USSR and instead forged links with the People's Republic of China. In 1968 it formally withdrew from the Warsaw Pact, which it had joined in 1955. In 1978 it severed economic and political links with China.

Under the long leadership of Enver Hoxha, who effectively ruled the country from the end of 1944 until his death in April 1985, Albania was a very closed country, with all travel in and out the country carefully supervised. The constitution did not guarantee freedom of movement and with the exception of official delegations and a few students, Albanian citizens were almost never permitted to leave their country. The frontiers were heavily guarded and people who tried to leave without official permission faced being shot by border guards or punished by long prison sentences.

Hoxha's successor, Ramiz Alia, has attempted a gradual relaxation of Hoxha's extreme isolationaist policies – the acceptance of foreign credits was forbidden by the constitution and punishable as treason in the criminal code. Thousands of Albanians left their country in 1990 following occupations in foreign embassies and there was a sharp increase in those crossing the border illegally in December and in early 1991, apparently due to a relaxation of the vigilance of border patrols. The authorities have promised to introduce freedom of travel in the future, and have relaxed the draconian anti-religious practices.

Religion

Religion has been, as elsewhere in the Balkans, of primary importance in self-identification in Albania. For both the Greek and the Orthodox Slav minorities, the Orthodox church has been essential in protecting (and often, especially for the Greeks, increasing, by assimilation through the past control of the education process) their numbers. As such, the Albanian authorities' attempt to ban all religious practices merits close attention.

Religion was officially attacked after World War II when the communists took power and in 1967, Albania was officially proclaimed 'the first atheist state in the world' and all forms of organized religious activity were banned. In September 1967, the government announced that it had closed all religious buildings, including 2169 mosques, churches, monasteries and other institutions.[366] Among these were 630 major Orthodox Chuches which were razed to the ground and an equal number converted to other uses such as grain depots, theatres, coffee shops and stables.[367] The constitution of 1976 expressly outlawed religion. Article 55 stated: 'The creation of any type of organization of a fascist, anti-democratic, religious, or anti-socialist character is forbidden. Fascist, religious, war- mongering, anti-socialist activity and propaganda are forbidden'. Article 55 of the 1977 criminal code was similarly worded and carried a sentence of between three and 10 years' imprisonment.

Religious holidays and private religious practices were also suppressed. During the anti-religious campaign, the authorities confiscated religious artifacts from individuals, including personal crucifixes, icons and bibles. Religious leaders were publicly denounced, shaven, defrocked, imprisoned and even killed.[368] In April 1967, the 40 Orthodox priests still alive were taken to the city of Delvino (some were taken from prison for this purpose) and shaved in public and had their vestments removed and spat upon.[369] One priest, Reverend Theodore Zisis, resisted being shaved and was consequently imprisoned for 10 years.

The government effectively eradicated formal religion. All the postwar East European communist regimes were initially very hostile to organized religion but none went as far as Albania. Why? As noted above, the majority of Albania's population were and probably remain Muslim and this helped delay the Albanian national awakening, as the Ottoman Empire was a theocratic (not a national Turkish) state, all Muslims were treated as first-class citizens with many Muslim Albanians, at times, occupying high posts in the Ottoman hierachy. Another factor of this Ottoman millet system was that the other religious denominations were seen as more important differentiators for population groups than ethnicity – this is still shown in the respective national (Greek, Macedonian, Serbian etc.) claims and counter-claims for the Orthodox populations, including Orthodox Albanians in the Greek case, in the former Ottoman territories. As such in the Albanian context, it could be argued that religion was a potential threat to the forging of an independent unified Albanian nation which would be able to resist past foreign incursions.

Combined with this was Enver Hoxha's personal ideological dogmatism, and it is no coincidence that the anti-religious campaign took place in Albania at the same time as the Cultural Revolution did in Albania's then ally China – indeed, in Albania, the campaign was part of what was called 'the Cultural and Ideological Revolution'.[370] The communist Albanian elite led by Hoxha was, compared to other communist elites in Eastern Europe at the time, well educated, and this, combined with the extreme backwardness of the Albania they inherited may have been a factor in the tendency of Hoxha – perhaps similarly to Pol Pot in Kampuchea in the mid 1970s – to indulge in such radical attempts at social engineering. However, despite this frontal attack on religion by the state, reports pointed to the continuation of private religious practice hidden from the watchful eyes of the authorities.

In 1990, Hoxha's successor, Ramiz Alia, began to reverse this policy. In part, this has been due to public pressure from within. About 1000 people demonstrated in Shkodra in northern Albania on 11 January and reportedly, one of the aims of the demonstrators was to get religious practice legalized again.[371] On 8 May, the parliament redefined 'religious propaganda' as a non-criminal activity and on 11 May, government officials reportedly promised UN Secretary General Javier Perez de Cuellar that churches would be reopened.[372] Further signs came in October with the opening of a kindergarten in Tirane named after Mother Teresa[373], the ethnic Albanian (she was born in Yugoslav Macedonia as Gonxhe Bojaxhi) Nobel Peace Prize winner. Also in October, Iran reported that prayers were being said again in mosques[374]. On 16 November, up to 5000 Catholics attended a mass in Shkoder conducted by Archbishop Simun Yubani who had been in prison from 1967 to 1989[375] and a number of other masses were held in the city and nearby towns with reports of many priests released after long years of detention.[376] Services were also reported in Orthodox villages in the south and Ramiz Alia announced at a Central Committee meeting that a commission would be set up to study amendments to the constitution involving lifting the ban on organized religion. In December, Mother Teresa's visit to Albania was widely publicized within the country when she met with Ramiz Alia.377 It appears that the long period of officially enforced atheism in Albania is over.

The Greeks

The Greek minority in Albania predominantly lives in the southern regions of the country. The minority's identity derives mainly from its adherence to the Orthodox Church and the use of the Greek language and names. As noted above, the post-war communist government attempted to eradicate religious practices; it has forbidden the use of 'foreign' and religious names; and reportedly, it has discouraged the use of the Greek language in public places. There are also allegations that the authorities have moved Albanians into Greek majority areas and moved Greeks out, thus dispersing the Greek community.[378] Albania is a highly centralized state which has attempted to exert a great measure of control over individuals' lives and many of the above measures are also applied to the entire Albanian population and as such are not explicitly aimed at the Greek or other minorities, but introduced purely for economic reasons.[379]

Additionally, the authorities have temporarily relocated individuals and families through legislation which was first introduced in 1949 and updated in the 1950s, 1960s and again as Decree 5912 of 26 June 1979. Such decrees have been widely used by the authorities. Decree 5912 specifies internment of those 'who represent a danger to the social system'. It also permits the internment of those persons whose relatives have fled Albania or gone into hiding within the country.[380] Reportedly, ethnic Greeks tended to be interned in the north of the country while ethnic Albanians were moved south.

Education

Although no recent statistics for ethnic minorities have been published in Albania, the Greek minority is officially recognized by the authorities. Greek emigre sources claim that some 400,000 ethnic Greeks live in Albania. This estimate is based on historical accounts of Greeks in Albania, Greek schools and churches formerly in Albania, and individuals formerly registered with the Autocephalous Orthodox Church of Albania (which predominantly used the Greek language).[381] It includes all those who are Greek Orthodox by religion – Slavs (Macedonians and Montenegrins), Albanians, Vlahs, as well as Greeks – and would therefore, appear to be very unreliable for assessing the ethnic Greek population. It is highly likely that the inflated estimate for Slavs claimed by Yugoslav sources is based on similar precepts, and with the prospect of Albania 'opening up', claims and counter-claims on ethnicity similar to those over Macedonia can be expected to take place.

Greek language schools have existed in Albania since the 16th Century. In 1922, the Albanian government reported that 36 Greek schools existed in southern Albania.[382] There is one Greek language teacher-training college serving the community, and schools are provided with some Greek language texts, apparently in Greek with Albanian instructions. The number of Greek schools today is unknown, although recent refugees suggest a significant decrease in their numbers in recent decades.[383] If a village is comprised of Greek minority residents then the village may obtain a Greek language school and other privileges. However, minority status is reportedly granted only to wholly Greek villages and once two or three Albanian families arrive, the village loses that status. Greek children attending Greek language schools are taught in Greek during the first four years, subsequent Greek instruction being only as a foreign language.

Names and language

In 1975, the government ordered name-changes for 'citizens who have inappropriate names and offensive surnames from a political, ideological, and moral standpoint.'[384] Local civil affairs offices were supplied with lists of government-approved names. According to refugees, this order did not affect Muslim names (Hoxha himself – his name means Muslim priest – should have had to change his name otherwise). However, non-Muslims – Albanians, Greeks and members of other ethnic minorites – with religious names, were reportedly obliged to change them. Muslim refugees stated that the name-changing campaign did not affect them while virtually all Greek escapees could recount at least one instance of an imposed name-change.

According to one former resident, the government circulated a list of 'acceptable' names to the Greek community as early as 1967-69. Some have seen the measure to be more 'for nationalistic reasons than religious reasons', namely to eliminate 'alien influences' in the names of persons, as well as places, and replace them with what the regime regards as 'purely Albanian names'.[385] Decree No. 225, also in 1975, ordered changing geographic place names with religious connotations. Towns named after Christian saints have been renamed.[386] This decree was also apparently applied to some non-religious Greek town names as well.[387] The name-changing campaign disrupted longstanding traditions of the Greek community. Greeks name their children after their grandparents, or saints, martyrs or other religious figures.[388] Parents sometimes registered an Albanian name with the government and used a Greek name at home. Such children were reportedly obliged to use their Albanian names at school.

Although there is no direct evidence of legal prohibitions against the use of Greek in public, many refugees have reported *de facto* restrictions in certain settings. A non-Greek escapee said that in his village, none of the minorites – Macedonian, Italian or Greek – were allowed to speak their own languages outside their homes. Some schools allegedly forbid children to speak Greek to each other, and Greeks in internal exile, a widely used punishment (see above), are reported to be forbidden to speak Greek outside their homes. Further reported restrictions on the use of Greek are when visiting prisoners in Albanian prisons[389] and during military service. There is, however, a weekly Greek language newspaper – *Laiko Vima*, organ of the Democratic Front of Gjirokaster for the Greek minority – which has been published since 25 May 1945[390], some Greek publications and radio broadcasts in Greek. In early 1991, following the internal liberalization which had taken place within the country, an ethnic Greek party, called Konkord, was reported to be in formation in southern Albania and the Democratic Union of the Greek minority known as Omonia was registered.

Relations with Greece

As noted above, under Enver Hoxha all foreign contacts were severely limited while his successor, Ramiz Alia, has begun to ease the restrictions. For example, visitors in 1988 report extensive restoration of churches and mosques as cultural relics and tourist sites. Albania has also opened its borders to allow Greek nationals to visit relatives in Albania and some Albanians are now allowed to travel to Greece with the prospect of free travel in the near future, following mass protests in December 1990. Numbers have increased steadily: in 1984, 87 Albanians travelled to Greece; in 1985 301; and in 1986, 535.[391] In 1985, 1265 Greeks travelled to Albania and in 1987 the figure was over 6000.[392] Cultural exchanges are also occurring between the two countries.

However, this easing of relations with Greece, symbolized by the agreement between the Albanians and the Greek government of Andreas Papandreou in 1987 (to end the formal state of war which had existed between the two countries since 1940) has become strained in the 1990s due to what the Albanians see as Greek Premier Mitsotakis's government's claims to southern Albania or, Northern Epirus, as the Greeks call the area. Deputy Prime Minister of Greece, Athanasios Kanellopoulos, at a conference in Ioannina at the end of August 1990, reportedly demanded the redrawing of the boundaries and the Greek government reportedly attacked the previous Papandreou administration for lifting the state of war and its general policy of good-neighbourliness towards Albania.[393] The ending of Albania's isolation looks certain to be marked by future polemics with Greece and Yugoslavia (or its successors) over contested areas.

The sudden change in the internal situation in 1990 resulted in thousands of Albanian citizens leaving the country. A proportion of those who fled the mountains to Greece would undoubtedly have been ethnic Greeks, although there are no figures available. In January 1991, the Greek authorities returned over 5000 Albanian citizens to Albania, leaving perhaps up to 10,000 others behind in Greece.[394] During the visit to Albania in January, the Greek Premier urged ethnic Greeks not to leave Albania.[395]

The Slav Macedonians and other minorities

The situation regarding the number of **Slav Macedonians** (Bulgarian sources claim they are Bulgarians), either Muslim or Orthodox by religion, living in Albania, is unclear due to the extreme secrecy of the Albanian authorities and the above noted tendency for rival ethnic groups to claim their co-religionists as their own. Estimates range from '3000 to 4000 distributed in nine villages of Prespa' – Enver Hoxha the then Albanian leader to the 7th Congress of the Albanian Labour Party in 1975 – to over 100,000 in a book published in Skopje in 1983.[396] This last figure appears to be exaggerated and most, non-Yugoslav, observers put the figure at between 10,000 and 20,000.

Equally exaggerated appears to be the figure of 100,000 **Muslim Macedonians** (Pomaks) claimed by the Yugoslav institution the Macedonian Association of Cultural and Scientific Manifestation of Macedonian Muslims.[397] While there was likely to be – similar to the case in Western Yugoslav Macedonia – considerable numbers of Pomaks in the area, such a large figure seems improbable at any time. Combined with the natural assimilationary tendency of Balkan Muslims towards the majority Muslim group, which is observable even in societes where the Muslims are not the majority population, this figure appears ridiculous. Both the Greek and Yugoslavs appear to be indulging in deliberate overestimation of their respective kinsfolk in readiness for possible future claims.

According to the British Vice-consul in Bitola (Manastir), C.C. Blunt, at the turn of the century in the area of Bilishta, Korcha (Korce), Borbot and Golo Brdo (Gorni Debar) there were some 11,000 Orthodox and Muslim Slavs.[398] In the 1930s, the Macedonian National Committee in Sofia put the figure at 27,500 for Slav Macedonians (called Bulgarians by the native Albanians) living in Albania.[399] In contrast to the Greek authorities after 1912, the authorities in the new Albanian state did not attempt to assimilate the Slav minority or forcibly change the Slav names of villages and towns. Similar to former Ottoman territories, especially Bulgaria, the battleground for national identity tended to be held in matters of the church with the Greek Orthodox Church and its attendant educational facitlities instrumental in checking Slav Macedonian/Bulgarian tendencies. In this the Greek metropolitan of Korce appears to have been particularly active, especially when, according to Yugoslav sources, Slavs from Boboshchitsa, Drevno and two districts of Korce tried to implement the 1870 Ottoman decree and escape the patronage of the Greek Orthodox Church (a Slav school was opened in Korce in 1888 but was quickly closed down).[400]

In 1945 at the end of World War II, 13 Macedonian schools were opened in villages with predominantly Slav populations and, in November 1945, a Yugoslav-Albanian agreement between the new communist authorities allowed a number of Macedonian teachers into Albania to facilitate the running of these schools which only taught Albanian for two hours a week in the fourth grade. However, after the Tito-Stalin break in 1948 and the corresponding Yugoslav-Albanian break, these schools apparently stopped and Albanian became the main language of instruction. While there were textbooks in the Macedonian language for 1st and 2nd grade pupils published in Tirane, all contact with neighbouring Yugoslavia and Greece was stopped. In October 1980, Blagoj Popov from the Yugoslav Republic of Macedonia visited Albania and reported that in Pustets in Mala Prespa there was a Macedonian school in operation, although in the local libraries there was not reportedly a single book in Macedonian.[401]

The abolition of organized religion and the Law on First and Last Names in 1975 whereby all religious names which were not Albanian were to be replaced, no doubt aided the gradual Albanianization of young Slavs – in Pustets, for example, which was entirely Slav, the whole population was renamed Licenas.[402] However, the Albanian authorities, while pursuing social policies at least as restrictive (and almost certainly more) as any in the region, have not indulged in attempted negation or outright assimilation policies as have Bulgaria and Greece. As such, the small Slav minority (Macedonian or Bulgarian or Pomak) is in a position to benefit from the changes currently taking place in Albania by way of contact with other communities outside the country. Increasing numbers were leaving for Yugoslavia in 1991.

There is very little information on other ethnic groups in Albania. There is a small **Italian** community and a small number of **Montenegrins** live in the north. A Montenegrin association was formed in Vraka in early 1991 with over 1000 members. A sizeable **Vlah** population lives in the country around Korce especially in Voskopolje and around Fier. Although no reliable figures are available, there are estimated to be perhaps as many as 35,000 Vlahs in Albania.[403] The same source gives a figure of 5000 **Roma** (Gypsies) although other sources give higher figures. The Roma are still at the basic stage of seeking permission for cultural organizations. There is also a small **Armenian** and **Jewish** population. Forty Jews fled the country on 30 December 1990 and Israeli sources stated that a further 350 Albanian Jews were planning to leave.[404]

Even though the authorities have at least recognized its minorities and, for the Greeks and the Macedonians, granted them certain minority rights, the human rights record of Albania has been bleak. While the government's harsh policies have affected all sectors of the population, minorities have been particularly affected. In its attempt to unify the country and its rigid ideological standpoints, the authorities have undercut some of the fundamental bases of minority identity. The attempted abolition of religion has been disruptive to all the minorities whose cohesiveness often depends on shared religious as well as ethnic ties. The name-changing campaign also focused on non-Muslims – predominantly members of the ethnic minorities. The government also attempted to eradicate the use of Orthodox and secular Greek names for people and places. Not all minority children can attend schools where their language is used for instruction, or even permitted among the pupils. Minority populations have also been apparently weakened by internal exile and other population movements. Former residents report that Greek and other minority languages cannot be used in most public institutions and that most minority members are afraid to speak their own language outside their homes. The government's attempts at forging a unified state and the extreme repressive policies have clearly affected the rights of its minorities.

15

A VANISHING MINORITY
– JEWS OF THE BALKANS

Separate mention should be made concerning the fate of the Jews in the Balkan countries. Large numbers of Spanish-speaking Sephardic Jews settled in the area after being expelled from Spain in the 16th Century and, until World War II, Salonika (Thessaloniki or Solon – the main city in Macedonia), was predominantly Jewish. The Jews were recognized as a separate millet by the Ottoman authorities and remained after the liberation of the area from Ottoman rule in the newly formed states of Bulgaria, Yugoslavia and Greece. The occupation of the area by Nazi Germany and her allies, Italy and Bulgaria, however, saw the Jews once more faced by intolerance from the West, this time of a genocidal character.

In Bulgaria itself the situation was somewhat different to the other areas under study. Under Nazi pressure the Bulgarian government in October 1940 proposed several restrictions on the Jews but, in contrast to German laws, applied religious rather than racial criteria which allowed Jews to convert to Christianity to avoid persecution, and the Bulgarian King delayed signing this obviously unpopular law until the end of January 1941 when Bulgaria's alliance with the Axis powers was inevitable. Stiffer legislation, including Jews having to wear the star of David, was introduced in early 1942 and in August a Commissariat for Jewish Affairs (KEV) was set up in Sofia under Aleksander Belev which was to prepare to transfer Jews to the death camps in Poland. However, massive opposition from prominent Bulgarians, including the King, deputies and leading church figures helped to save the Jews of Bulgaria from deportation and death and instead they were settled temporarily in the provinces and assembled in labour camps. As a result nearly all of Bulgaria's Jews, estimated at some 51,500, survived the war. However, the period from 1946 to 1956 saw a mass exodus to Israel when almost 40,000 left Bulgaria and the population has dwindled to about 5000, and some observers say, only 3000. The Sephardic Jews still remain larger than the Ashkenazim.[405]

205

The fate of the Jews in occupied Yugoslavia and Greece was very different. Deportations began in March 1943. The overwhelming majority perished in Treblinka concentration camp in Poland. The Jewish population of Greece, for example, was 63,200 in 1928, almost entirely Spanish-speaking, according to official Greek statistics, but in 1951 the number was only 6325, while in Macedonia the census of 1953 recorded only 55 Jews. In Yugoslavia as a whole some 16,000 out of the 75,000 pre-war Jewish population survived.

In the Bulgarian occupied territories, responsibility for the transfer of the Jews to Nazi authority rested with KEV, and it appears that, despite Bulgarian claims to the contrary, the Jews in Macedonia and Thrace were knowingly transferred to their deaths by the Bulgarians – perhaps sacrificed for the sake of the Bulgarian Jews. The Nazi crime investigator, Simon Wiesenthal, confirmed on Skopje television in February 1986 that Aleksander Belev and Bulgarian ministers who signed documents on the liquidation of the Macedonian Jews in February and March 1943 were included in his list of war criminals.[406]

CONCLUSION

THE FUTURE FOR MINORITIES IN THE BALKANS

The issues concerning minorities in the Balkans are acute. The most serious problems are currently in Yugoslavia where the recent reassertion of the disparate nationalities has put the state under severe stress so that its very existence is threatened. In Bulgaria the situation has ameliorated greatly since the fall of Todor Zhivkov in November 1989 and the subsequent changing of the authorities' policies of extreme coercive measures to forcibly assimilate most of the country's minorities. Despite this great improvment there is as yet no sign of recogition from any of the main political parties in Bulgaria of the possibility that some of its citizens espouse an identity, Macedonian, separate from Bulgarian. In addition there has been a serious nationalist backlash from sections of the Bulgarian majority against the relaxation of the harsh measures imposed against the ethnic Turkish minority compounded by a continuing fear of a future scenario akin to that of Cyprus occurring within Bulgaria.

In Greece the authorities remain adamant in their apparent refusal to recognize any minorities other than religious ones within the country, and appear to be, similarily to the Bulgarian authorities under Todor Zhivkov, pursuing a policy of creating a one-nation state by assimilation, using education and economic pressure to achieve this. Although the situation in Greece is not comparable to that which recently took place in Bulgaria in the level of violence used by the authorities, the aim appears to be the same. Perhaps the high levels of state-violence in Bulgaria in this recent period was due to the shorter time-scale of the assimilations which while starting in the mid-1950s against the Macedonians (a special case for the Bulgarians), only really began in earnest in the late 1960s and early 1970s, while in Greece the assimilation of the Macedonians for example has beeen in operation since Greece acquired the territories in 1913 after the Balkan Wars and even earlier.

While Greece and until recently Bulgaria have opted for total assimilation, Yugoslavia, due to its inherent multi-nationalism and lack of a majority people, opted for cultural diversity – in modern parlance the salad-bowl approach rather than the melting pot. However, as elsewhere in Eastern Europe, the political relaxation following the retreat from total power of the various communist parties has allowed the virulent nationalism, which always existed but was to some extent controlled by the communist authorities, to come into the open. The whole area of post-communist Eastern Europe is experiencing an explosion of nationalist forces which are filling the power vacuum vacated by the mostly discredited former official ideology of Marxist-Leninism. It is somewhat ironic that as Western Europe appears to be slowly heading towards greater political unity, Eastern Europe is threatened with ethnic fragmentation and none more so than Yugoslavia.

Yugoslavia appears to have the most serious problems: the aspirations of its large ethnic Albanian minority which run against Serbian intransigence over what they perceive as their ancient homeland of Kosovo; a share in the perennial 'Macedonian Question'; the age-old Serb-Croat rivalry now compounded by a seemingly total impasse between Serbia and Slovenia; an inability to cleanly divide up the country should it fall apart – especially the existence of large vocal Serb minorities outside of Serbia proper; a large population which in the oft-contested heartlands of Bosnia-Hercegovina constitutes the largest group and which defines itself not on ethnic-national criteria but on religious ones. All these pose a serious threat of civil war and a worst case scenario of 'Lebanonization' of Yugoslavia which would be disasterous for all concerned – including the rest of Europe.

Albania, while allowing certain rights for its minorities, has had a dismal individual human rights record, and has pursued draconian social policies, apparently from ideological standpoints which attacked the very foundations on which minority identity in the country was based, predominantly religion. The country's apparent awakening from many years of almost total isolationist policies, and the beginnings of internal relaxation are encouraging. However, this relaxation is liable to further exacerbate the Yugoslav/ Albanian problem while opening up new ones especially in the shape of Greek claims to its southern borders.

Throughout the entire region, almost all the borders are looking increasingly temporary especially with the break up of the Warsaw Pact with its unwritten policy of Pax Sovetica for the USSR's erstwhile allies. The NATO partners of Greece and Turkey have been more outright enemies than allies in the past. It will take great patience and diplomacy, so far singularly lacking, in stopping the already acute internal national problems from becoming internationalized with the concommitant threat of regional war(s). The role of the European Community and Turkey in particular, due to the Turkish minorities in Bulgaria and Greece, will be crucial in keeping the peace.

The growth of religious or national militancy poses major problems to governments throughout the world. Often they are symptoms of the denial of rights of minorities over many years, a feeling of exclusion from the benefits of the state and a belief that as there is little to lose, militant action offers the best chance of success. It is essential to tackle these root causes and not to heighten the feelings of injustice and exclusion through repression. Regrettably, armies and police forces are rarely subtle in their approach, while politicians are rarely sufficiently self-confident and far-sighted to respond positively.

Throughout the Balkans religion has been and continues to be an important factor. Smaller Islamic minorites like the Pomaks have tended to become assimilated by larger Islamic groups within the relevant countries – the Turks in Bulgaria and Greece, or, in Yugoslav Macedonia, the Albanians who have also tended to assimilate the Turks there, resulting in the authorities encouraging these smaller Islamic groups to assert their separate identities. Minorities in all four countries who share the religion of the dominant group, Orthodoxy, have been or are being assimilated with far greater ease than the Muslims. This is not so in northern Yugoslavia due to the Hapsburg as opposed to the Ottoman legacy.

However, it may be a mistake to merely divide Yugoslavia on a historic Hapsburg/Catholic north, and a historic Ottoman/Orthodox south. Current events indicate that the Serbs show greater attachment to the old unified state than their compatriots, whether they be Catholic Croats and Slovenes, or Orthodox Macedonians. The results of the elections, with the success of nationalist parties everywhere except in Serbia and Montengro, where the old communist authorities succeeded in playing the nationalist card and, for the time being, remaining in power, are significant.

This book may be seen by some as being anti-Serb, especially in its criticism of the Serbian intelligentsia. It may be argued that all the national elites in Yugoslavia and elsewhere in the region are acting in similar fashion so why pick on the Serbs? It has not been the intention to be 'anti-Serb', it is a great mistake in the Balkans, and one often committed in the past, to favour one group over others. However, the Serbs, while not a numerical majority, have effectively been a power majority in the post-war Yugoslavia, shown in their over-representation in the Communist Party, the army and the police outside their own republic. The elections have tended to confirm this. As such, they have been, despite often claiming the reverse, in a position of power over other minorities and, in such circumstances it is essential that such power majorities do not abuse this position – something the Serbs have significantly failed to do in Kosovo at least.

Similar charges can be brought against the Greeks with their refusal to recognize ethnic minorities on Greek soil. While the assimilation of the Orthodox Macedonians, Vlahs and Albanians in Greece has apparently so far been successful, it remains to be seen whether the Muslim Turks and Pomaks of Western Thrace will be assimilated so easily.

Throughout the whole area the Roma remain at the bottom of the social scale although their very position has to an extent protected them from greater assimilation in the past. Developments beginning in Yugoslavia, but also taking place in Bulgaria, make the formation of greater self-awareness and corresponding political clout for the Roma a possibility – albeit only a distant future one.

Peaceful assimilation is to a large extent a natural process whereby an ethnic group, usually a small minority, over a period of time gradually coalesces from choice with another group, usually a dominant majority. At the other extreme is forceable assimilation whereby an ethnic group is usually denied to exist and its members are forced by pain of death or imprisonment to declare themselves to be part of another group and to abandon their customs and culture and adopt new ones. Between these two poles are a variety of others usually involving assimilation not so much by force as by control of the education system and the corresponding denial or restriction of education rights to a particular minority. In the Balkans almost every type of assimilation from the utilization of extreme force to that of apparent peace has been or is being pursued.

It is clear that the greatest threat to the security of many states is their internal conflicts with minorities and their failure to find strength in diversity. The repression of minorities has been shown to be an unsuccessful strategy fuelling conflicts and retarding development. It would be wise, therefore, for all the governments in the region, as a matter of urgency, to review their practices towrds minorities, and to work towards greater mutual understanding in the difficult times that lie ahead.

FOOTNOTES

Information available on minorities in Yugoslavia is enormous. In contrast, there is considerably less published on minorities in Bulgaria, and even less on minorities in Greece where the whole idea of any minorities in the country is still taboo. There is little information regarding Albania at all, due to the country's extreme isolationist policies pursued by the authorities there which have continued until recent times. This imbalance in available information is reflected in the large number of footnotes for Yugoslavia in contrast to the other countries.

Much of the information regarding the situaton of the ethnic Turks in Bulgaria comes from over 100 interviews made, in the course of a number of trips to Turkey and Greece between January 1985 and June 1989, with recently arrived refugees from Bulgaria. The author is indebted to the Minnesota Lawyers International Human Rights Committee (MLIHRC) for information regarding ethnic Greeks in Albania. Obtaining reliable figures for different ethnic groups is hampered by the competing aspirations of the various nationalities/ethnic groups and their supporters abroad which has made statistics in the area, especially in Macedonia, notoriously suspect over a long period (see 'Maps and Politics' by H.R. Wilkinson). All census figures, unless indicated, are official ones.

RFE = Radio Free Europe, Munich
BTA = Bulgarian Telegraph Association
SWB = BBC Summary of World Broadcasts
KNS = Keston News Service, Keston, Kent, UK.

YUGOSLAVIA

Serbs

[1] The Declaration by the Bishops of the Serbian Orthodox Church against the genocide inflicted by the Albanians on the indigenous Serbian population, together with the sacrilege of their cultural monuments in their own country – 14 September 1988.
[2] Michelle Lee – 'The end of an era' – *Labour Focus on Eastern Europe*, Vol 8 No 3, London, November 1986.
[3] Vienna home service, 6 September 1990, in SWB EE/0864 B/8, 8 September 1990.
[4] *The International Herald Tribune*, 28 December 1990.
[5] Tanjug, 7 January 1991 in SWB EE/0965 B/12, 9 January 1991.
[6] Tanjug, 30 January 1991 in SWB EE/0986 B/13, 2 February 1991.
[7] Figures from; 'Nationalities in the LCY: Ethnic composition of the membership of the League of Communists in Major Cities and Republics and Provinces', Vuskovic, Boris, *Nase Teme*, No 3-4 March-April 1986, Zagreb.
[8] Boris Vuskovic quoted in *Intervju*, Belgrade, 8 June 1984.
[9] Kokan, J., 'Where even toddlers know hatred', *Index on Censorship* 8/1990, London.
[10] *Op. cit.* as note 1.
[11] Bousfield, J.,'Voting to the finish', *East European Reporter*, Vol 4 No 3, Autumn/Winter 1990, London.
[12] *NIN*, Belgrade, 20 July 1990.
[13] Tanjug, 11 October 1990, in SWB EE/0895 B/6, 15 October 1990.
[14] Tanjug, 12 December 1990, in SWB EE/0948 B/18, 15 December 1990.
[15] *Op. cit.* as note 12.
[16] Belgrade home service, 25 January 1991 in SWB EE/0982 B/11, 29 January 1991.
[17] *The Independent*, 18 April 1990, London.
[18] *Danas*, Zagreb, 6 February 1990.
[19] Andrejevich, M., 'Croatia between Stability and Civil War' (Part 1), *RFE Report on Eastern Europe*, 14 September 1990.
[20] Goldstein, I., 'Serbs in Croatia', *East European Reporter*, Vol 4 No 3, Autumn/Winter 1990.
[21] *Politika*, Belgrade, 5 July 1990.
[22] *Op. cit.* as note 19.
[23] *Politika Weekly International*, Belgrade, No 21, year 1, 11-17 August 1990.

[24] Andrejevich, M., 'Crisis in Croatia and Slovenia', *RFE Report on Eastern Europe*, 2 November 1990.
[25] Tanjug (citing Radio Zagreb), 29 September 1990, in SWB EE/0833 i, 1 October 1990.
[26] Tanjug, 20 October 1990, in SWB EE/0866 B/16.
[27] Tanjug, 1 October 1990, in SWB EE/0885 B/8.
[28] Tanjug, 13 December 1990, in SWB EE/0948 i, 15 December 1990.
[29] Tanjug, 4 January 1991 in SWB EE/0963, 7 January 1991.
[30] Tanjug, 26 January 1991 in SWB EE/0982 B/8, 28 January 1991.
[31] *Op. cit.* as note 19.
[32] *Op. cit.* as note 20.
[33] KNS No 365, 20 December 1990.
[34] BBC World Service, 5 January 1991.
[35] BBC World Service, 5 January 1991.

Croats

[36] 'Yugoslavia: Prisoners of Conscience – *Amnesty International*, EUR/48/20/85.
[37] Statistical Year Book SFRJ, 1973.
[38] Op. cit. as note 7.
[39] Tanjug, 8 December 1990, in SWB EE/0947 B/14.
[40] *The Independent*, 18 April 1990.
[41] *RFE Weekly Record of Events*, 18 March 1990.
[42] Zagreb radio, 10 October 1990, in SWB EE/0893 B/11, 12 October 1990.
[43] *Slobodna Dalmacija*, Split, 22 July 1990.
[44] Tanjug, 8 November 1990, in SWB EE/0918 B/14, 10 November 1990.
[45] Tanjug, 9 September 1990, in SWB EE/0868 B/10, 13 September 1990.
[46] Tanjug, 12 December 1990, in SWB EE/0948 B/18, 15 December 1990.
[47] Zagreb, 21 January 1991, in SWB EE/0977 B/4, 23 January 1991.

Slovenes

[48] Tanjug, 20 November 1990, in SWB EE/0627 B/22, 30 November 1990.
[49] Tanjug, 29 November 1990, in SWB EE/0627 i, 30 November 1990.
[50] Tanjug, 28 January 1990, in SWB EE/W0114 A/10, 8 February 1990.

51 Tanjug, 13 December 1989, in SWB EE/0642 B/6, 18 December 1990.
52 Tanjug, 4 February 1990, in SWB EE/0681 i, 6 February 1990.
53 RFE Weekly Record of Events, 2 July 1990.
54 Tanjug, 27 September 1990, in SWB EE/0882 B/10, 29 September 1990.
55 Tanjug, 6 September 1990, in SWB EE/0864 B/6, 8 September 1990.
56 RFE Weekly Record of Events, 5 October 1990.
57 RFE Weekly Record of Events, 5 October 1990.
58 Tanjug, 6 and 7 November 1990 in SWB EE/0917 A1/3, 9 November 1990.
59 RFE Weekly Record of Events, 23 October 1990.
60 Tanjug, 14 November 1990, in SWB EE/W0156 A/7.
61 Tanjug, 22 November 1990, in SWB EE/0931 B/14, 26 November 1990.
62 Tanjug, 26 December 1990.
63 Agence France Press in *The Independent*, 16 February 1991.
64 For further information on the Slovene minorities in Italy and Austria, see Minority Rights Group (Ed.), *World Directory of Minorities*, Longmans, 1989, pp.99-101.

Muslims

65 Pawlowich, S.K., *The Improbable Survivor – Yugoslavia and its Problems 1918-1988*, C. Hurst and Co, London, 1988.
66 *Danas*, Zagreb, 6 March 1990, in JPRS-EER-90-073, 29 May 1990.
67 Ramet, S.P., 'Islam in Yugoslavia Today', in *Religion in Communist Lands*, Keston College, Vol 18, No 3, August 1990.
68 *Ibid.*
69 For the full text see *The South Slav Journal*, London, Spring 1983.
70 Amnesty International, op. cit.
71 *Ibid.*
72 Tanjug, 12 December 1990, in SWB EE/0948 B/18, 15 December 1990.
73 *Borba*, Belgrade, 3/4 March in KNS No 347, 5 April 1990.
74 Belgrade home service, 6 February 1991, in SWB EE/0991 B/11, 8 February 1991.
75 Belgrade domestic service, 6 February 1990, quoted in op. cit. as note 65.
76 Belgrade radio and Tanjug, 9 September 1990, in SWB EE/0866 i, 11 September 1990.

Macedonians

77 Barker, E., Macedonia: its Place in Power Politics, *Register of research in the Social Sciences in progress and in plain* No 7, 1949-50, Cambridge, London, 1950.
78 The most comprehensive refutation is 'Edinstvoto na Balgarskiya Ezik b Minalato i Dnes', The Bulgarian Academy of Sciences, Sofia, 1978.
79 Eg. *Istorija za VII Oddelenie*, (IV Isdanie), Skopje, 1980.
80 KNS No 349, 3 May 1990.
81 Amnesty International, op. cit.
82 Tanjug, 31 August 1990.
83 *Politika*, Belgrade, 27 October 1989.
84 *Borba*, Belgrade, 4/5 November 1989.
85 Tanjug, 4 February 1990, in SWB EE/0682 B/11, 7 February 1990.
86 RFE Weekly Record of Events, 16 July 1990.
87 RFE Weekly Record of Events, 20 February 1990.
88 *Oslobodjenje*, Sarajevo, 23 June 1990.
89 RFE Weekly Record of Events, 2 August 1990.
90 Sofia home service, 4 August 1990, in SWB EE/0837 A2/3, 8 August 1990.
91 Tanjug, 2 September 1990, in SWB EE/0861 B/17, 5 September 1990.
92 *Oslobodjenje*, Sarajevo, 5 September 1990.
93 RFE Weekly Record of Events, 2 June 1990.
94 RFE Weekly Record of Events, 3 November 1990.
95 Tanjug, 5 November 1990, in SWB EE/0916 B/7, 8 November 1990.
96 BTA, 18 January 1991, in SWB EE/0975 A2/3, 21 January 1991.
97 Tanjug, 1 February 1991, in SWB EE/0987 B/12, 4 February 1991.
98 Tanjug, 4 and 5 February 1991, in SWB EE/0990 A2/3, 7 February 1991.
99 BTA, 25 January 1991, in SWB EE/0983 A2/3, 30 January 1991.
100 Tanjug, 19 November 1990, in SWB EE/0928 B/19, 22 November 1990.
101 Tanjug, 21 December 1990, in SWB EE/0955 B/20, 24 December 1990.

Muslim Macedonians

102 *Duga*, Belgrade, 8 May 1982.
103 Tanjug, 13 August 1990, in SWB EE/0843 B/10, 15 August 1990.
104 Tanjug, 6 November 1990, in SWB EE/0916 B/7, 8 November 1990.

[105] Tanjug, 27 November 1990 in SWB EE/0934 B/15, 29 November 1990.

Albanians of Kosovo

[106] Biberaj, E., 'Kosovo: The Struggle for Recognition', and Pawlowich, S.K.,'Kosovo: An Analysis of Yugoslavia's Albanian Problem', both in Conflict Studies No 137/138, 1982.

[107] *Opstina*, Belgrade, No 8-9, August-September 1983.

[108] *Rilindja*, Pristina, 25 June 1984.

[109] Amnesty International, op. cit., and 'Adem Demaci – Deset tisuca dana robije' by Radoncic, F., *Danas*, Zagreb, 1990.

[110] *Komunist*, Belgrade, 28 August 1981.

[111] Amnesty International, *op. cit.*

[112] *NIN*, Belgrade, 6 September 1981.

[113] Amnesty International, *op. cit.*

[114] Tanjug, 10 July 1982, in SWB EE/7075 B/9, 12 July 1982.

[115] *NIN*, Belgrade, 20 November 1983.

[116] *Op. cit.*, as note 109.

[117] *Rilindja*, Pristina, 17 June 1979.

[118] Amnesty International, op. cit.

[119] Memorandum – The Albanian Kosovar Youth in the Free World, New York, 20 September 1990.

[120] *Jedinstvo*, Pristina, 1 March 1984.

[121] Yugoslavia: Recent Events in the Autonomous province of Kosovo, Amnesty International, EUR 48/08/89.

[122] Tirana home service, 2 February 1990, in SWB EE/0680 A2/1, 5 February 1990.

[123] Tirana home service, 15 December 1990, in SWB EE/0953 A2/1, 21 December 1990.

[124] *Nova Makedonija*, Skopje, 25 December 1990.

[125] Amnesty International, *op. cit.*

[126] RFE Weekly Record of Events, 9 February 1990.

[127] *Danas*, Zagreb, 22 May 1990, pp.22-27.

[128] Belgrade home service, 24 September 1990, in SWB EE/0897 B/10, 26 September 1990.

[129] RFE Weekly Record of Events.

[130] RFE Weekly Record of Events, 4 April 1990.

[131] SWB EE/0836 B/15, 7 August 1990.

[132] Tanjug, 8 February 1991, in SWB EE/0992 B/6, 9 February 1991.

[133] SWB EE/0742 i and EE/0744 i, 21 April 1990.

[134] RFE Weekly Record of Events, 14 May 1990.

[135] Andrejevich, M., 'Kosovo and Slovenia declare their sovereignty', *RFE Report on Eastern Europe*, 27 July 1990.
[136] *East European Newsletter*, Vol 4 No 18, 10 September 1990, London.
[137] *Student*, Belgrade, May 1990, in JPRS-EER-90-103.
[138] Tanjug, 4 February 1991, in SWB EE/0989 B/14, 6 February 1991.
[139] Tanjug, 13 September 1990, in SWB EE/0872 B/10, 18 September 1990.
[140] Tanjug, 14 September 1990, in SWB EE/0872 B/12, 18 September 1990.
[141] Belgrade home service, 24 September 1990, in SWB EE/0879 B/10, 26 September 1990.
[142] Zagreb radio, 27 October 1990, in SWB EE/0909 B/16, 31 October 1990.
[143] *Index on Censorship* 8/1900, London.
[144] *East European Newsletter*, Vol 4 No 7, 2 April 1990, London.
[145] RFE Weekly Record of Events, 18 March 1990, and 1 May 1990.
[146] *Borba*, Belgrade, 14-15 December 1985, in JPRS-EER-034, 11 March 1986.
[147] *Vjesnik*, Zagreb, 24 March 1990.
[148] *Op. cit.*, as note 136.
[149] *Vjesnik*, Zagreb, 10 February 1990.
[150] KNS No 363, 22 November 1990.
[151] KNS No 358, 13 September 1990.

Albanians in Montenegro and South Serbia

[152] *Danas*, Zagreb, 15 March 1983.
[153] *NIN*, Belgrade, 20 December 1981.
[154] *Duga*, Belgrade, 30 January 1982.
[155] Tanjug, 17 December 1990, in SWB EE/0951 B/11, 19 December 1990.
[156] *Jedinstvo*, Pristina, 6 February 1982.
[157] *Duga*, Belgrade, 19 November 1983.

Albanians of Macedonia

[158] Figures from 'Much Discomfort in Macedonia', Meier, V., *Frankfurter Allgemeine*, 23 June 1983, p.10.
[159] From Kantardzhiev, R. and Lazaroski, L., in 'Schools and Education' in Apostolski, M. and Polenkovich, H., 'The Socialist Republic of Macedonia', Skopje, p.110.
[160] *Op. cit.*, as note 7.

[161] Tanjug, 28 August 1981.
[162] Tanjug, 7 May 1984, in SWB EE/7639 B/9, 10 May 1984.
[163] Belgrade home service, 23 February 1988, in SWB EE/0084 B/5, 25 February 1988.
[164] Jankovic, D., in *Vjesnik*, Zagreb, 12 October 1986, p.7.
[165] IRNA (Iranian report), 13 December 1986, in SWB EE/8444 B/19, 17 December 1986.
[166] Josifovski, I., 'Opshtestvenite Promeni na Selo: Makedonskoto, Albanskoto i Turskoto Naselenie na Selo vo Polog: Sotsioloshka Studija', published by the Institute of Sociological, Political and Juridicial Research, Skopje, 1974.
[167] RFE Weekly Record of Events, 1 February 1990.
[168] Tanjug, 19 June 1990, in SWB EE/0796 B/15, 21 June 1990.
[169] RFE Weekly Record of Events, 28 August 1990.
[170] Tanjug, 16 August 1990, in SWB EE/0846 B/5, 18 August 1990.
[171] Tanjug, 25 August 1990, in SWB EE/0853 B/19, 27 August 1990.
[172] *East European Newsletter*, Vol 4 No 23, London, 19 November 1990.
[173] Tanjug, 1 September 1990, in SWB EE/0861 B/18, 5 September 1990.
[174] *Intervju*, Belgrade, 31 August 1990.
[175] Tanjug, 19 September 1990, in SWB EE/0876 B/6, 22 September 1990.
[176] *Op. cit.*, as note 174.
[177] Tanjug, 17 November 1990, in SWB EE/0928 B/19, 22 November 1990.

Roma (Gypsies)

[178] Tanjug, 23 October in SWB EE/0598 B/8, 27 October 1989.
[179] Tanjug, 30 May 1980.
[180] Tanjug, 12 January 1980.
[181] KNS No 366, 10 January 1991.
[182] RFE Weekly Record of Events.
[183] Tanjug, 1 September 1990, in SWB EE/0681 B/17, 5 September 1990.
[184] AFP, 15 March 1986.
[185] *The New York Times*, 30 July 1990.
[186] *Politika*, Belgrade, 10 April 1990.
[187] *Der Spiegal*, September 1990.
[188] Tanjug, 6 August 1990, in SWB EE/0837 B/10, 8 August 1990.
[189] Tanjug, 21 October 1990, in SWB EE/0902 B/13.
[190] Tanjug, 24 September 1990, in SWB EE/0879 B/10, 26 Sept 1990.

Turks

[191] Shoup, P., *Communism and the Yugoslav National Question*, New York, 1968, pp. 181/2; and Palmer, S., and King R., *Yugoslav Communism and the Macedonian Question*, Hamden, Connecticut, Archon Books, 1971, p.178.

[192] *Op. cit.* as note 102.

[193] Tanjug, 21 September 1987, in SWB EE/8683 B/7, 26 September 1987.

[194] *Op. cit.* as note 102.

[195] *Op. cit.* as note 159.

Hungarians, Slovaks, Romanians, and Ruthernians/Ukrainians

[196] Tanjug, 19 October 1990, in SWB EE/0902 B/13.

[197] Budapest home service, 24 January 1991, in SWB EE/0982 B/12, 29 January 1991.

[198] *Magyar Nemzet*, Budapest, 2 June 1990, in JPRS-EER-90-116, 14 August 1990.

[199] *RFE Report on Eastern Europe*, 12 October 1990, pp.43-44.

[200] *Magyar Hirlap*, Budapest, 1 March 1990.

[201] Budapest home service, 5 February 1991, in SWB EE/0991 B/13, 8 February 1991.

[202] RFE Weekly Record of Events, 12 May 1990.

[203] Budapest home service, 25 March 1990, in SWB EE/0726 B/4, 30 March 1990.

[204] *Romania Libera*, Bucharest, 28 November 1990.

Vlahs

[205] *Op. cit.* as note 7.

[206] For a recap of Dr Trifunoski's findings in Ovce Polje and other references see 'Tzintzari in Ovce Polje in S.R. Macedonia' by Dragoslav A., Balkanica V, Belgrade, 1975.

Others including 'Yugoslavs'

[207] *Danas*, Zagreb, 22 May 1990.

[208] Tanjug, 20 October 1990, in SWB EE/0902 B/14, 23 October 1990.

[209] BTA, 15 October 1990, in SWB EE/0897 B/13, 17 October 1990.

[210] Tanjug, 26 March 1990, in SWB EE/0726 B/4, 30 March 1990.

The Army (JNA)

[211] *Vecernje Novosti*, Belgrade, 15 August 1990.
[212] Milan Andrejevich – 'Military Attemptes to File Charges Against Slovenian Presidential Candidate', *RFE Report on Eastern Europe*, 27 April 1990.
[213] *East European Newsletter*, Vol 5 No.3, 4 February 1991.
[214] *East European Newsletter*, Vol 4 No 21, London, 22 October 1990.
[215] Tanjug, 11 April 1990, in SWB EE/0741 B/7, 18 April 1990.
[216] Open Letter by Idriz Ajeti, Chairman of the Defense of Human Rights in Pristina, to Federal Secretary of Defence, published in DELO, 1 June 1990, Ljubljiana.

Emigres

[217] *Narodna Armija*, Belgrade, 21 June 1990.
[218] *Vjesnik*, Zagreb, June 1976.
[219] Amnesty International, op. cit.
[220] *Ibid.*
[221] *East European Newsletter*, Vol 4 No 7, London, 2 April 1990.
[222] *Narodna Armija*, Belgrade, 1 February 1990.

BULGARIA

[223] Statisticheski Godishnik na Naraodna Republika Bulgaria 1985 (all census figures unless indicated are official ones.

Macedonians

[224] Pedrag Vukovic, 'U Sluzbi Starog', *Politika*, Belgrade, 7 December 1975.
[225] Bulgaria: Imprisonment of Ethnic Turks, Amnesty Internatiornal EUR/15/03/86, p 26.
[226] King,R., *Minorities under Communism, Nationalities as a source of tension among the Balkan Communist States*, Cambridge, Mass., Harvard University Press, 1973, pp 188/9.
[227] Amnesty International, op. cit., p 26.
[228] *NIN*, Belgrade, 5 January 1975.
[229] RFE Research Bulgaria SR/2, 12 March 1985, p.5.
[230] BTA, 22 February 1990, in SWB EE/0697, 24 February 1990.
[231] BTA, 11 March 1990, in SWB EE/0711 B/2, 13 March 1990.

232 BTA, 14 May 1990, in SWB EE/0765 B/3, 16 May 1990.
233 BTA, 22 April 1990, in SWB EE/0747 B/1, 25 April 1990.
234 BTA, 15 May 1990, in SWB EE/0767 B/1, 18 May 1990.
235 BTA, 23 May 1990, in SWB EE/0774 B/2, 26 May 1990.
236 BTA, 18 July 1990.
237 BTA, 31 July 1990, in SWB EE/0832 B/2, 2 August 1990.
238 Sofia home service, 2 August 1990, in SWB EE/0836 B/5, 7 August 1990.
239 Sofia home service, 4 August 1990, in SWB EE/0837 A2/3, 8 August 1990.

Pomaks

240 Amnesty International, op. cit., p.27.
241 *Ibid.*
242 Huseyin Memisoglu, *Bulgarian Oppression in Historical Perspective*, Ankara, 1989, p.26.
243 Amnesty International, *op. cit.*, p.28.
244 *Ibid.*
245 *Minority Name Studies in the Balkans – the Pomaks of Hadjiyska, The Final Report of the Field Study* 'Hadjiyska, 90'. Konstantinov, Y., Igla, B., and Alhaug, G., currently unpublished but available from Professor Konstantinov, ul. Latinka No. 6, bl.43, vh.B, 1113 Sofia, Bulgaria, or Dr. Igla, Sprachwissenschaftliches Institut, Ruhr-Universitat, D- 4630, Bochum, Germany.

Roma, Albanians, Tatars, Vlahs, Sarakatsani, and others

246 BTA, 18 October 1990, SWB EE/0902 B/6, 23 October 1990.
247 Sofia home service, 7 January 1990, in SWB EE/0658 B/3, 10 January 1990.
248 BTA, 18 March 1990, in SWB EE/0718 B/3, 21 March 1990.
249 Reuter, 18 June 1990.
250 BTA, 11 November 1990, in SWB EE/0921 B/2, 14 November 1990.
251 *Demokratsiya*, Sofia, 29 October 1990.
252 Memisoglu, *op cit.*, p.26.
253 Bahnev, Y., 'Muslims with Turkish Ethnic Identity', 15 February 1990, paper presented to MRG Conference in Copenhagen, 30 March-1 April 1990.
254 European Parliament Working Document 2-119/85.
255 KNS, No 347, 5 April 1990, and BTA, 17 March 1990.

[256] Troebst, S.,'Nationale Minderheiten' in *Sonderdruck aus Sudosteurope-Handbuch, Bulgarien,* Herausgegeben von Klaus-Detlev Grothusen, Gottingen, 1990.

[257] 'Foreign Workers in Eastern Europe', complied by Reed, H., in RFE, Vol 1 No 27, 6 July 1990.

[258] BTA, 18 December 1990, in SWB EE/0953 A3/1, 21 December 1990

Turks

[259] Amnesty International, *op cit.*, pp 3-4 and Simsir, B., *The Turks of Bulgaria,* London, 1988, pp.245-264.

[260] Tanjug, 28 March 1985, in SWB EE/7914 B/1, April 1985.

[261] *Rabotnicheski Delo,* Sofia, 19 April 1971.

[262] From paper by Hoepken, W., Institute of Southeast European Studies, Munich, for Refugee Studies Programme, Oxford University, 8 February 1988.

[263] *Ibid.*

[264] Amnesty International, *op cit.*, p.6.

[265] Op. cit., as note 260.

[266] Amnesty International, *op cit.*, p.16.

[267] RFE Bulgaria SR, 8 April 1988.

[268] BTA, 22 January 1991, in SWB EE0979 B/6, 25 January 1991.

[269] Amnesty International, *op cit.*, p17.

[270] BTA, Sofia, 5 April 1988.

[271] *Bulgaria: Continuing Human Rights Abuses Against Ethnic Turks,* Amnesty International, EUR/15/01/87, p.5.

[272] , as note 260.

[273] *Otkrito Pismo na Grupa Balgari ot Narodni Republika Balgaria Vazstanovili Svoite Balgarski Imena,* Sofia Press, 1985.

[274] See statement by Valentin Bojilov, Deputy Permanent Representative of Bulgaria, to UN in Geneva, at the Sub-Commission on the Prevention of Discrimination and Protection of Minorities, 38th Session, 26 August 1985.

[275] Troebst, S., 'Stories from the Polotburo and 1001 Nights: the Aggravation of the Bulgarian Assimilation Politics against the Turkish Minority.

[276] Tanjug, 8 January 1986, in SWB EE/8153 B/3, 10 January 1986.

[277] Memorandum and Press Release, March 1985 from the Bulgarian Press Office in London.

[278] BTA, 2 April 1986.

[279] Amnesty International, *Imprisonment of Ethnic Turks,* p.13.

[280] *Ibid.*, p 20.

[281] Deputy Foreign Minister Ivan Ganev at Sofia Press Conference reported in the *Guardian Weekly*, 2 July 1985.

[282] Reuter, 18 May 1989.

[283] Turgat Ozal reported in BBC World Service. 18 June 1989.

[284] RFE Weekly Record of Events in Eastern Europe, 1-7 June 1989.

[285] Bahnev, *op cit.*, as note 253.

[286] BBC World Service, 23 June 1989, and *Guardian Weekly*, 2 July 1988.

[287] Ozal, *op cit.*, as note 258.

[288] Bahnev, *op cit.*, as note 253.

[289] RFE Weekly Record of Events in Eastern Europe, Bulgaria, 18-24 May 1989.

[290] Amnesty International, UA 173/89 EUR 15/04/89, 9 June 1989.

[291] Amnesty International, 'Bulgaria: Imprisonment of Ethnic Turks and Human Rights Activists', EUR 15/01/89.

[292] RFE Weekly Record of Events in Eastern Europe, Bulgaria, 8-14 June 1989.

[293] Ashley, S., 'Ethnic Unrest During January', *RFE Report on Eastern Europe*, 9 February 1990.

[294] BTA, 10 January 1990, in SWB EE/0662 B/7, 15 January 1990.

[295] BTA, 2 January 1990, in SWB EE/0653 B/1, 4 January 1990.

[296] Ashley, *op cit.*, as note 293.

[297] Reuter, 18 November 1989.

[298] BTA, 9, 10,11 and 12 January, in SWB EE/0622 B/2-5, 15 January 1990.

[299] *Ibid.*

[300] Amnesty International, 'Bulgaria: Amnesty International's remaining concerns regarding ethnic Turks in Bulgaria', in EUR 15/03/90.

[301] RFE Weekly Record of Events, 18 January 1990.

[302] BTA, 14 May 1990, in SWB EE/0765 B/1, 16 May 1990.

[303] BTA, 8 June 1990, in SWB EE/0787 B/3, 11 June 1990.

[304] Reuter, 9 November 1990.

[305] BTA, 20 November 1990, in SWB EE/0928 i, 22 November 1990.

[306] BTA, 30 November 1990, in SWB EE/0937 B/7, 3 December 1990.

[307] Reuter, MFB HP SB (no date).

[308] BTA, 6 June 1990, in SWB EE/0785 B/5, 8 June 1990.

[309] Reuter, 4 June 1990.

[310] RFE Weekly Record of Events, 28 June 1990.

[311] BTA, 14 June 1990, in SWB EE/0794 B/3, 19 June 1990.

[312] BTA, 14 November 1990, in SWB EE/0925 C1/1, 19 November 1990.

[313] *Otechestvan Front*, Sofia, 9 May 1990.

[314] BTA, 26 May 1990, in SWB EE/0776 B/1, 29 May 1990.

[315] BTA, *op cit.*, as note 312.

[316] Bahnev, *op cit.*, as note 253.

[317] BTA, 26 April 1990, in SWB EE/0752 B/3, 1 May 1990.

[318] BTA, 1 May 1990, in SWB EE/0754 B/5, 3 May 1990.

[319] BTA, 1 October 1990. in SWB EE/0855 i, 3 October 1990.

[320] *Index on Censorship*, Vol. 20 No 1 1991, London.

[321] BTA, 11 October 1990, in SWB EE/0895 B/4, 15 October 1990.

[322] *Demokratsiya*, Sofia, 26 October 1990.

[323] BTA, op. cit. as note 312.

[324] BTA, 22 November 1990, in SWB EE/0932 B/1, 27 November 1990, and *Demokratsiya*, Sofia, 23 November 1990.

[325] BTA, 24 November 1990, in SWB EE/0932 B/2, 27 November 1990.

[326] BTA, 5 February 1991, in SWB EE/0990 B/5, 7 February 1991.

[327] Perry, D., 'The New Prime Minister and the Moslems', *RFE Report on Eastern Europe*, 18 January 1991.

GREECE
Slav Macedonians

[328] Simovski, T., 'The Balkan Wars and their Repercussions on the Ethnical Situation in Aegean Macedonia', *Glasnik*, Vol.XVI, No.3, Skopje, 1972.

[329] Andonovski, H., 'Macedonian National Minorities in Greece, Bulgaria and Albania', in *The Socialist Republic of Macedonia*, Apostoloski, M. and Polenakovich, H. (Eds), Skopje 1974, p.192; and Barker, op. cit.

[330] Popovski, T., 'Makedonskoto Natsionalno Maltsinstvo vo Bulgarija, Grtsija i Albanija', Skopje, 1981, p.72.

[331] *Op. cit.* as note 323, pp.198/9.

[332] *Istorijata na Makedonskiot Narod*, Kniga III, published by NIP Nova Makedonija, Skopje, 1969, pp.271/5.

[333] *Ibid.*, p.274.

[334] Hoppe, H-J., 'Bulgarian Nationalities Policies in Occupied Thrace and Aegean Macedonia', in *Nationalities Papers*, Spring-Fall 1986, Vol XIV, No 1-2, pp.89-100.

[335] Some give a figure as high as 50%: see Kofos, E., 'The Impact of the Macedonian Question on Civil Conflicts in Greece (1943-49)', published by Hellenic Foundation for Defense and Foreign Policy, *Occasional Papers* No 3, Athens, 1989, pp.20-22.

[336] According to Greek newspaper 'Elefteron Vima', 19 October 1952, referred to in as note 330, p.76.

337 See Kofos, E., 'The Macedonian Question, the Politics of Mutation', Institute for Balkan Studies, Thessaloniki, 1987.
338 Lazo Mojsov 'Okoly Prashanjeto na Makedonskoto Natsionalno Maltsinstvo vo Grtsija', published by the Institute for National History, Skopje, 1954, p.17.
339 *Op. cit.* as note 330, p.223.
340 *Op. cit.* as note 329, p.196.
341 'The Way Ahead for Macedonian Human Rights – Report of the Europe 89 Delegation', prepared by Radin, M., and Popov, Dr. C., Central Organizational Committee for Macedonian Human Rights, Thessaloniki (no date).
342 Clogg, R., *A Short History of Modern Greece*, CUP, 1979, p.164.
343 *Op. cit.* as note 329, p.196.
344 Tanjug, 6 June 1988, in SWB EE/0712 A1/3, 8 June 1988.
345 Reuter 201651 GMT of 30 June 1988.
346 Tanjug, 15 May 1986, in SWB EE/8262 A1/6, 19 March 1986.
347 *Ibid.*
348 Tanjug, 19 April 1986, in SWB EE/8238 A1/1, 21 April 1986.
349 *Vecernje Novosti*, 10 June 1988, in SWB EE/0177/ i, 14 June 1988.
350 Tanjug, in SWB EE/0795 i, 20 June 1990.
351 Tanjug, 3 June 1990, in SWB EE/0784 B/10, 7 June 1990.

Turks and Pomaks

352 De Jong, F., 'Names, Religious Denomination and Ethnicity in Western Thrace', E.J. Brill, Leiden, 1980.
353 See 'Greeks of Turkey' in *World Directory of Minorities*, op. cit.
354 For this and following section see De Jong – 'Muslim Minorities in Western Thrace', in *World Minorities in the Eighties*, Ashworth, G. (Ed), Quartermaine House Ltd. and MRG, 1980. (out of print)
355 Amnesty International, *Greece: Dr. Sadik Ahmet and Ibrahim Serif*, EUR 25/02/90.
356 *Dateline*, London, 28 October 1989.

Roma and Albanians

357 *Roma: Europe's Gypsies*, MRG Report, 1987, p.8.
358 J.G. Nandris, The Thracian Inheritance, *The Illustrated London News*, June 1980, p.10.
359 Information, Federal Union of European Nationalities, Flensburg, Austria, 29 March 1990, p.7.

[360] 'The Situation of the Albanian Minority in Greece', Democratic League of Chameria, Illinois, USA, 18 March 1990.

Vlahs

[361] *Op. cit.*, as note 359.
[362] For this and the following sections see a series of articles by Balamaci, N., 'One View from the Diaspora', in *The Greek American*, 12, 19, 26 September and 3 October 1987; 26 August and 2, 9, 16 September 1989.
[363] See Averoff-Tossizza, E., *The Call of the Earth*, Caratzas Brothers, New Rochelle NY, 1981, and review of the above by N. Balamaci, N., in the 'Newsletter of the Society Farsarotul', Vol II Issue 2, August 1988, pp.19-22.

ALBANIA

[364] Prifti, P., 'Socialist Albania since 1944: domestic and foreign developments, 1978.
[365] *Ibid.*, citing Marmullaku, R.,'Albania and the Albanians', 1975.
[366] Amnesty International, *Albania: Political Imprisonment and the Law*, AI EUR/11/04/84, p.13, 1984.
[367] *Human Rights in Albania: Hearing Before the Sub-committee on Human Rights and International Organizations of the House Committee on Foreign Affiars*, 98th Congress, 2nd Session, 14, 25 January 1984, statement by Nikolaos. A. Stavrou.
[368] Amnesty International, *Op. cit.*, p.13.
[369] Since beards are associated with Orthodox priests, the wearing of beards was outlawed. Until 1983, foreign visitors with beards were shaved at customs.
[370] Amnesty International, *Op. cit.*, p.13.
[371] KNS, No 347, 5 April 1990.
[372] Ens, D., 'Growing religious freedom in Albania', News Netweork International, 17 May 1990.
[373] KNS, No 361, 25 October 1990.
[374] SWB EE/0902, 23 October 1990.
[375] Belgrade radio, in SWB EE/0925 i, 19 November 1990.
[376] KNS, No 363, 22 November 1990.
[377] KNS, No 365, 20 December 1990.

Greeks

[378] MLIHRC interview with former resident. See also the International Federation for the Protection of the Rights of Ethnic, Religious, Linguistic and other Minorities, (IFPRERLM), 'The State of Religious and Human Rights in Albania', submitted at the 39th Session of the UN Sub-Commission on Prevention of Discrimination and Protection of Minorities, Geneva, pp.3-5, 1987.

[379] Op. cit., as note 367, testimony by Sami Repishti reprinted in part in Albanian *Catholic Bulletin* 63, 64, Nos 1 and 2, 1984.

[380] Amnesty International, *Op. cit.*, pp.26-7.

[381] MLIHRC interview with Konstantin Gigas of the Committee for the Struggle of Northern Epirus, Athens, March 1988.

[382] Report from the Albanian Minister for Foreign Affairs, Tirana, 7 July 1922, reprinted in 'Minority Schools in Albania', (Alb), 1935 PCIJ, Ser C, No 76, Pleadings pp.40-42.

[383] One former resident told MLIHRC of two school closings in particular. Also see note 378.

[384] Administrative Decree 5339, cited in Prifti, *Op. cit.*, p.164.

[385] Ibid.

[386] Eg. Agios Nikolaos ('Saint Nicolas'), an ethnically Greek village whose name was changed to Drita ('Light').

[387] Stavrou statement, op. cit., as note 367, eg. Mavropoulo ('Black City' in Greek) became Buronjq ('Shield' in Albanian).

[388] *Ibid.*

[389] Amnesty International, *op. cit.*

[390] ATA, 26 May 1990, in SWB EE/0775 B/5, 28 May 1990.

[391] MLIHRC interview with Helena Smith, AP, Athens, March 1989.

[392] Cowell, 'A Hint of Change in the Albanian Air', *New York Times*, 20 June 1988.

[393] Tirana Radio, 3 September 1990, in SWB EE/0861 i., 5 September 1990.

[394] Tanjug, 29 January 1991, in SWB EE/0983 i, 30 January 1991.

[395] Athens home service, 14 January 1991, in SWB EE/0971 A1/2, 16 January 1991.

[396] Budimovski, D.K., 'Makedontsite vo Albanija', NIP 'Studenski Zbor', Skopje, 1983.

[397] Tanjug, 31 January 1990, in SWB EE/0680 A2/2, 5 February 1990.

[398] Andonovski, H., 'The Socialist Republic of Macedonia', Skopje, 1974, p.203.

[399] *Makedoniya* No 8, III, Sofia, 1932.

[400] Andonovski, *op. cit.*, p.202.

[401] Popovski, *op. cit.* as note 330, pp.247-248.

[402] *Ibid.*, p.251.

[403] Horak, S.M.,'National Minorities in Albania, 1919-1980', in *East European National Minorities: 1919-1980*, Horak, S.M., (Ed) Colorado, 1985.

[404] BBC World Service, 31 December 1990.

JEWS

[405] See, *op. cit.*, as note 334, for Bulgaria's treatment of the Jews in World War II.

[406] Tanjug, 20 February 1986, in SWB EE/8190 A1/2, 22 February 1986.

Very Select Bibliography

ALEXANDER, Stella, *Church and State in Yugoslavia Since 1945*, Cambridge University Press, 1979.

AMNESTY INTERNATIONAL, *Albania: Political Imprisonment and the Law*, AI Eur/11/04/84, 1984.

BARKER, Elizabeth, *Macedonia: Its Place in Balkan Power Politics*, London, 1950.

CLOGG, Richard, *A Short History of Modern Greece*, Cambridge University Press, 1979.

CRAMPTON, R.J., *A Short History of Modern Bulgaria*, Cambridge University Press, 1987.

DODER, Dusan, *The Yugoslavs*, Random House, New York 1978 and Allen and Unwin, London, 1979.

JELAVICH, Barbara and Charles, *Nationalism in the Balkans 1804-1920*, University of Washington Press, Seattle/London.

LENDVAI, Paul, *Eagles in Cobwebs; Nationalism and Communism in the Balkans*, Doubleday, New York, 1969.

PALMER, Stephen and KING, Robert, *Yugoslav Communism and the Macedonian Question*, Hamden, Connec, Archon Books, 1971.

PAWLOWICH, Stevan, *The Improbable Survivor – Yugoslavia and its Problems: 1918- 1988*, C. Hurst and Co., London, 1988.

PRIFTI, Peter, *Socialist Albania since 1944: Domestic and Foreign Developments*, MIT, Cambridge, Mass./London, 1978.

PUXTON, Gratton, *Roma: Europe's Gypsies*, MRG Report, 1987.

RUSINOW, D., *The Yugoslav Experiment: 1948-1974*, The Royal Institute of International Affairs, C. Hurst and Co., 1977.

SHOUP, Paul, *Communism and the Yugoslav National Question*, New York, 1968.

STAVRIANOS, L.S., *The Balkans since 1453*, New York, 1958.

SUGAR, P., *South Eastern Europe under Ottoman Rule 1354-1804*, University of Washington Press, Seattle/London.

SWIRE, J., *Bulgarian Conspiracy*, London, 1939.

WACE, A.J.B. and THOMPSON, M.S., *Nomads of the Balkans*, Methuen, 1914.

WILKINSON, H.R., *Maps and Politics, A Review of the Ethnographic Cartography of Macedonia*, Liverpool, 1951.

WINNIFRITH, Tom, *The Vlachs*, Duckworth, 1987.

INDEX

assimilation of, 112-15, 129, 130, 143, 168
Bulgarian Roma, 13, 87, 105, 116-17, 119, 122, 167, 210
Bulgarian Slavs, 111-15, 164
Bulgarian Social Democratic Party, 109
Bulgarian Socialist Party, 117, 166, 168, 170
Bulgarian Turks, 77, 83, 105, 111, 117, 119-21, 122-25, 168-71, 209; emigration of, 112, 114, 119, 129, 134, 146, 147, 153, 157-60, 164, 169; forced assimilation of, 17, 79, 93, 115, 121, 127-28, 129-51, 157, 160, 163, 165-66, 171, 207; resistance of, 134, 139-49, 153-57, 160, 163-64, 169
Bulgarian Vlahs, 117-18, 189
Bulgarians, 47-48, 109, 110, 126, 150, 164, 171, 190; support for ethnic Turks, 17, 160, 165; of Yugoslavia, 5, 47, 54, 97, 110
Burukov, Ahmet, 156
Busik, Bruno, 102, 103
Byzantine Empire, 2, 87, 175, 183

Cana, Zekeria, 66
Catholicism, 71; in Albania, 57, 71, 82, 193; Croatian, 7, 23, 27, 29, 33, 34, 72-73, 209; Slovene, 4, 7, 35, 37, 209; Yugoslav attitude to, 41, 42
Catholicism
Celaj, Zenon, 70
Central Committee for Macedonian Human Rights, 179
Central Europe, 38
Chakirov, Abdullah, 148
Cherkez people, 117
Chetnik movement, 17, 59, 104
China, People's Republic of, 195, 197
Circassians, 117, 183
Comecon, 161
Comintern, 49, 104, 177
Commissariat for Jewish Affairs (KEV), 205, 206
Committee for the Defence of National Interests (KZNI), 165, 170
Committee for the Protection of Human Rights, 70
Committee for Religious Rights, 160

Committee for the Truth about Kosovo, 70
Communist Party Marxist-Leninist of Yugoslavia (PKMLSHJ), 62
Congress of Berlin, 46
Constantinople, 2
Cosic, Dobrica, 19
Council of Elders of the Islamic Community of Macedonia, 55
Council of Europe, 179, 186
Council for the Protection of Human Rights and Freedoms in Kosovo, 66
Crimean War, 117
Croatia, 1, 23, 29, 35, 41
Croatia, Yugoslav Republic of, 6, 10, 19, 29, 37, 38, 44, 45, 53, 58, 97, 99, 100; and struggle with Serbia, 22, 24-27, 31-35, 37, 72-73
Croatia-Slavonia, 5
Croatian Defence Ministry, 34
Croatian Democratic Party (HDZ), 24, 32-33
Croatian Democratic Party of Bosnia-Hercegovina, 33-34, 44
Croatian League of Communists, 21, 24, 31, 32-33
Croatian Muslims, 41, 44
Croatian National Council (HNV), 101
Croatian nationalism, 6, 7, 10, 24, 29, 31-34
Croatian Peasant Party (HSS), 7, 102
Croatian Roma Assembly, 89-90
Croatian separatism: see also Ustasha movement
Croatian Serbs, 13, 15, 20, 23-27, 29, 32, 35, 97, 208
Croats, 1, 4, 101-2, 103, 104; Catholic, 4, 7, 23, 27, 29, 33, 34, 72, 209; as Yugoslav nation, 5, 21, 24-25, 27, 29-35, 39, 44, 93, 97
Csorba, Zoltan, 94
Cyprus, 161, 166, 173, 184; partition of, 183
Czechs, 118; of Yugoslavia, 5, 97

Dalmatia, 5, 100
Dalmatian coast, 1, 29, 35
D'Almeido, Vidal, 133
Damatoglu, Ahmet, 184
Danube river, 1, 116, 142, 189
Dapcevik-Kucar, Savka, 31

Panhellenic Romani Association, 188
Pan-Hellenic Vlah Cultural Society, 192
Papagos government, 179
Papandreou, Andreas, 173, 180-81, 182, 200-1
Papazisi-Papatheodorou, Zoitsa, 191-92
Paroja, 62-63
Pan-Serbian Council of National Salvation, 20, 54
Partisans, 32, 41, 42, 43, 45, 48-49, 277
Party of Democratic Action (SDA), 43-45, 72
Party for Democratic Prosperity of Macedonia (PDPH), 55-56, 85, 86, 90
Party of Yugoslavs, 98
Parvomay, Bulgaria, 109
PASOK Socialist party, 173, 180-81
Pazardzhik, Bulgaria, 112
Peasant Democratic Party of Kosovo, 70
Pec Initiative Council, 71
Penev, Pancho, 168
People's Militia Law, 108, 143, 163
Perez de Cuellar, Javier, 197
Perinovic, Davor, 33
Petar, Bishop of Prespa and Bitolj, 51
Peterle, Alojz, 38
Petrov, Professor Petar, 149-50
Petrich, Bulgaria, 109
Petrovar, Tanya, 17
Petrinja, Croatia, 26
Pindus mountains, 189
Pirin Macedonia, 49, 107, 108; autonomy movement in, 108, 109-11
Pirin Macedonians, 109
Pirker, Pero, 31
Pitu Guli Cultural Association, 96
Philip of Macedon, 107
Plovdiv, Bulgaria, 116, 117, 118, 129, 122, 134, 138, 146, 147, 164
Pol Pot, 197
Poland, 127, 160, 205, 206
Poles, 5
Political prisoners; in Bulgaria, 112, 113, 142-43, 145, 147, 148, 151, 154-55, 163, 165, 166; in Yugoslavia, 64-65, 68, 69

Politica, 19, 20, 87
Pomaks, 2, 209; of Albania, 201, 203; of Bulgaria, 111-15, 122, 123-24, 129-30, 143, 159, 163, 167-78, 170; of Greece, 175, 176, 183, 185
Popov, Blagoj, 202
Popov, Dimitar, 54
Popov, Prokopi, 97
Popovski, Ante, 52
Popular Fronts, 177
Poturs: see Pomaks
Pravoslavlje, 41
Praxis, 19
Preporod, 41, 44
Pristina, Kosovo, 6, 21, 41, 60, 62, 68, 70, 71, 80, 90-91, 101; TV station of, 89
Pristina University, 60-61, 65
Prizren League, 103-4
Protectors of Northern Greece, 178
Protestant Christianity, 7
Proto-Bulgarians, 1
Pucnik, Joze, 36, 99-100

Quaranta, Mario, 97

Rabotnichesko Delo, 126, 138
Radio Belgrade, 89
Radio Deutsche Welle, 155
Radio Free Europe, 147, 155
Radio Knin, 26
Radio Skopje, 79
Radio Tetovo, 89
Radio Titograd, 75
Radio Zagreb, 24
Rajic, Simo, 24, 27
Rankovic, Alexander, 16, 59-60, 78
Raskovic, Dr. Jovan, 24, 26-27
Razgrad, Bulgaria, 134, 135, 138-39, 140, 155-56, 157
Razgrad Committee for the Defence of National Interests, 170
Red Cross, 180
Red Front, 62
Redzepi, Jusuf, 86
Redzepi, Remzi, 85
Reis-ul-ulema, 41
Republican Secretariat for the People's Defence, 80
Reuters news service, 139

About Minority Rights Group Reports

The Minority Rights Group began publishing in 1970. Over two decades and ninety titles later, MRG's series of reports are widely recognized internationally as authoritative, accurate and objective documents on the rights of minorities worldwide.

Over the years, subscribers to the series have received a wealth of unique material on ethnic, religious, linguistic and social minorities. The reports are seen as an important reference by researchers, students, campaigners and provide readers all over the world with valuable background data on many current affairs issues.

Around six reports are published every year. Each title, expertly researched and written, is approximately 30 pages and 20,000 words long and covers a specific minority issue.

Recent titles in our report series include:

Europe
Romania's Ethnic Hungarians
Refugees in Europe

Middle East
Beduin of the Negev
The Kurds

General
Language, Literacy and Minorities

Americas
Maya of Guatemala

Africa
The Sahel
Somalia

Southern Oceans
Maori of Aotearoa-New Zealand
The Pacific: Nuclear Testing and Minorities

Asia
Afghanistan
Bangladesh

If you have found this book informative and stimulating, and would like to learn more about minority issues, please do subscribe to our

243

report series. It is only with the help of our supporters that we are able to pursue our aims and objectives – to secure justice for disadvantaged groups around the world.

We currently offer a reduced annual rate for individual subscribers – please ring our Subscription Desk on 071 978 9498 for details. Payment can be easily made by MasterCard or Visa over the telephone or by post.

All enquiries to: Sales Department
                    The Minority Rights Group
                    379 Brixton Road
                    London
                    SW9 7DE
                    United Kingdom.

Customers in North America wishing to purchase copies of our reports should contact:
                    Cultural Survival
                    53 Church Street
                    Cambridge
                    MA 02138
                    USA